Cézanne

PORTRAITS

Cézanne
PORTRAITS

John Elderfield

WITH

Mary Morton
Xavier Rey

CONTRIBUTIONS BY

Alex Danchev
Jayne S. Warman

NATIONAL PORTRAIT GALLERY, LONDON

Contents

Directors' Foreword

THIS IS THE FIRST EXHIBITION to be devoted exclusively to Cézanne's portraits, an important, yet often neglected, aspect of his art. As such, it provides an unrivalled opportunity to reveal the extent and depth of his achievement in portraiture, arguably the most personal, and therefore most human, aspect of his work.

Paris in the second half of the nineteenth century was a place of great vitality in artistic and literary circles. The official Académie des Beaux-Arts, which upheld the academic style of the day, was being challenged; the newly initiated Salon des Refusés reflected the revolutionary spirit that heralded Impressionism and inspired a young Paul Cézanne. Yet although he may have employed techniques similar to those of the Impressionists, his aim was quite different, his vision unique, informed by a desire to see through appearances to the underlying structure of things – whether a portrait or a landscape or still life – by means of mass, line and shimmering colour. And nowhere was this more evident than in his portraits.

Like all exhibitions with equivalent ambitions, *Cézanne Portraits* has been a long time in gestation. It began in 2007 with a conversation at the Clark Art Institute in Williamstown, Massachusetts, between the former Director of London's National Portrait Gallery, Sandy Nairne, and the Senior Curator of European Paintings at Washington's National Gallery of Art, Philip Conisbee. Why had there not been an exhibition of Cézanne's portraits? Subsequently, while historian Alex Danchev was working on his biography of the artist, the question was again raised. Sadly, both these early advisers on the project – Philip and Alex – have since died, and we would like to take this opportunity to remember their contributions.

In the summer of 2009 Sandy Nairne invited John Elderfield to be the lead curator of the exhibition. He agreed enthusiastically, and at the same time partner organisations – the Musée d'Orsay, Paris, and the National Gallery of Art, Washington, D.C. – were approached. John outlined three principles that would

inform the selection of works aside from obvious considerations of quality. The exhibition would explore Cézanne's creation of pairs or series of portraits of the same sitter, something previous curators have tended to avoid (with the exception of the 2014–15 exhibition of portraits of Madame Cézanne at the Metropolitan Museum of Art in New York). It would trace Cézanne's portrait output chronologically, so revealing changes in style and method. And it would show the full range of his sitters and the extent to which they inflected the development of his practice.

We are enormously grateful to John for his exceptional leadership and dedication in bringing together these outstanding examples of Cézanne's oeuvre, drawn from public and private collections worldwide, and for his insightful and authoritative research into the artist's work, as reflected in this accompanying publication. Mary Morton, Curator and Head of the Department of French Paintings at the National Gallery of Art, Washington, D.C., has contributed her scholarship, as has Xavier Rey, now Directeur des musées de Marseille but formerly Directeur des collections at the Musée d'Orsay, Paris (with particular reference to the French publication). Collectively, all three bring to life the artist's working techniques and his search for intellectual solutions to the problem of representation. Through Alex Danchev's 'Dramatis Personae' we are introduced to the cast of sitters that constituted Cézanne's portraiture: his father and son, wife and uncle; artists and writers; his patron and dealer; and the working people of his native Aix-en-Provence, many of them virtually unknown. Jayne S. Warman, author of the online catalogue raisonné of Cézanne, has contributed a newly researched chronology to this publication. Mary Tompkins Lewis served as scholarly reviewer of catalogue texts and Matthew Simms made a final review before the texts were finalised. We are most grateful to them all.

Colleagues from each of our institutions also deserve our sincere thanks. At the National Portrait Gallery, Sarah Tinsley, Director of Exhibitions and Collections, was closely involved in the development of the exhibition from an early stage, while Michelle Greaves, Exhibitions Manager, has skilfully coordinated what has been a very complex project, the later stages of which have been managed by Andrew Horn. Peter Funnell, Head of Research and Senior Curator, has had curatorial input at the Gallery, while Jude Simmons led the creative design work. We are also grateful to Denny Hemming for editing and project-managing the exhibition catalogue, overseen by Christopher Tinker, the Gallery's Managing Editor; to Ruth Müller-Wirth, the Gallery's Production Manager; to Mark Lynch for his picture research; and to Philip Lewis for his thoughtful and elegant design.

Other colleagues at the National Portrait Gallery we wish to acknowledge are Pim Baxter, Robert Carr-Archer, Andrea Easey, Jenny Foot, Jessica Litwin, Laura McKechan, Justine McLisky, Nicola Saunders, Fiona Smith, Liz Smith, Denise Vogelsang, Helen Whiteoak and Rosie Wilson.

At the National Gallery of Art, we wish to thank Franklin Kelly, Deputy Director and Chief Curator; D. Dodge Thompson, Chief of Exhibitions; Ann Robertson, Exhibition Officer; Elizabeth Dent, Exhibition Associate; Susan M. Arensberg, Head of Exhibition Programs; Margaret Doyle, Deputy Head and Associate Curator of Exhibition Programs; Mark Leithauser, Senior Curator and Chief of Design; Donna Kirk, Senior Architect; Nathan Peek, Production Coordinator; Theresa Beall, Registrar for Exhibitions; Bethann Heinbaugh, Head of Preventive Conservation; Jamie Gleason, Associate Preventive Conservator; Barbara Berrie, Head of Scientific Research Department; John Delaney, Senior Imaging Scientist; Michael Swicklik and Ann Hoenigswald, Senior Conservators; Christine Myers, Chief Development and Corporate Relations Officer; Giselle Obermeier, Senior Development Officer; Patricia Donovan and Cathryn Scoville, Senior Development Officers for Major Gifts; Anabeth Guthrie, Chief of Communications-Converged Media; Kimberly Jones, Curator of Nineteenth-Century French Paintings; and Michelle Bird, Curatorial Assistant, Department of French Paintings.

For the Musée d'Orsay, this exhibition is the result of the enthusiasm of Guy Cogeval, who until 2017 was Président of both the Musée d'Orsay and the Musée de l'Orangerie, Paris, and embraced the project presented to him by John Elderfield. We owe much to the unstinting efforts of the exhibition department, headed by Hélène

Flon, and especially to Pascale Desriac. It would not have been possible without the research of Annabelle Mathias (now responsible for the archives of the Musée de l'Armée, Paris). Estelle Bégué made a major contribution by drawing up a dynamic visual chronology as part of the exhibition design, while Isabelle Gaétan contributed to the selection and presentation of Cézanne portraits, drawn from French national collections and conserved by Leïla Jarbouaï. The French edition of the catalogue was made possible by the creativity and rigour of the publications team, headed by Annie Dufour, and especially Flore Toffoli, who has been involved with the book from its inception, including the translation of texts originally written in English. We would also like to mention the ever-demanding work of the Collections Commission, which enables us to receive and present masterpieces from all over the world.

We are indebted to the many people who have offered valuable information, advice, and support in matters both curatorial and scholarly, as well as to those who have facilitated the loan of crucial works to this exhibition. In particular, we would like to thank Christopher Riopelle, Curator of Post-1800 Paintings at the National Gallery, London, and Ernst Vegelin, Head of the Courtauld Gallery, London, for their encouragement from the outset. In addition, we would like to thank Scott Allan, William Allman, Helga Aurisch, Ronni Baer, Laurence des Cars, Keith Christiansen, Guy Cogeval, Moriah Evans, Walter Feilchenfeldt, William E. Freedberg, Davide Gasparotto, Michael Govan, Gloria Groom, Katie Hanson, Diana Howard, Frederick Ilchman, Yuko Katada, Sam Keller, Simon Kelly, Irene Koenfal, Dorothy Kosinski, Ulf Kuster, Eric Lee, Christophe Leribault, Glenn Lowry, Patrice Marandel, Line Clausen Pedersen, Adriano Pedrosa, Salvador Pons, David Pullins, Joseph Rishel, James Rondeau, Timothy Rub, Scott Schaefer, Karen Serres, George Shackelford, Jill Shaw, Phaedra Siebert, Susan Stein, Elizabeth Szancer, Jennifer Thompson and Gary Tinterow. To all of them and to those whose help was anonymous, we extend our deep gratitude.

Finally, we would like to extend our warmest thanks to all those public and private owners of works who have lent so generously to the exhibition, thus making these exceptional portraits accessible to a wider audience.

We extend our deep gratitude to the Anna-Maria and Stephen Kellen Foundation for its generous sponsorship of the exhibition in Washington. We also would like to thank Marina Kellen French and her family for their enthusiastic support of this project.

NICHOLAS CULLINAN
Director, National Portrait Gallery, London

EARL A. POWELL III
Director, National Gallery of Art, Washington, D.C.

LAURENCE DES CARS
Président, Musée d'Orsay and Musée de l'Orangerie, Paris

Acknowledgements

I OWE A GREAT DEBT of gratitude to Sandy Nairne and Sarah Tinsley of the National Portrait Gallery, London, who visited me in New York in 2009 with the invitation to be the lead curator of an exhibition devoted to Cézanne's portraits. I am also grateful to Nicholas Cullinan, now Director of the Gallery, for his support and encouragement, and to all those members of staff at the Gallery who have been involved in this project. Their names are listed in the Directors' Foreword, but I especially want to acknowledge the indispensable work of Michelle Greaves, who managed an extremely complex exhibition, its later stages managed by Andrew Horn, and Denny Hemming, who managed and edited this equally complex volume. The enthusiasm of Rusty Powell at the National Gallery of Art, Washington, D.C., and Guy Cogeval at the Musée d'Orsay, Paris, was essential for the development of the project, and made possible the curatorial collaboration of Mary Morton and Xavier Rey, respectively, who have been constantly thoughtful and insightful colleagues in the shaping of the exhibition and catalogue. It was also a great pleasure to have the late Alex Danchev as a contributor to the catalogue. And to Jayne Warman, the final contributor, I owe particular thanks: she gave me access to the online catalogue raisonné of Cézanne's paintings, of which she is a co-author, even as it was being prepared, which made the selection for the exhibition so much easier than it would otherwise have been; and she

was my constant interlocutor throughout the latter part of the project as we debated the place and date of the creation of every work in this volume. In her scholarly review of texts as they were written, Mary Tompkins Lewis became a de facto member of the working group, making important suggestions, as did Matthew Simms in his final review.

My own work additionally benefited from discussions with students in my autumn 2015 seminar on Cézanne at Princeton University; with Carol Armstrong, Yve-Alain Bois, Richard Shiff, Matthew Simms and Jayne Warman, who participated in a colloquium associated with that seminar; and with Dita Amory and Charlotte Hale on the subject of their work on the 2014–15 exhibition of portraits of Madame Cézanne at the Metropolitan Museum of Art. More specifically, in writing my texts for this volume, I am indebted to Delphine Huisinga for her careful and assiduous research support; and, as always, to Jeanne Collins, who reviews and makes editorial improvements to everything I write, and who accompanied me in looking at many of the paintings illustrated in this volume. Finally, I am pleased to acknowledge the influence on my understanding of Cézanne of John Rewald and Lawrence Gowing, who introduced me to the study of his art some forty years ago, and whose pioneering work on it resonates to this day.

JOHN ELDERFIELD, CURATOR

FRONTISPIECE
Self-Portrait with Bowler Hat, 1885–6 (detail, cat. 10.2)

PAGE 4
Madame Cézanne, 1885–6 (detail, cat. 11.2)

PAGE 8
Self-Portrait, Rose Ground, c.1875 (detail, cat. 5.2)

Introduction:
The Reading of the Model

JOHN ELDERFIELD

La lecture du modèle, et sa réalization,
est quelquefois très lent à venir pour l'artiste.
Cézanne to Charles Camoin, 9 December 1904[1]

Paul Cézanne was born in Aix-en-Provence on 19 January 1839, and died there aged sixty-seven on 23 October 1906. He made almost 1,000 paintings, of which around 160 are portraits.[2] This publication accompanies the only exhibition exclusively devoted to these works since 1910, when Ambroise Vollard, who had been the artist's dealer, showed twenty-four 'Figures de Cézanne'. The present, much larger selection was chosen with the aims of providing a guide to the range and development of Cézanne's portraits, the methods of their making, and the choice of their sitters. Also, more broadly, it is intended to raise the question of what the practice of portraiture meant for Cézanne when he was painting – or, as he said, reading and 'realising' – the model.

OLD RULES

When Cézanne began painting portraits in the early 1860s, portraiture in France had long been acknowledged as a genre second in importance only to paintings of historical and mythological subjects. It was growing in popularity, and it would continue to do so during the period of Cézanne's career: in the late 1880s, a National Portrait Gallery would be proposed for Paris, as well as a special gallery for portraits in the Louvre.[3] It was during the 1860s and 1870s, however, that many ambitious painters found themselves enquiring what a portrait should aim to do. They no longer needed to ask, as they had in earlier times, what comprised a landscape painting, a still life, or a figure composition. But what was a portrait? That was the question they had to address.

The first reason that they had to do so was a matter of historical change. A traditional notion of portraiture, based on precisely detailed, idealised images of the public faces of people who lived public lives, had all but come to an end – at least, the followers of Jean-Auguste-Dominique Ingres had dragged out this approach beyond plausibility. What remained by default was the rudimentary understanding that a portrait, still a social art, should provide a physical and psychological likeness of its sitter. But this was complicated by the emergence of new, highly personalised

Paul Alexis Reading a Manuscript to Emile Zola, 1869–70
(detail, cat. 3.3)
Museu de Arte de São Paulo
Assis Chateaubriand

11

approaches to portraiture by artists such as Gustave Courbet, Edouard Manet, Edgar Degas and, among others, Cézanne. They raised the issue as to whether the claims of painting overall were being elevated over those of portraiture in particular; and, if so, whether invocation of the individuality of the sitter was being supplanted by expression of the individuality of the artist. Also open to interpretation was whether muting a sitter's individuality in favour of that of the artist depersonalised, or even objectified, the sitter. Such charges, first made against Manet's portraits, were also made against Cézanne's.

Conversely, the question arose as to whether acceptance of a commission to paint a portrait would compromise both the claims of painting and the individuality of the artist. This, however, was a perennial problem: the art historian E.H. Gombrich described it crudely as 'quarrels between great artists and pompous sitters whose stupid wives insist there is still something wrong around the mouth'.[4] Stupid husbands and friends, too. The English painter-critic Walter Sickert, writing in 1910, more carefully divided portraits into two kinds: 'pictures painted by artists as servants of their customers' and 'pictures painted by artists who are masters of their customers'.[5] But aspiring French painters of the 1860s and 1870s, Cézanne included, had long mastered a third kind: pictures not painted for customers, but rather of people they knew.

An additional reason why portraiture needed to be redefined came as the result of an invention. The enormous popularity of photographic portraits, especially of small, informal *cartes-de-visite*, did not compromise the viability of portrait painting – a common claim – but did offer what historian Carol Armstrong nicely calls a 'boldly strange' alternative to the painted portrait that caught the attention of many critics and artists, such as Cézanne; and worried others.[6] The example of photography, a young, mechanical, reproductive medium opposed to but influencing the old, personalised, imaginative one, expanded the question of depersonalised representation, attaching it to concerns about modern alienation and loss of identity in an age of mass production. Cézanne, although attracted to photography and himself accused of depersonalisation, was traditional in his views of the world and highly suspicious of modernisation, famously complaining about the introduction of electric street lighting in Marseille because it spoiled the twilight.[7]

This meant that the subject of modern life was of no interest to Cézanne, separating his practice of portraiture from its urban, social locus as practised by most of the Impressionists. The poet and critic Charles Baudelaire contended that fashionable dress was appropriate to modern life;[8] there are at best a half-dozen portraits of fashionably dressed women, and the same of men, among Cézanne's portraits. Manet's portraits effectively tell us that there is no self except a social one;[9] Cézanne's that there is no self within a social one.

In an ambitious essay on Impressionist portraits, focused mainly on the work of Degas, art historian Linda Nochlin asserted that they 'should not on the whole be considered as portraits but rather should be seen as part of a broader attempt to reconfigure human identity by means of representational innovation'.[10] This innovation included 'liberating portraiture from restrictions of categorization' and 'overturning the conventions of the portrait pose'. The former meant, for example, that a painting by Manet of nightlife in Paris was also a portrait of his friends; portraiture thus escaped from the studio into the social world. Cézanne was utterly uninterested in thus liberating portraiture: he made some figure compositions based on portraits, but it remains fairly clear which genre is which;[11] and portraiture firmly belonged in the studio or in the domestic interior. The only exceptions were a group of fantasy figure compositions, painted in the early 1870s, into which Cézanne inserted his own likeness, and his occasional attempts at painting portraits out of doors, of which more to follow.

The other representational innovation to which Nochlin refers was the discarding of the 'morally and posturally upright' way of showing a portrait subject; for example, by painting a portrait of a man with his feet propped up on chair, of a woman powdering her nose, of another pretending to be a bullfighter. Cézanne will have none of this. He paints his father reading a newspaper (cat. 4.1) and his future wife Hortense Fiquet sewing (cat. 7.2), but apart from these and very few other exceptions, nobody does anything in Cézanne's portrait paintings, except pose motionless for Cézanne. There is no lounging. Everyone has to follow the rules – the old rules.

By this point, it should be obvious that Cézanne was traditional not only in his life but also in his notion of portraiture. He was, however, the very opposite of traditional in the making of his portraits – more so than any of his fellow artists – not despite but because he accepted portraiture as it was. (Only Vincent van Gogh, among his ambitious contemporaries, shared the same indifference to reforming the species.) The Impressionist painter whom Cézanne most admired, Camille Pissarro, would write in 1884: 'Don't bother trying to look for something *new*: you won't find novelty in the subject matter, but in the way you express it.'[12] Some fifty years later, the poet and critic T.S. Eliot would rephrase this thought, asserting: 'The perpetual task of poetry is to *make all things new*. Not necessarily to make new things.'[13] Both precepts apply to Cézanne's portraiture. Initially, though, they did so because Cézanne learned from what was new; not only from new painting in Paris by Courbet and Manet, but also from photography.

NEW MEANS

Cézanne's first portrait was a self-portrait (cat. 1.1) made from a photograph (p.44), which exaggerated the 'boldly strange' character of the source in the harshly lit appearance that he gives himself. More than forty years later, the painter-critic Emile Bernard observed, 'To my great astonishment, Cézanne had no objection to a painter's use of photography; but in his case, it was necessary to interpret this exact reproduction just as he would interpret nature itself.'[14] In 1862, interpretation meant hyperbole – and soon thereafter hyperbole not in the depiction of a face but in the means of realising it.

The year 1866 was critical; before it ended, Cézanne had found his own artistic voice through the practice of portraiture. However, as late as in the autumn he was momentarily deflected by the radical idea, shared by Impressionists including Claude

INTRODUCTION: THE READING OF THE MODEL

FIG. 1
A group of photographs of portraits
by Cézanne, as exhibited at the Salon
d'Automne, 1904
Ambroise Vollard, *Paul Cézanne* (1914)

Monet and Fréderic Bazille, of going one big step further than Manet's studio-painted *Le Déjeuner sur l'herbe* of 1863, and making portraits out of doors in natural light. By mid-October, he had produced an oil sketch of his friends Antoine-Fortuné Marion and Antony Valabrègue heading out to paint a landscape (fig. 100). As he wrote to his closest friend, Emile Zola:

> All the paintings done indoors, in the studio, will never be as good as things done outdoors. In showing outdoor scenes, the contrasts between the figures and the ground are astonishing, and the landscape is magnificent. I see some superb things, and I must resolve to paint only out of doors.[15]

Cézanne's aim was to create a large composition from the oil sketch, but it was either never made, or did not survive. And so suddenly did he then drop *plein-air* portraiture that we can only conclude, given what followed, that this one attempt to paint figures in the magnificence of an outdoor setting was enough to show that it was impossible – impossible for him, at least – to produce a sufficiently potent reading of them as individuals. Over the decades that followed, he would sporadically return to the problem and find that time and again it defeated him.[16] But then, at the very end of his life, he more than succeeded by all but eliminating 'the contrasts between the figures and the ground' in outdoor portraits of his gardener Vallier (cats 26.2, 26.3).

Towards the very end of 1866, the portraits that followed this failed experiment were explicitly studio productions. They were akin to photographs in their restriction to monochrome, in their abrupt contrasts and suppression of internal modelling, and in the frank matter-of-factness of their imagery.[17] The series of portraits that Cézanne painted of his uncle, Dominique Aubert, in 1866–7 (cats 2.1–2.6, figs 22–5) may also owe something to grids of portrait photographs of the same person being made in Paris (fig. 2)[18] – an arrangement that Cézanne's dealer Ambroise Vollard would recapitulate some forty years later by exhibiting a grid of photographs of portraits by Cézanne (fig. 1). That said, the early portraits are also very far from being photographic, sharing with Cézanne's landscapes, figure paintings and few still lifes of the period an effacement of the detail and a repudiation of the slick surfaces that made photographs as popular as Salon paintings. Their highly personalised, bulging impasto showed disregard of conventional niceties and an unmitigated assertion of the physicality of the medium, often carried to the point of sheer coarseness.

These works have commonly and quite rightly been characterised as rebellious. But rebellion is less the cause of their motivation than the effect, which presents itself as the same intense need to externalise an inner experience, whether of the actual or the imagined, that had produced the sado-masochistic, erotic poems in his youthful letters to Zola, and would soon produce his violent and erotic figure paintings. Art historian André Dombrowski has argued that, rather than resulting from Cézanne's personal fixations, they comprise an alternative, law-breaking version of how modern experience could be translated into paint.[19] In fact, whether personal or social in impetus, both the matter-of-factness and the crude treatment of the early portraits may be seen as setting back painted portraiture to a primitive stage.

FIG. 2
Portrait photographs of Eugène Chevreul
by Nadar (Félix Tournachon), 1886
Le Journal illustré, 5 September 1886

Their search for truth-to-experience, although indebted to the Realism of Courbet (fig. 3), is more basic and rudimentary; although modelled on the objectivity of Manet (fig. 4), it is not cool and impersonal. It was, perhaps, because Cézanne's portraits of the 1860s were so elemental, appearing to occupy a point zero of portraiture, that it was by making these works in particular that he found his own, individual artistic voice. At the end of that decade he would say, 'I paint as I see, as I feel – and I have very strong sensations.'[20] The young painter was determined that the subjectivity of his response to his subjects be noticed. And no matter how apparently depersonalised his paintings might become, he would always speak in the first person singular.

The materiality of his early paintings was certainly noticeable. In fact, that term is hardly adequate, especially for the palette-knife portraits of 1866–7 (cats 2.1–3.1). At the very beginning of the decade, Zola had admonished his friend, writing, 'As I've told you before: in the artist there are two men, the poet and the worker. One is born a poet, one becomes a worker.'[21] However, these portraits are not merely the result of working hard. Seeing how Cézanne had built figure and ground alike from heavy slabs of paint, his friend and portrait subject Valabrègue called it 'mason's painting',[22] implying not merely a worker's but a working man's art. That is closer to what they are, but it is too dry a description. Even in their present desiccated state, their surfaces remember something of the wet stickiness of 150 years ago. The patches of paint were, in fact, pockets of liquid paint, together forming a plenum held in place by a drying skin. Imagining what they were like when Cézanne painted them, Jean-Paul Sartre's extended paean to *le visqueux*, the viscous and slimy, comes to mind;[23] and, with it, the realisation that their representation of bodily substance was a matter of creating not only a resemblance but also an analogy in the paint, its surface an epidermis implying flesh beneath.[24] It was body work that Cézanne was doing.

FIG. 3
Gustave Courbet, **Portrait of Champfleury**, 1855
Musée d'Orsay, Paris

FIG. 4
Edouard Manet, **The Smoker**, 1866
Minneapolis Institute of Art, Minnesota

Cézanne's often-remarked brutalising and coarsening of his social and personal presentation was the corollary of his approach to portrait painting. His famous refusal to shake hands with Manet because his own were dirty was, I think, prompted not by concern for Manet's personal hygiene but to avoid being infected by debonair Parisian painting any more than he already was.[25]

It is unsurprising, then, that those identifiable sitters of Cézanne's early portraits are all family and friends from Aix. He was as proprietorial about his subjects as his manner of portraying them. That is to say, he was beginning to realise how description could be complicit with and analogous to ownership.[26] He wanted his very own language, one that would differentiate his strong sensations about the world he occupied from those – less strong, is the implication – experienced by the owners of the practice of painting in Paris. That meant portraying people in his own immediate circle: also being suspicious of outsiders to it, the staid locals in Aix as well as figures from the Parisian art world. He was happy to see his method of painting become a house style for other young *Aixois* artists. Another friend, Fortuné Marion, observed that it was spreading 'like the germ of an epidemic, and all the painters, even the glass-makers, are beginning to work with a thick impasto'.[27] On the other hand, Cézanne would always be on the lookout for outside predators: his later, continuous complaining that Gauguin had stolen his style from him became legendary.[28] A much later portrait subject, the critic Gustave Geffroy (cat. 17.1), recalled Cézanne's consuming 'desire to possess the things he sees and admires'; to possess them in 'the restricted [*restreint*] space of a canvas'.[29]

This synergy of personally felt images, an aggressively material style, and familiar portrait subjects set the pattern for Cézanne's subsequent portraiture, which overwhelmingly comprises people whom he knew, and local working-class people with whom he felt comfortable. Portraiture does imply reciprocity of some kind between artist and sitter. Cézanne's refusal to be pictorially ingratiating required subjects who didn't expect it. But how to do that? His two early portraits of Valabrègue are especially telling. In the first portrait, dated 1866 (cat. 3.1), Valabrègue does his best not to appear to be posing, but the clenched hands are a giveaway;[30] rather, Cézanne finds himself not quite able to hide his friend's self-consciousness. In the beautiful second canvas, 1869–70 (cat. 3.2), Valabrègue is self-absorbed rather than self-conscious. Cézanne has learned how empathy may be depicted without a cloying effect. But the elemental quality has gone.

'There are two ways of understanding portraiture – either as history or fiction.' Baudelaire's epithet in his 'Salon de 1846' is well known; less so is how he defined the two alternatives. History uncontroversially meant exactness of representation, but not excluding idealisation; Cézanne knew how to avoid that. Fiction, however, meant 'to transform the portrait into a picture – a poem with all the accessories, a poem full of space and reverie'.[31] The poet Rainer Maria Rilke, thinking about Cézanne's work of the later 1870s, would dismiss this in a parenthesis, saying 'that's how the painting of moods came about (which is in no way better than the painting of things)'.[32] But, ten years earlier, Cézanne was tempted. It takes nothing away from the beauty of the second Valabrègue portrait to say that it is a painting of fiction, but the first is a painting of fact. In 1869–70, he was painting not, or not only, 'the thing regarded, but the thing remembered, imagined, desired';[33] which is to say, he was getting perilously close to Parisian notions of what portraiture should be. Had he continued in this vein, he would be remembered as the last of the great Realist portrait painters. Instead, in 1872, in order to learn how to paint out of doors, he joined forces with Pissarro, the elder statesman of the Impressionists, soon to become a very different kind of artist – and, initially, hardly a portrait painter at all.

EXPERIMENTATION

The patient record of light and shade on landscape that Cézanne learned from Pissarro unsettled the stillness and solidity that he had been building into his paint; it was not easy to know quite how to shape an obdurate human presence with means designed to record a continuous, ever-changing, visual array. It wasn't until the mid-1870s that the first new kinds of portraits began to appear. In an extraordinary rush of experimentation, he had moved through three radical approaches by 1880.

Again, self-portraiture begins the process. In the 1860s, the expressive materiality of the surface had been somewhat at odds with creating a sense of rounded volume in the painting of heads; and Cézanne only got that right when he adapted his palette-knife technique to the brush, modelling with irregular swathes of usually beige-brown paint. The first new self-portraits (cats 5.1, 5.2), painted around 1875, picked up on that approach, ratcheting up the palette in emulation of the portrait that Pissarro had just painted of him (fig. 5),[34] while maintaining enough of the earlier, charged handling to distinguish it from portraits by any Impressionist. And now the creation of volume had a new subject, his own prematurely bald head. Of this, art writer Adrian Stokes was right not to joke that, 'considering the wonderful volume he always achieved for the dome of his skull', being bald on top 'was very fortunate for the artist'.[35] And Rilke was even more right, and droll, when, speaking of the 'utter primitivity' of one of these portraits (cat. 5.2), he observed how, 'without even remotely interpreting his expression or presuming himself superior to it, he reproduced himself with humble objectivity, with the unquestioning, matter-of-fact interest of a dog who sees himself in a mirror and thinks: there's another dog.'[36]

Then Cézanne experimented with a new kind of handling. In the head of his friend Victor Chocquet, 1876–7 (cat. 6.1), he recovered in an exaggerated form the weaving of strands of colour by Eugène Delacroix, whose work they both loved, which lay behind the optical mixtures of Impressionist painting. It is – and was received as – an aggressively physical work; in its own way, as much a construction of paint built to form a homogeneous, corporeal surface as the palette-knife paintings of a decade before. And that is its link to the startlingly different next step that Cézanne took, notably in a portrait of Hortense Fiquet, of c.1877, with whom he had been living since 1869 (cat. 7.1).

Rilke admired this work even more than the self-portrait; and, in the letter that he wrote about it, he made a tiny drawing of the wallpaper pattern in the background – 'a cross with the centre left out ✚', he called it.[37] This motif quietly implies a gridded substructure, a multicoloured pattern – half billowing tapestry, half jigsaw – of bands, blocks and curved pieces of varying sizes. The consistency of the composition lies in part in that settled order, and in part in the density of the pictorial surface, the method of its building revealed in the less finished lower-right corner. Within this splendour Hortense sits, cool and composed. There is nothing quite like this in the previous history of portraiture.

The ruthlessness of finding and then surrendering, or at least modifying, a new means of proceeding continued into the early 1880s. This included Cézanne's use in his portraits of a technique he had begun to use when making landscapes, that of so-called 'constructive brushstrokes': patches of paint of a similar size applied in a parallel, usually diagonal, direction running more or less continuously across facial features, and across figure and ground alike. As uniform aggregated units, they create,

FIG. 5
Camille Pissarro,
Portrait of Paul Cézanne, 1874
National Gallery, London

FIG. 6
Portrait of the Artist's Son, *c.*1878
Private collection; FWN 457

FIG. 7
Portrait of the Artist's Son, 1875
Henry and Rose Pearlman Collection,
on loan to Princeton University Art
Museum; FWN 456

more explicitly than the continuous surface of the Chocquet portrait, an updated, potentially livelier form of the palette-knife method. Cézanne used this technique for the figure but not for the ground in a self-portrait of 1879–80 (fig. 39), but was using it for both in self-portraits painted shortly thereafter (cats 8.1, 8.3). And, wanting to try out the approach on heads close in shape to his own, he explored it in a series of small, close-up studies of the head of his young son, Paul, begun in the mid-1870s and continuing through the first half of the following decade.[38]

Unlike previous pairs or sets of portraits, these were explorative works of comparison, none completely finished. They contrasted the new constructive brushstrokes method (fig. 6) with the quieter blending of patches of colour of a similar value (fig. 7), in both cases using paint more thinly applied than in his self-portraits. And they also considered how, modelled in either way, the oval shape of his son's head – charmingly in reverse of his own, covered on top but clean around the chin – could be preserved. How best to attach the ears was critical; and the conclusion Cézanne reached was that they should not interfere with the integrity of the oval, to which end perhaps one of them could be dispensed with (see fig. 7). The constructive touch was judged to be optional. An equal visual texture, especially one implying a field of arrested movement and somewhat mechanically applied across carefully balanced compositions, risked producing 'resolutions of things already resolved', to borrow a phrase by art critic Clement Greenberg on the later Monet.[39]

In another experiment of the early 1880s, Cézanne tested how necessary was the presence of the sitter (Chocquet) in comparative portraits painted from life (fig. 8) and from a photograph (figs 9, 97), and in a self-portrait made by copying a pastel portrait that Renoir had made of him (figs 10, 11). It may be significant that it was in the copies, and not in the portrait painted from observation, that he used the more mechanical, constructive brushstrokes.

The early and mid-1880s produced two pairs of self-portraits that may be thought to extend the Chocquet photography experiment: in each case a painting in full colour succeeded by one in almost monochrome (cats 8.1, 8.3; 10.2, 10.3). But while both comprise a modernist *paragone*, comparing the merits of two means of objective representation, the second pair also makes a traditional painting comparison between an explorative *esquisse*, or painted sketch, and a fully realised *tableau*. Cézanne would repeat neither the *paragone* experiment, if it is one, nor the traditional method. But he did paint another self-portrait from a photograph in the mid-1880s (cat. 10.1), and he did continue the practice of comparing differing treatments of the same subject. Indeed, the 1880s was a decade of serial, comparative portraiture.

FIG. 8
Portrait of Victor Chocquet, *c.*1880
Simonow Collection, France; FWN 453

FIG. 9
Portrait of Victor Chocquet
(after a photograph), 1880–5
Private collection; FWN 454

INTRODUCTION: THE READING OF THE MODEL

FIG. 10
Pierre-Auguste Renoir,
Portrait of Cézanne, 1880
Private collection

FIG. 11
Portrait of Cézanne after Renoir, 1881–2
State Hermitage Museum, St Petersburg;
FWN 461

COMPARATIVE PORTRAITURE

Of the some 160 portraits that Cézanne painted, Hortense Fiquet was the subject
of twenty-eight or twenty-nine. Fully seventeen of these he painted in five years,
during the second half of the 1880s, the most intense, continuous examination of the
features of any one person that he ever made. This compares to roughly the same
number of self-portraits that he made in the twice-as-long period that preceded and
just overlapped the start of this sequence of works. Art historian Joseph Rishel
suggested that Cézanne's self-portraits are about 'taking inventory'.[40] We might
reasonably ask ourselves why Cézanne ceased his self-inventory to take up an
inventory of Hortense.

There is a practical explanation. After a lengthy period with more separation than
cohabitation, the couple spent a year together in Gardanne before and after their
marriage there in April 1886; then, after another period of frequent separation, they
spent another year mostly together in Paris in 1888–90. Hortense was now Madame
Cézanne and was there to be painted – many times, in many different ways.[41]

This said, Hortense's availability allowed, but does not explain, either the systematic
manner in which Cézanne proceeded from canvas to canvas to form short sets of two

to four closely related portraits; or the character of the changes from one canvas to the next. We have seen that, in 1866–7, he made an extended series of portraits of his uncle, Dominique Aubert. In taking up serial imagery again, one influence must certainly have been its increasing popularity in Paris among printmakers and photographers, whose mediums facilitated its production, and among Impressionist painters.[42] This new fashion affected Cézanne's landscapes, still lifes and, notably, his Bathers compositions, which in the mid-1880s were assuming a grander form. Like them, and unlike, say, Monet's series paintings, the multiple portraits of Hortense were painted neither to meet market demands (Cézanne was hardly selling anything at the time) nor to complement each other in a display (he had virtually stopped exhibiting). They were new vehicles of experimentation; each work a variation of another. In the case of the portraits, the experiment was initially in the depiction of affect.

The depiction of emotions and expressions had been a topic of great interest among French artists since the seventeenth century, first gaining currency in Charles Le Brun's posthumously published *Conférences sur l'expression* of 1698, and in appreciation of the expressive heads of Cézanne's admired Nicolas Poussin, which may have been in his mind as he set about painting his own.[43] Moreover, the term *tête d'expression*, describing portraits depicting emotion and the subject of a national competition established in the late eighteenth century, remained in currency.[44]

Notwithstanding the suggestions, mentioned earlier, that new French painting privileged expression of the individuality of the artist over that of the sitter, there is plenty of personality in Impressionist portraits – by Degas, Monet, Renoir, and even in Manet's work, despite the often-repeated claim that he always objectified his sitters. Likewise, Cézanne's portraits had nearly always invoked a sense – and, in the case of the self-portraits, a vivid sense – of the character of the person painted. However, it is usually a sense of a settled permanence of character rather than of someone caught in a particular mood; therefore, not a 'fictional' portrait in Baudelaire's sense of the word. Complaining of such 'painting of moods', Rilke had commended Cézanne for keeping emotion, meaning expressed emotion, out of his work. I don't think he would have liked Cézanne's portraits of Hortense made in 1885–6 (cats 11.1–11.4).

This set of four paintings, and the sets that followed it through the remainder of the 1880s, do reveal expressed emotion. Moreover, they reveal alterations in emotion from portrait to portrait across the first set, and from set to set in those that follow. However, unlike traditional *têtes d'expression*, designed to specify a single emotion – anger, joy, pain, sorrow, fright – these paintings obstruct such single readings. Especially so in the case of the first set: what Hortense is feeling is all but impossible to specify. Was Cézanne projecting his own feelings into what appear to be depictions of hers? It raises the unanswerable question: did Cézanne ask Hortense to assume particular expressions when he posed his wife? Whether he did so or not, he obviously controlled the portrait's mode of address. Yet, in doing so, he seemed also to be offering Hortense a means of presenting herself, for we feel no clear line between the painter's control and the sitter's self-presentation.[45] Such a portrait – one that affords the sitter, with the cooperation of the painter, the means of presenting him- or herself – speaks of a quality of intimacy between the two, whether or not the presentation they collaborate to produce also expresses mutual affection.

Taking the pair of portraits that followed (cats 13.2, 13.3), it is commonly understood that it doesn't, but rather expresses a sullenly alienated Hortense; while the final four (cats 14.1–14.4) suggest an automaton rather than a person. Perhaps they do. Still, any hope that Cézanne might start to conceive of portraiture as a charitable art is bound to be continually dashed. The closer the subject to him, the more condescending a benevolent painting would be. And Hortense is painted as extremely close. A large majority of these portraits address the viewer, a privilege previously reserved mainly for Cézanne's self-portraits; and they also face the viewer, something reserved mainly for family portraits, but a recent feature of the photography experiment with Chocquet. In the first set, Cézanne compares a pair of two facing portraits with a pair in which Hortense looks away. After that, though, the frontality of address in these portraits is commensurate with the quality of isolation they convey. The figure regarded is painted as coolly disregarded, neither imagined nor desired.

The systematic grouping and development of these portraits contributes to what Rilke called both 'humble' and 'limitless' objectivity.[46] Insistent repetition may reinforce a common identity despite changes of affect and appearance. Hence, Cézanne's experiments with the oval of his own head, then his son's, found their consummate resolution in his studies of his wife's. Creating an unimpeded oval for her head became an increasing obsession – that is not too strong a word – as one set of portraits succeeded another. It came to mean flattening both ears, to a somewhat discomforting effect if one notices it (see cat. 11.1); or exposing a continuous, sculptural contour on one side, usually her right, eliminating the ear on that side if necessary, to achieve a more noticeable, audacious effect that delivers the uncanny purity of a head by Brancusi (see cat. 11.2). In the final set of these 1880s portraits of Hortense, four works that show her wearing a red dress, the form of her head, like that of a cast sculpture, appears to be voluminous without being solid; that is to say, hollow.

Repetition that reveals comparative differences in a single portrait subject may also impose an awareness of how changes have been made. To follow the oval head as transformed from one painting to the next is to experience it not only as a figural motif but also as a pictorial one, carried upon Hortense's neck much like a sculpture on a base. And another, more radical example of Cézanne's manipulation of the subject image occurs in these four portraits. He appears to have painted one of them, and most probably two, not directly from Hortense, but by copying them in her absence from other works in the series. And in the copies, the head of Hortense noticeably grows in importance, actually swelling in size.[47] Writing about Cézanne in 1907, the painter-critic Maurice Denis quoted a remark by a fellow artist, Paul Sérusier: 'The subject disappeared; there is only a motif.'[48] He didn't mean it literally, but sometimes it was literally true.

NAMES AND NO NAMES

Shortly after 1890, Cézanne began to live more or less continually apart from his wife and son. Even while they were also living in Aix, he no longer asked them to be painted, or they no longer chose to be. Instead, he turned for subjects to various farmhands, local workmen and domestic servants, engaged by his mother and sister at the Jas de Bouffan, the family estate, or working for acquaintances. As Mary Tompkins Lewis has observed, appreciation of the rural population of France as its 'granite foundation' had been growing since the mid-1880s;[49] and Cézanne, long

FIG. 12
Edouard Manet,
Portrait of Emile Zola, 1868
Musée d'Orsay, Paris

fiercely attached to his native Provence, and increasingly conservative, was quickly making highly sympathetic portraits of his new subjects. However, his major focus in the early 1890s were his Card Player paintings – the serial approach applied to figure compositions – which, to a considerable extent, subsumed and replaced his portraiture to picture the community rather than the individual. But whether painting one or many figures, nearly all of them are anonymous. Before this point, the subjects of nearly all Cézanne's portraits can be identified. Now he was mainly painting portraits without names.

At mid-decade, however, this changed. Cézanne's first solo exhibition, at Ambroise Vollard's gallery in Paris in 1895, brought him increasingly wide attention, to his definite discomfort at times.[50] In any event, he found himself again painting names, mainly in Paris, as well as no names in Aix; and more prominent names than he had painted before.

In 1895–6, he painted his portrait of Gustave Geffroy (cat. 17.1), a portrait almost without precedent in Cézanne's art: almost, because it picks up from the final portrait in the final set of the 1880s portraits of Hortense Fiquet (cats 14.1–14.4). In that canvas, for the first time, figure and interior are equally components of a portrait that is also a composition with a figure. The same is true of the Geffroy portrait, and of one no-name portrait, *Woman with a Cafetière* (cat. 17.2), painted around the same time.

Cézanne invariably reminds us of his aims with regard to painting as well as to portraiture, but rarely does his allegiance to the former go so far as to challenge the plausibility of the latter. Yet it does here. We can, and I think do, believe that these scenes existed, and that Cézanne stood in front of them. But we cannot, I think, believe that Geffroy actually arranged the shelving of his books in the upright, slightly slanting, strongly diagonal, then back to the vertical sequence that so impressed Roger Fry;[51] or that the coffee pot stood so much to attention as to match the stiff uprightness of the domestic servant; or that parts of the room flew in space around Hortense in her portrait.[52] Modernist taste admires such anomalies, but they were something that Cézanne chose not to pursue. These three works are so uniquely, consciously staged that we must wonder if he deliberately tried out this approach using these three very different portrait subjects. We don't know. If the Geffroy portrait was the last of the three, the difficulties he had with it may have discouraged him from attempting something so ambitious again.

Still, the problems that Cézanne had with the Geffroy portrait were not directly related to such anomalies, but with implications of the form that the painting took. It followed the example of canvases by Manet and Degas in showing a man of letters in his library; the former shows Cézanne's childhood friend Zola (fig. 12), the latter the critic Edmond Duranty (see fig. 61). Degas's painting may be thought of as the conceptual, as well as compositional, model of Cézanne's portrait insofar as both embody Duranty's ideas on portraiture, promulgated in his *La Nouvelle peinture*, published on the occasion of the second Impressionist exhibition of 1876. For Duranty, the painter needed to leave his studio and come 'out into the real world'; should 'no longer separate the figure from the background of an apartment or the street', but be shown surrounded by 'the furniture, fireplaces, curtains, and walls that indicate his financial position, class, and profession'; and this appearance should 'reveal temperament, age, and social condition', especially in the face and the hands.[53]

The face and especially the hands of Cézanne's portrait of Geffroy are unfinished. It is as if he had tried to follow Duranty's instructions, and managed to do so wonderfully, but couldn't bring himself to complete the painting. As Mary Tompkins Lewis has explained, portraits of journalists and writers had become popular in the early 1890s, which may have prompted this work.[54] So may the fact that, a year earlier, Geffroy had written a glowing article about Cézanne and the two had recently met in Claude Monet's home.[55] But Cézanne had never before painted anyone with whom his relationship was primarily a professional one; neither had he before painted anyone in a context that would indicate his sitter's 'financial position, class, and profession'. He had also never accepted a commission; and this came perilously close to one.

The Geffroy-Duranty experiment, once tried, was never repeated. The other portraits of names – of the *Aixois* poet and critic Joachim Gasquet (cat. 20.1), of Gasquet's father, Henri, an old friend (fig. 69), of Vollard (cat. 20.2), and of a young Norwegian painter, Alfred Hauge (cat. 20.3) – would be done in the studio, the sitters posed against the 'neutral or vague backgrounds' that Duranty wanted to prohibit.[56] The ways in which the sitters are dressed divide those portraits made in the capital and those made in Provence. However, the dark formality of the Parisian men's jackets and the shapeless, earth-toned no-name Provençal clothes were equally appropriate to the darkness that descended on Cézanne's portraiture in the 1890s. And the occasional brighter and more colourful settings were there for both city and country dwellers.

A problem, though, was that Cézanne admired his working-class sitters not only for what they were, but also for what they were not. As he came to view particularly elderly working people as unselfconsciously heroic figures, people who lived in the old ways, the urban professionals seemed inauthentic, resisting the laws of time. [57] Cézanne, like Jonathan Swift, could admire the individual while disliking the species; otherwise he would not have painted professionals at all. However, perhaps it was because he was less comfortable with them than with his working-class subjects that they gave him problems. Like the Geffroy portrait, those of Gasquet and Vollard were left incomplete, and Cézanne cut the Hauge portrait into pieces with a knife.

WHAT VOLLARD SAID

Cézanne's acts of painting comprise so large a subject that only those most relevant to his portraiture have been mentioned in this account of its development. However, Vollard's famous description, published in 1914, of Cézanne painting his great 1899 portrait allows us to highlight the most important and controversial aspects of his procedures. One of these concerns the time it took him to paint his portraits, Vollard observing that Cézanne required 115 sittings for his, only to remain dissatisfied with it and to abandon it unfinished.[58]

This remark passed quickly into the mythology of modern picture-making, validating the importance of canvases that had taken (or were claimed to have taken) Pablo Picasso and Henri Matisse almost as long to paint.[59] A year after the artist's death, Maurice Denis had written rapturously of Cézanne's 'labour', with St Paul in mind, as evidence of a struggle of flesh and spirit. (A 'Chardin of decadence', he called him.)[60] Cézanne's principal lesson, it seems, was that a worrying, revisionary process could have an intrinsic value. As Picasso said in 1935, it was Cézanne's anxiety that mattered, not what he did.[61] In 1945, the philosopher Maurice Merleau-Ponty felt it was Cézanne's doubt that mattered, opening his now-celebrated essay on this subject with the gratuitous statement that Cézanne required 150 sittings to paint a portrait, and 100 for a still life.[62]

Delacroix, whom Cézanne passionately admired, wrote that 'easy won pleasure ceases to be pleasure, and easy works of art are like easy pleasures; they make little impression on those who look at them and also on those who have made them'.[63] However, even leaving aside as examples of youthful exuberance his small portraits of his Uncle Dominique, each one supposedly painted in a single afternoon, we find not only canvases that Cézanne must have reworked and reworked, but also others that appear to have been made fairly quickly and with which he seems to have been satisfied. But the question remains: why did Cézanne, according to Gasquet, 'sometimes remain still for twenty minutes between two strokes of the brush'?[64]

I think the art historian T.J. Clark's answer is a good one. To simplify what he said, Cézanne was trying to recreate the structure of experience out of the units of that experience. The brush mark seems precisely to match one unit of visual experience, yet it will be – from start to finish – one of many, with none guaranteed to retain that match as they accumulate.[65] The seriality of this approach is, in miniature, equivalent to that of Cézanne's painting-to-painting seriality, sharing its implications of a manipulation of what is experienced by the artist for the artist; and, if the marking is in the form of 'constructive brushstrokes', of manipulation by mechanical means. To complicate things further, the 'non-identity of mark and marked', as Clark puts it, is exacerbated by the mind's dreaming and imagining, even as it is seeking (in Cézanne's celebrated phrase) 'the logic of organised sensations';[66] and even as the eye is looking and the hand is recording, the hand will stray.

This brings us to an aspect of Cézanne's practice as famous as his long, revisionary process: he failed to complete many of his canvases. In another often-repeated remark, Vollard tells of Cézanne warning him that if he arbitrarily filled in the few unfinished patches on the hands, he would have to start all over again.[67] This, however, was in 1899. Only two or three portraits made around 1890 and a half-dozen made after 1895 reveal small unpainted patches, some very minor, of the kind to which Cézanne referred.[68] The unfinish of his canvases is often intrinsically admired, and we rightly cannot help but admire those of Gasquet, Geffroy and Vollard, with their unfinished patches. However, we cannot pretend that Cézanne was satisfied with them.

Neither can we pretend that he was satisfied with canvases entirely without unfinished areas, witness his attempted destruction of his portrait of Alfred Hauge (cat. 20.3). The portrait of Vollard came perilously close to this end, too. Here again, Delacroix's experience aids our understanding:

> At the start of any work, one's imagination catches fire and promises something very different from what it can actually achieve. So that when one has finished one can only cast a regretful glance at the shapeless blend of good and bad, which is called an artist's production.[69]

Delacroix also spoke of how 'putting the finishing touch is a most difficult matter', adding: 'The danger consists in reaching the point where remorse no longer serves any useful purpose, and I am much addicted to remorse.' [70] Cézanne was an addict, too. For Cézanne, the crux of the warning was, better to leave a work without its finishing touches than risk creating something gratuitous, after which remorse becomes useless and the canvas has to be repainted, discarded, or destroyed.

Vollard's third and most celebrated report on sitting for his portrait included the words of the artist when he started fidgeting: 'Do I have to tell you again you must sit like an apple? Does an apple move?' [71] This has two implications: first, that Cézanne required the sitter's continual presence; second, that he required the sitter's immobile presence, as he wanted to paint a portrait much as he would paint an apple, the most central and controversial issue in his portraiture.

To take the first implication, the evidence is contradictory. On the one hand, we have reports like Vollard's of very many sittings; and we have statements by the artist himself such as, 'Two sittings a day with the model are more than enough to wear me out. And that is how it has been for several weeks.' [72] On the other, we have Gasquet saying that he sat for his portrait only five or six times, then adding this remarkable postscript:

> I thought that he had given up the picture. Later, I discovered that he had spent roughly sixty sessions on it … that he worked on it after I had left … During numerous sittings, Cézanne would seem to make but a few brushstrokes, but he was constantly boring into his model with his eyes … I emphasise that, since it has often been claimed that Cézanne was only able to paint directly from the model, and never worked in any other way. He had a memory for colours and lines like almost no one else. [73]

Gasquet is known for embroidering, perhaps inventing, statements by Cézanne, but this is a factual account that deserves careful consideration.[74] As we saw earlier, he appears to have made revised versions of one and possibly two of the portraits of Hortense without her presence. He also worked simultaneously on two portraits of his gardener, Vallier (cats 25.1, 25.2), presumably not always with Vallier there.[75] The visual evidence of certain paintings and watercolours suggests that Cézanne advanced from memory frameworks drawn directly from a motif;[76] and paintings for which there are studies in oil or watercolour may also have been executed partly or entirely without the presence of the model.[77] If Cézanne could paint from a photograph, he could paint from a study that he himself had made – but apparently not from his sketchbook drawings; they were lessons in the reading of the model rather than precursors to a painted realisation.[78]

Another and clear indication that Cézanne did not only paint direct from the model are the signs of revision revealed by the surfaces of the later portraits in particular.[79] The *Old Woman with a Rosary* (cat. 18.1) was clearly revisited a number of times.[80] So were the dark-toned portraits of Vallier (cats 25.1, 25.2), with their deeply encrusted surfaces and – as in other paintings – narrow, drawn lines of paint set down on top of a dried paint surface, their purpose being mainly to revise contours.[81] Moreover, since Cézanne usually built up his surfaces gradually on the basis of a thinly painted foundation, we cannot discount the possibility that, on occasion, time elapsed between the initial laying-in of paint and the more developed surface: many canvases show areas of both.[82]

The fifth of Cézanne's celebrated 'opinions' that Bernard recorded in 1904 reads: 'There are two things in the painter, the eye and the mind [*cerveau*]; the two should aid each other. It is necessary to work at their mutual development; in the eye for the vision of nature, in the mind for the logic of organised sensations, which provide the means of expression.'[83] Mutual does not necessarily, or exclusively, mean simultaneous.[84]

STILL LIFE

To return to the essential, yet most radical, aspect of Cézanne's portraiture, the Parisian critic Charles Morice wrote in 1905: 'Cézanne takes no more interest in a human face than in an apple.'[85] Nine years later, however, Vollard would claim that Cézanne had said to him that, while the subject 'must sit like an apple', nonetheless 'the goal of all art is the human face.'[86]

There are logical and ethical objections to Morice's claim,[87] but neither answers the practicalities. One reason was that Cézanne couldn't concentrate if the sitter moved.[88] Another was that he didn't want the sitter even to think about posing. Baudelaire, one of those who thought photography's influence on painting was pernicious, wrote in his 'Salon de 1859' that photography encouraged people to grimace and play theatrical roles in front of the camera – and, therefore, in front of the painter.[89] However, the photographer A.A.E. Disdéri, and perhaps others, apparently scolded sitters for grimacing, even for smiling, and loudly insisted that they did not move.[90] Cézanne, like such a photographer, demanded stillness and did not want any role-playing from his subjects. And he didn't want people playing themselves, either. Gasquet tells a perhaps apocryphal story of Cézanne abandoning a portrait of the radical statesman Georges Clemenceau because Clemenceau was basically too full of himself.[91] This was why, as Bernard observed in 1904, Cézanne had come to prefer painting 'good, local people' in Aix as opposed to 'dandies and socially polished types whose corrupt taste and worldly insincerity he loathed'.[92] No posing, no acting, no reaching out to the beholder, nothing demonstrative, that was the rule. The single communicative gesture in all of Cézanne's portraits is the limp raised hand of Uncle Dominique playing at being a lawyer (cat. 2.5). And if we were to place a more typical, Cézannean non-pose, say, that of himself in his *Self-Portrait with Palette* (fig. 13), next to the eager-to-please appearance of James Tissot in Degas's portrait (fig. 14), the point is obvious.

Zola said that while Manet was painting his portrait (fig. 12) he 'had forgotten about me, he no longer knew I was there, he copied me as if he were copying any human creature'.[93] It is often said that Zola, in this portrait, is treated no differently from the inanimate objects that surround him; and that Manet – and Cézanne followed his example – did not merely redefine but repudiated the traditional humanistic premises of portraiture in acts of depersonalisation. Rilke, as usual, saw the matter differently, writing in 1907 that 'it is this limitless objectivity, refusing any kind of meddling in an alien unity, that strikes people as so offensive and comical in Cézanne's portraits'.[94] (This is also a warning to us not to meddle in the alien unity of the portraits by pressing upon them our own feelings.)[95]

Expanding on this position, the writer and amateur painter D.H. Lawrence not only defended Cézanne for his 'be an apple' approach, but also realised that 'while he was painting the appleyness, he was also deliberately painting *out* the so-called humanness, the personality, the "likeness", the physical cliché'. By doing so, Cézanne

FIG. 13
Self-Portrait with Palette, 1886–7
(see also cat. 12.2)
Foundation E.G. Bührle Collection,
Zurich; FWN 499

FIG. 14
Edgar Degas, **Portrait of
James Tissot**, 1867–8
Metropolitan Museum of Art,
New York

FIG. 15
Rembrandt van Rijn,
An Elderly Man as St Paul, *c*.1659
National Gallery, London

could 'make the human form, the *life* form, come to rest. Not static – on the contrary. Mobile but come to rest.'[96] This quality of coming to rest, which was there almost from the beginning, was especially conspicuous as his career was coming to an end.

There were no more urban portraits of named people after 1900. During his last six years, Cézanne seems to have been comfortable painting only people he knew, or who had no reason to expect anything from him except a pittance for posing. Stillness had become meditative on earlier occasions, but in the late portraits its enhanced application to working-class subjects is an ennoblement of them. Defenders of the fact that Cézanne simply objectified his sitters claim that he did not depict 'human beings who do normal human things like talk, laugh, or move'.[97] Do we think that these labourers are incapable of such things? Surely not; rather, that they have refrained from such actions out of respect for being painted by a venerable old man who, in turn, respected them. The reciprocity between artist and sitter expressed in these portraits includes that of a shared sense of community; and it is this, expressed in the dignity of these dark canvases, that justifies their comparison to works by Rembrandt (fig. 15).[98]

FIG. 16
The Gardener Vallier, 1902–6
(see also cat. 25.2)
Private collection; FWN 544

Still, we need to resist either sentimentalising these portraits or pathologising them. On occasion, Cézanne would test how far sentiment could be expressed without falling into sentimentality (see *Old Woman with a Rosary*); at other times, he would explore the gestures of an old man, perhaps Vallier's open hands resting upon his knees, and show that they need not be read as a supplication (cats 25.1, 25.2); and, in his self-portraits, although sick and tired, he demonstrated how resilient he remained (cat. 22.1, fig. 76). Much has been made of a premonition of death in Cézanne's late works, and his letters confirm his awareness of his infirmity and mortality.[99] Nonetheless, we do injustice to the continuing, vital invention of these canvases to place them all in a waning light. In fact, in Cézanne's last years, he did not have what is commonly called a 'late style'. He had two.

In portraiture, these are exemplified by the darker- and the lighter-toned sets of paintings of Vallier (cats 25.1, 25.2; 26.1, 26.2). The two sets invoke not only two different people, but also two different conceptions of portraiture. Those that Cézanne painted in the studio may be thought to show a dark harbinger; those painted outside show a figure whose body is infused with the patterns of landscape. The dark style looks to the past, producing portraits as sunless as his youthful palette-knife pictures. The light style looks further back, to Cézanne's earlier, frustrated attempt to paint portraits out of doors in natural light, finally achieving that early aim by keeping these canvases as openly composed and luminous as his recent *plein-air* watercolours. Nothing is gained, though, by slotting these works into the simple, alternative categories popularly understood to be characteristic of late styles: complex and difficult (Beethoven's late string quartets) or harmonic and resolved (Matisse's late cut-outs); an artist who abhorred cliché deserves better than having clichés applied to him. Was he not, recapitulating his beginnings as a portraitist, keeping his options open to the very end?

The critic and essayist Elaine Scarry has written of how, in Jean-François Millet's paintings of farm labourers, 'the labourer's physical presence stops not at what would be conventionally understood as the boundaries of his or her body, but at the boundaries of the canvas'.[100] These paintings illustrate 'the recognition that the land and the tool are a literal prolongation of the working body', something confirmed by phenomenological experience: you can 'feel' the action of the tool you are working with. 'The recognition of this same reach of sentience, and the unity of sentience with the things it reaches,' Scarry suggests, is to be found in Karl Marx's under-standing of the body's presence in both agriculture and a made object. For Marx, writing when Cézanne was beginning painting, 'the activity of "making" comes to be the activity of "animating the external world", either described as a willed projection of aliveness … or as a more passive occurrence arising from sheer proximity to real human tissue.'

Unlike Millet, Cézanne very rarely showed labourers at work, only resting afterwards. His completed paintings record their suspended labour along with his, which (it is implied) at once recapitulates and relieves theirs. The 'mobile but come to rest' quality that D.H. Lawrence noticed in Cézanne's portraits in general is especially present in these late works. The activity of their making may be thought to have animated both them and the external world – and brought both to rest. Clark claims that the late portraits are 'rigid, and ineffectual, against the surrounding pressure of the void'.[101] Yes, they are. But there is also a fiercely willed projection of still-aliveness about them, in their presence and in their analogy of real human tissue, which colours even the darkest and stiffest of them all.

Everything definite, nothing definitive, seems to be the rule. The realisation of the reading of the model is specific; the reading itself is not. It is apt that Cézanne leaves us in Vallier's hands (fig. 16), hands unable or unwilling to grasp either something or nothing at all.

Notes

Abbreviated works are those specific to Cézanne that were consulted in the preparation of this publication. Full details can be found in the Select Bibliography on p.246. For a key to other abbreviations, see Note to the Reader, p.43.

1 'The reading of the model, and its realisation, is sometimes very slow in coming for the artist.' Camoin, a friend of Henri Matisse, was a young artist, who visited and corresponded with Cézanne, receiving pithy advice from the elderly painter.

2 This is far fewer than Cézanne's landscapes (roughly 320), but not many less than his still lifes (almost 190) and more than either his figure compositions (about 130) or his Bathers (80 paintings). See *The Paintings of Paul Cézanne*, online catalogue raisonné (Walter Feilchenfeldt, Jayne S. Warman and David Nash) for precise numbers; http://www.cézannecatalogue.com.

3 Neither proposal was accepted, though. Useful accounts, some brief, of the nineteenth-century status of portraiture, to which I am indebted, appear in Linda Nochlin, 'Impressionist Portraits and the Construction of Modern Identity', in Colin B. Bailey, *Renoir's Portraits. Impressions of an Age* (Yale University Press, New Haven and London, 1997), pp.53–75; Heather McPherson, *The Modern Portrait in Nineteenth-Century France* (Cambridge University Press, New York & Cambridge, 2001), pp.1–13; Tamar Garb, *The Painted Face. Portraits of Women in France, 1814–1914* (Yale University Press, New Haven and London, 2007), pp.1–17; Dombrowski 2013, pp.91–105 and ff.; Jane Block and Ellen Wardwell Lee, *Face to Face: Neo-Impressionist Portraits, 1886–1904*, exh. cat., Indianapolis Museum of Art, Indianapolis, 2014, pp.1–4 (with a good bibliography on p.23, n.2); George T.M. Shackelford and Xavier Rey, *Faces of Impressionism: Portraits from the Musée d'Orsay*, exh. cat., Kimbell Art Museum, Fort Worth, 2014, pp.15–29. However, rather than fill my summary of the situation with footnotes, only quotations and reports of things said will be cited.

4 E.H. Gombrich, 'The Mask and the Face', *The Image and the Eye. Further studies in the psychology of pictorial representation* (Cornell University Press, Ithaca, 1982), p.105. Gombrich is embroidering on John Singer Sargent's reputed statement: 'A portrait is a picture in which there is just a tiny little something not quite right about the mouth.'

5 Anna Gruetzner Robins (ed.), *Walter Sickert. The Complete Writings on Art* (Oxford University Press, Oxford, 2000), p.219.

6 Carol Armstrong, 'Manet at the Intersection of Portraits and Personalities', in *Manet: Portraying Life*, exh.cat., Toledo Museum of Art, Toledo, and Royal Academy of Arts, London, 2012–13, p.42.

7 See Cézanne's letter to Paule Conil, 1 September 1902.

8 MaryAnne Stevens, 'Manet: Portraying Life. Themes and Variations', in Toledo–London 2012–13 (as note 6), p.21.

9 Dombrowski 2013, p.102.

10 Nochlin in Bailey 1997, as note 3, p.55.

11 A portrait of his son and one of his friends could form the basis of a Mardi Gras composition of Harlequin and Pierrot; a farmworker, whose portrait Cézanne had painted, could be asked to pose in a Card Players composition. However, FWN places the double portrait included here (cat. 3.3) in the category of Figure Compositions; and in Portraits some paintings excluded here on principle, for example one of a studio model naked from the waist up (FWN 422): there is bound to be some ambiguity.

12 Camille Pissarro to his son Lucien, 17 February 1884. *Correspondance de Camille Pissarro*, ed. Janine Bailly-Herzberg, vol.1 (Presses universitaires de France, Paris, 1980), p.285 (present author's translation).

13 T.S. Eliot, 'Tradition and the Practice of Poetry' (1936), in James Olney (ed.), *T.S. Eliot. Essays from the Southern Review* (Clarendon Press, Oxford, 1988), p.13.

14 When Bernard visited Cézanne in 1904, the display of works by the artist at that year's Salon d'Automne included not only nine portraits but also photographs of nine others in a single frame (fig. 1). According to Bernard, Cézanne said he wanted to replace the figure of his friend Victor Chocquet in an *Apothéose de Delacroix* he had painted earlier (FWN 687; see p.146) with Bernard's figure and 'even had a photograph made of me in the proper pose, but he died before he could complete the project.' Bernard 1907, p.609, reprinted in Doran 1978, p.129; Doran 2001, p.69.

15 Cézanne to Zola, c.9 October 1866.

16 Most of these works were made in the 1870s and are, like the 1866 painting, small oil sketches. A somewhat larger work (FWN 674, of c.1890) bypasses the figure-ground problem by showing a figure reclining in the grass. In one of the two full-size canvases (FWN 455, *Madame Cézanne in the Garden*, of 1879–80), the canvas was abandoned before the outdoor setting was painted; in the other (FWN 498, *Portrait of Victor Chocquet*, of c.1889), the outdoor setting is no more than a single background screen of foliage. Worth noting here is that Cézanne's early deflection from straight portraiture into another area of Impressionist interest – interior genre scenes with portrait subjects – fared only a little better: of the two most ambitious such works, the so-called *Overture to Tannhäuser* of 1869–70 (fig. 21) caused him enormous difficulty, while *Paul Alexis Reading a Manuscript to Emile Zola* of the same date (cat. 3.3) was abandoned, unfinished. Again, it was much later that Cézanne found his own, individual solutions to this kind of subject: in his Mardi Gras paintings of 1888–90 (FWN 668–71) and his Card Players series of 1890–96 (FWN 680–6).

17 These features associate Cézanne's emulation of photography with that of Manet, on whose relation to photography see Michael Fried, *Manet's Modernism or, The Face of Painting in the 1860s* (University of Chicago Press, Chicago and London, 1996), pp.323–6, and the sources he cites there.

18 The image reproduced here was illustrated in Charles Stuckey, 'The Predications and Implications of Monet's Series', in *The Repeating Image: Multiples in French Painting from David to Matisse*, exh.cat., The Walters Art Museum, Baltimore, 2007, p.117. It originally appeared in the historic 5 September 1886 issue of *Le Journal illustré* honouring the 100th birthday of the great scientist Eugène Chevreul, and bears an interesting comparison to Cézanne's costume studies of Uncle Dominique, painted some two months later. We know that Cézanne did read the Parisian illustrated magazines, and may well have seen this image. Stuckey also illustrates a twelve-photograph grid by Nadar, p.96, with multiple views of the photographer's own head, a project not too dissimilar to that of the small Uncle Dominique heads. This subject awaits study, as does the relationship to Cézanne's practice of the full-plate portrait photographs of the period.

19 Dombrowski 2013, p.4. Andrea Callen, *The Work of Art. Plein-air Painting and Artistic Identity in Nineteenth-century France* (Reaktion Books, London, 2015) is an exemplary study of the methods of the worker-painters, beginning with Courbet, the source of this interpretation of Cézanne.

20 Rewald 1954, p.8; Rewald 1986, pp.85–6.

21 Emile Zola to Cézanne, 16 April 1860.

22 Aix-en-Provence 1984, p.120.

23 Jean-Paul Sartre, *Existential Psychoanalysis* (Philosophical Library, New York, 1953), pp.168–9, 180–3. This associates 1860s Cézanne with 1960s Willem de Kooning: see John Elderfield in *de Kooning: A Retrospective*, exh.cat., Museum of Modern Art, New York, 2011, pp.37–8.

24 Cézanne would have read later (in the original French, of course) Delacroix's comment, commending the visible 'epidermis' in the work of Pierre-Paul Prud'hon, that 'that side of the artist's talent which people call material... is wholly a matter of feeling'. Eugène Delacroix, *The Journal of Eugène Delacroix*, trans. and ed. Walter Pach (Grove, New York, 1961), p.566. Entry for 25 January 1857.

25 Marc Elder, *A Giverny, chez Claude Monet* (Bernheim-Jeune, Paris, 1924), p.48.

26 These comments on Cézanne and ownership are indebted to Adam Phillips's on the 'peasant poet' John Clare: 'John Clare's Exposure', *On Flirtation* (Harvard University Press, Cambridge MA, 1994), p.209.

27 Fortuné Marion to Zola, in Rewald 1936, p.71; reprinted in Callow 1995, p.126.

28 Maurice Denis, *Journal*, vol. 2, 1905–20 (La Colombe, éditions du Vieux Colombier, Paris, 1957), p.46.

29 'Paul Cézanne' in Gustave Geffroy, *La Vie artistique*, vol.3 (E. Dentu, Paris, 1894), p.253; quoted by Richard Shiff in Hamilton–Philadelphia 2014–15, p.193, n.95.

30 Dombrowski 2013, p.103. The question of whether or not a sitter shows awareness of having been painted is integral to Michael Fried's discussions of the relationship between the portrait and the beholder in nineteenth-century French painting. See, for example, Fried 1996 (as note 17), pp.189–91, 266–7. Cézanne's portraits frequently raise questions about the nature of that relationship: I touch only briefly on them in what follows, but interested readers may wish to read Fried's arguments with these works in mind.

31 Charles Baudelaire, *The Painter of Modern Life and Other Essays*, trans. and ed. Jonathan Mayne (Phaidon, London, 1964), p.88.

32 Rilke 2002, p.46.

33 This is Henry James on the painter Alexandre-Gabriel Decamps: *The Painter's Eye,* ed. John L. Sweeney (University of Wisconsin Press, Madison, 1956), p.74; quoted in Bernard Richards, 'Henry James and the Artistic Conscience', *Essays in Criticism*, vol.65, no.2, 2015, pp.187–205. I thank Christopher Ricks for drawing this article to my attention.

34 As long recognised, this painting contains an acknowledgement of Courbet, a caricature of whom is depicted in the background, and Manet, being generally based on Manet's portrait of Zola (fig. 12).

35 Stokes 1947, p.22.

36 Rilke 2002, pp.74–5.

37 Rilke 2002, p.70.

38 FWN is imprecise on the dating of these works, but Jayne Warman, in an email to me, proposed the following plausible dates on the basis of the likely age of Paul *fils* in each case: FWN 456: *c.*1875 (aged three or four); 457: *c.*1878 (aged about six); 458: 1878–80 (aged about six to eight); 459: 1881–2 (aged nine or ten); 460: *c.*1882 (aged ten); 465: 1883–4 (aged eleven to twelve); 469: *c.*1882–3 (aged ten to eleven); 470: 1883–4 (aged eleven to twelve).

39 'The Later Monet', *Art and Culture* (Beacon Press, Boston, 1961), p.43.

40 Paris–London–Philadelphia 1995–6, p.210.

41 The *Boy in a Red Waistcoat* paintings, contemporaneous with the final series of portraits of Hortense, when taken as a group (cats 14.1–14.4, 15.1), comprise something akin to a serial development from the former to the latter.

42 See Stuckey in Baltimore 2007 (as note 18), pp.83–125, which meticulously plots this development, including Claude Monet's first documented display of series art, which took the form of seven *Gare Saint-Lazare* paintings in the third Impressionist exhibition of 1877 (pp.106–8). Cézanne also showed his own works there, was friendly with Monet, and would have seen these canvases.

43 For the seventeenth-century background, see Jennifer Montagu, *The Expression of the Passions. The Origin and Influence of Charles Le Brun's Conférence sur l'expression générale et particulière* (Yale University Press, New Haven and London, 1994).

44 At the Salon d'Automne of 1907, within which Cézanne's famous memorial exhibition was featured, Henri Matisse exhibited a portrait utterly devoid of emotion under that title with a straight face. We must wonder whether, given Matisse's worship of Cézanne, this gesture was intended, or at least read, as a homage to the then-famous lack of expression in Cézanne's portraits. Matisse's painting, in the Barnes Foundation, is now known as *The Red Madras Headdress*, a title that nicely distracts our attention from the subject's face. The following year, Matisse's famous 'Notes d'un Peintre' followed Cézanne in explicitly rejecting expression understood as 'passion bursting from a human face or manifested by violent movement'. See Jack Flam, *Matisse on Art* (University of California Press, Berkeley and Los Angeles, 1995), p.38.

45 A general point made in Michael Podro, *Depiction* (Yale University Press, New Haven and London, 1998), p.91, in a fine discussion of portraiture, pp.87–106. The reciprocal relationship of painter and model in Cézanne's work awaits comparison with that extensively discussed in the work of Manet. See, notably, Fried 1996 (as note 17), pp.336–42; and Carol M. Armstrong, *Manet. Manette* (Yale University Press, New Haven and London, 2002) on the many faces of Manet's model Victorine Meurent.

46 Rilke 2002, pp.58, 74.

47 Cézanne is reported to have said in January 1905, 'If a head interests me, I make it too large.' R.P. Rivière and J.F. Schnerb, 'L'atelier de Cézanne', *La Grande revue*, 25 December 1907; reprinted in Doran 1978, French edition, p.155; 2001, English edition, p.86. A later, notably large head, also an elongated oval, is that of Vollard (cat. 20.2).

48 Maurice Denis, *Théorie: 1890–1910. Du symbolisme et de Gauguin vers un nouvel ordre classique* [1912] (Rouart et Watelin, Paris, 1920), pp.245–61; reprinted in Doran 1978, p.284; Doran 2001, p.172.

49 Lewis 2000, p.269.

50 See Cézanne to Joachim Gasquet, 30 April 1896.

51 Fry 1927, pp.69–70.

52 Michael Fried discussed drawings of bookcases by Edgar Degas and Adolph Menzel in the context of seeing and knowing, with reference to a text by John Ruskin: Michael Fried, *Menzel's Realism. Art and Embodiment in Nineteenth-Century Berlin* (Yale University Press, New Haven and London, 2002), pp.1–4. Cézanne's painting of Geffroy's bookcase with its slanted books is subsumable within neither category alone: it may be thought to impose the clarity afforded by knowledge; to respect the indistinctness of detail in seeing; to mobilise the pictorial field in the shifts in direction of the books from shelf to shelf; and to represent Geffroy's use of them, as does the drawing of Menzel, in Fried's view.

53 Louis-Edmond Duranty, *La Nouvelle peinture* (E. Dentu, Paris, 1876), pp.24, 26–7.

54 Lewis 2000, pp.276–7.

55 See Doran 2001, pp.3–6.

56 Duranty 1876 (as note 53), p.38.

57 'I love above all things the aspect of people who've grown old without changing their ways, abandoning themselves to the laws of time. I hate the efforts of those who resist these laws.' Jules Borély, 'Cézanne à Aix', *L'Art vivant*, 1 July 1926, p.493, reprinted in Doran 1978, p.52; Doran 2001, p.23.

58 Vollard 1914, p.105; Vollard 1937, p.86.

59 These were the former's 1905–6 *Portrait of Gertrude Stein* (more than 90 sittings) and the latter's 1913 *Portrait of Madame Matisse* (over 100). Although Vollard's reminiscences of Cézanne were not published until 1914, both Matisse and Picasso knew him, and it is very likely that he shared the best stories with them.

60 Denis 1920, as note 48, pp.245–61, reprinted in Doran 1978, pp.286, 294; Doran 2001, pp.173, 179.

61 Picasso in Richard Friedenthal, *Letters of the Great Artists, from Blake to Pollock*, 2 vols (Random House, New York, 1963), p.259.

62 Maurice Merleau-Ponty, 'Cézanne's Doubt', *Sense and Non-Sense* (Northwestern University Press, Evanston, 1964), pp.9–25. Originally published as 'Le Doute de Cézanne,' *Fontaine*, no.47, December 1945.

63 Delacroix to Frédéric Villot, 15 September 1838. *Eugène Delacroix: Selected Letters 1813–1863*, ed. Jean Stewart (Eyre & Spottiswoode, London, 1971). For this and the reference to Delacroix cited in notes 69 and 70, I am indebted to Richards's article, see note 33.

64 Gasquet 1921, p.57; Gasquet 1991, p.114.

65 T.J. Clark, 'Phenomenality and Materiality in Cézanne', in Tom Cohen, Barbara Cohen et al., *Material Events. Paul de Man and the Afterlife of Theory* (University of Minnesota Press, Minneapolis and London, 2001), pp.106–10. This is a crude paraphrase

of a lengthy, rich argument within a study with also other concerns.

66 'Fifth Opinion to Bernard'. Bernard 1904, pp.17–30; reprinted in Doran 1978, p.76 and Doran 2001, p.38.

67 Vollard 1914, pp.95–6; Vollard 1937, p.79.

68 Vienna–Zurich 2000 is the fullest consideration of its subject, too large to discuss in depth here. However, three points deserve noting. First, as opposed to Cézanne's portraits, larger areas of exposed canvas, and fewer small empty patches, are to be found in his still lifes, and especially his landscapes, from around 1890 onwards. Second, Cézanne may be referring to the two different kinds of unfinish when, writing to Bernard on 23 October 1905, he refers to how 'the colouring sensations [*sensations colorantes*] that create light are the abstractions that do not allow me to cover my canvas, nor to pursue the delimitation of objects when their points of contact are subtle, delicate; the result of which is that my image or painting is incomplete.' Third, in this same letter, he attributes the problem to his old age; there are other reports of his having problems with his eyes.

69 Delacroix to Théophile Thoré, 2 March 1837. See *Eugène Delacroix* 1971 (as note 63), and for the following quotation.

70 To Constant Dutilleux, 2 April 1859.

71 Vollard 1914, p.92; Vollard 1937, p.77.

72 Cézanne to Emile Solari, dated 25 February, Paris, and thought by Rewald and others to have been written in 1899.

73 Gasquet 1921, pp.56–7; Gasquet 1991, pp.113–14.

74 True, Emile Bernard observed that 'Cézanne's imagination was not great, but he had a very refined sense of composition. He did not know how to draw without a model – a serious obstacle to credible creation.' Bernard 1907; reprinted in Doran 1978, p.129; Doran 2001, p.69. However, this does not disqualify the possibility that Cézanne advanced a drawn framework from memory. But, complicating the question of Gasquet's veracity, he writes also of Cézanne proceeding in a similar way in the painting of his father, which he appears to have witnessed, and that of Vollard, which it is extremely unlikely he did. See Gasquet 1921, p.57; Gasquet 1991, pp.113–14.

75 Vollard reported that Cézanne dressed himself in Vallier's clothes. See Gasquet 1921, p.67; Gasquet 1991, p.132. But he may have been embroidering on Cézanne having taken away the clothes that he himself posed in, so that he might continue working on his portrait. The discovery of a wooden head in the Lauves studio (illustrated in London–New York 2010–11, p.39) may mean that Cézanne set up mannequins from which to paint.

76 This topic awaits fuller discussion. I have studied the Pearlman watercolours at the Princeton University Art Museum: some (notably RW 634) do allow that interpretation.

77 For example, FWN 482, for which there is an oil study, FWN 481; the head of FWN 514, for which there is an oil study, FWN 513; FWN 547, for which there is a related watercolour, RW 638; and FWN 548, for which there are two related watercolours, RW 639, 640.

78 There are very few drawings that unquestionably can be related to painted portraits, and it is uncertain whether these few unquestionably are studies for their related portraits.

79 This is on record for other studio compositions: visitors in January 1905 reported Cézanne as having said that he had been working on a large Bathers composition since 1894; an earlier visitor that he said he had been painting a still life full-time for a month. Rivière and Schnerb 1907, pp.811–17; Bernard 1907, reprinted in Doran 1978, pp.109, 162; Doran 2001, pp.58, 90. Yet another spoke of a typical Cézanne painting, 'most often unfinished, scraped with a knife, overlaid with turpentine-thinned pentimenti, repainted several times, encrusted to a state of relief'. Denis 1920 (as note 48); Doran 1978, pp.285–6; Doran 2001, p.173.

80 See Reissner 2008, pp.14–23, in an indispensable conservator's study.

81 Ibid., pp.17–18.

82 Here, we must remember that, since Cézanne hardly exhibited or sold canvases in the almost twenty years between his showing at the third Impressionist exhibition in 1877 and his first solo exhibition at Vollard's gallery in 1895, he would have had a lot of paintings in his possession tempting revision until Vollard bought the contents of his studio in 1899.

83 Doran 1978, p.76; Doran 2001, p.38.

84 However, Denis – relating the two ways of seeing to Poussin's *Aspect* (receiving light rays in the eye) and *Prospect* (applying reason and judgement to them) – says that in Cézanne 'the two operations … are no longer separate'. Denis 1910, p.280.

85 Charles Morice, 'Le XXe Salon des Indépendants', *Mercure de France*, 15 April 1905, p.522.

86 Vollard 1914, p.101; Vollard 1923, English edition, p.133. This is the common English translation, but the French is ambiguous. Vollard writes: 'L'aboutissement de l'art, disait-il, c'est la figure.'

87 First, logically the contrary is therefore true. Second, as Richard Shiff points out, it is demeaning for an interpreter as well as disparaging of the artist to suggest that Cézanne was treating a person like a piece of fruit. R. Shiff, 'Ingemination', in *Theorizing Imitation of the Visual Arts: Global Contexts* (Wiley, Chichester, 2015).

88 'The minute [Vollard] moves, Cézanne complains that he makes him lose his *line of concentration*.' Maurice Denis, *Journal*, vol.1 [1884–1904] (La Colombe, éditions du Vieux Colombier, Paris, 1957), p.157.

89 Armstrong in Toledo–London 2012–13 (as note 6), p.45.

90 Zacharie Astruc, 'Spectres solaires, II. Disdéri', *Le Salon*, no.4, 5 May 1863, quoted in Fried 1996, as note 17, p.585, n.171; the relationship of painting and photography in the 1860s is addressed on pp.323–6 and 584–5, n.170–2.

91 Gasquet 1921, pp.117–18; Gasquet 1991, p.212.

92 See Paris–London–Philadelphia 1995–6, p.38; also Gasquet on Cézanne and his relationship with Aix, Gasquet 1921, pp.72–3; Gasquet 1991, p.141.

93 Zola, 'Mon Salon' [1866], p.199, quoted in Dombrowski 2013, p.122, in a discussion of Manet's painting and its relationship to the genre of still life, pp.117–28.

94 Rilke 2002, pp.58–9.

95 A startling instance of the extent to which their objectivity can actually encourage such meddling is the painter Elizabeth Murray's response to the final red dress portrait of Hortense (cat. 14.4): 'Hortense is regarding her husband, not with disdain, but as if she's saying, "You old fool." And all this emotion, this angst, this frustration is in the picture.' Quoted in Danchev 2012, p.175.

96 D.H. Lawrence, 'Introduction to these Paintings', *The Paintings of D.H. Lawrence* (Mandrake Press, London, 1929), excerpted in Wechsler 1975, pp.91–2. Lawrence's highly perceptive (and eccentric) essay, pinpointing the come-to-rest quality of Cézanne's portrait subjects, aids an understanding of their difference from the static, 'frozen or immobilized' appearance of Manet's models (Fried 1996, as note 17, p.340).

97 Julian Barnes recently argued that they don't when Cézanne is painting them, in a review of Danchev 2012: *The Times Literary Supplement*, 21 and 28 December 2012, p.4.

98 Comparisons made between the work of the two artists is the subject of Richard Verdi, 'Rembrandt and Cézanne', *Burlington Magazine*, CLVII, September 2015, pp.610–14. See also Alison McQueen, *The Rise of the Cult of Rembrandt. Reinventing an Old Master in Nineteenth-Century France* (Amsterdam University Press, Amsterdam, 2003).

99 Most recently and eloquently in Clark 2001, as note 65, pp.110–12.

100 Elaine Scarry, *The Body in Pain. The Making and Unmaking of the World* (Oxford University Press, Oxford and New York, 1985), p.248; and pp.246–8 for the argument surrounding this illustration of it.

101 Clark 2001, as note 65, p.111.

Cézanne Portraits

Note to the Reader

Illustrated works are by Paul Cézanne unless otherwise specified.

The plates record the exhibition, *Cézanne Portraits*. Not all works are shown in all exhibition venues; in these instances, the captions are accompanied by the following abbreviations:

P   Paris, Musée d'Orsay
L   London, National Portrait Gallery
W   Washington, D.C., National Gallery of Art

(Works without any such indication appear in all three venues.)

Titles of works by Cézanne are given in English translation, wherever possible following those in the online catalogue raisonné of Cézanne's paintings, FWN (see top right). Since similar and sometimes identical titles are commonly used for paintings of the same portrait subject, such works are identified in the catalogue entries by the city in which the collection in question is located. This information will also be found in the captions of the works illustrated.

Dates of execution derive mainly from FWN, any newly proposed dates being explained in the relevant catalogue entries. [Where two dates appear, separated by a dash (–), the work in question is thought to have been created at some point within the span of the years given. The abbreviation 'c.' (for 'circa') preceding a year, or years, indicates uncertainty: while there is evidence to give a work's creation this date, it is inconclusive.]

Details of the medium and dimensions of works will be found in the List of Works on pp.249–52.

The standard catalogues of Cézanne's works are referred to as follows:

A   Wayne Andersen, *Cézanne's Portrait Drawings* (MIT Press, Cambridge MA, 1970)
C   Adrien Chappuis, *The Drawings of Paul Cézanne: A Catalogue Raisonné*, 2 vols (New York Graphic Society, Greenwich CT, 1973)

FWN   Walter Feilchenfeldt, Jayne S. Warman and David Nash, *The Paintings of Paul Cézanne: An Online Catalogue Raisonné*; www.cezannecatalogue. com/catalogue/index.php
R   John Rewald, with Walter Feilchenfeldt and Jayne S. Warman, *The Paintings of Paul Cézanne: A Catalogue Raisonné*, 2 vols (Harry N. Abrams, New York, 1996)
RW   John Rewald, *Paul Cézanne: The Watercolours, A Catalogue Raisonné* (Little, Brown, Boston, and Thames & Hudson, London, 1983)
V   Lionello Venturi, *Cézanne: Son Art, Son Oeuvre*, 2 vols (Editions Paul Rosenberg, Paris, 1936)

Cézanne's letters are cited by date and recipient. The reader may consult the original French in John Rewald (ed.), *Cézanne: Correspondance* (Grasset, Paris, 1978). The most recent English translations are published in Alex Danchev, *The Letters of Paul Cézanne* (Thames & Hudson, London, 2013); in the present volume they are at times freely adapted.

References to publications on Cézanne and his work are cited by author and date of publication. Early references collected in Michael Doran, *Conversations avec Cézanne* (Macula, Paris, 1978) are additionally cited to its English translation, *Conversations with Cézanne* (University of California Press, Berkeley, 2001). Again, some of these translations have been freely adapted, as have others not in Doran for which there are English translations. References to exhibitions of Cézanne's work are cited by location and date of exhibition. All references given in abbreviated form will be found in full in the Select Bibliography, pp.246–7.

Contributors to the entries are indicated by the following initials:

JE   John Elderfield
MM   Mary Morton
XR   Xavier Rey

1 Defiant Beginnings

1862–72

Paul Cézanne, photographer unknown, 1861

PAUL CÉZANNE, born in Aix-en-Provence in 1839, made his first portrait in the early 1860s: a dark self-portrait of a brooding, discontented young man in his early-to-mid twenties. He was also painting fanciful allegories, an occasional still life and a lot of landscapes, having convinced himself that canvases painted outside were bound to be better than those made in the studio. Then, quite suddenly in 1866, portrait painting grasped his attention, and it was largely through working on portraits, more than anything else, that he found his own artistic voice.

From the beginning, this meant painting for his own satisfaction people in whose presence he felt comfortable. His early such works were influenced in style by the Parisian portraits of Gustave Courbet and Edouard Manet, but Cézanne's subjects were exclusively local, which meant family and friends. The family paintings included large, commanding portraits of his father, smaller ones of his mother and sisters, and nine or ten portraits of his uncle, the bailiff Dominique Aubert, painted entirely with a palette knife in a magnificently crude technique that he later described as a *manière couillarde* (from *couilles*, testicles). Uncompromisingly provocative paintings of his friends the poet and art critic Antony Valabrègue and the artist Achille Emperaire were rejected by the official Paris Salon; unsurprisingly so, as they were meant deliberately to challenge the debased genre of Salon portraiture.

These works cemented a perception of Cézanne among colleagues in both Paris and Aix – he spent more or less alternate years in the two cities – as someone as combative in his art as in his deliberately provincial personal behaviour. By the end of the 1860s, though, the point had been made, and his portraits became at once more refined and more sympathetic, notably in a second painting of Valabrègue. Cézanne's life was then disrupted by the outbreak of the 1870–1 Franco-Prussian War. In order to avoid conscription, he left Paris and he did not return until the libertarian Commune that succeeded it was crushed. Before he went into hiding, though, he was making more landscapes and still lifes, and would soon begin a new kind of imaginative painting with violent and erotic subjects. As these absorbed his attention, his interest in portraiture waned. JE

CAT. 1.1
Self-Portrait, *c.*1862–4
Private collection, New York; FWN 390

First Portraits

Cézanne's first portrait is thought to have been a self-portrait painted from a photograph apparently taken in 1861, when he was twenty-two years of age (cat 1.1 and p.44). But this cannot be verified,[1] and the chronology of his early portraits is likely to remain uncertain. Prior to his portraits of 1866, documented by Cézanne and his friends and discussed in the following catalogue entries, the single portrait that can be firmly dated is one of his closest childhood friends, Emile Zola, begun in Paris in June 1861, which some two months later the artist said that he had destroyed.[2] Complicating matters is the fact that the dense, curving and snaking brushstrokes of some of the eight portraits traditionally ascribed to the years 1861–5, which distinguishes them from the palette-knife portraits that followed in 1866, also appear in paintings known to have been made

after 1866.[3] Hence, an early portrait such as *Head of an Old Man* (fig. 17), composed of curling pieces of pigment, could have been made either before or after the palette-knife paintings.[4]

Unsurprisingly, Cézanne's return to the brush in 1867 initially reflected his earlier brush handling, but then grew in sophistication – and depictive assuredness – throughout the remainder of the 1860s. By contrast, the group of pre-1866 paintings has the unconnected, experimental quality of a young man still learning to acquire a habit of working.

One thing that Cézanne did not have to learn, however, was psychological intensity. Most evident in his contemporaneous figure compositions, it nonetheless runs through his early portraits in a more subdued form in two parallel, and sometimes merging, currents

FIG. 17
Head of an Old Man, *c.*1865
Musée d'Orsay, Paris; FWN 414

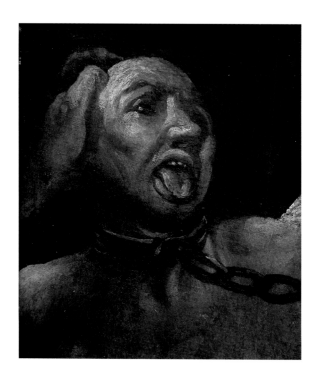

FIG. 18
Chained Woman, 1862–4
Private collection, Aix-en-Provence; FWN 576-TA

of disturbed and disturbing emotion: one, melancholic and tending to the sentimental; the other, excessive and verging on the wild. The former, exemplified in Cézanne's portraiture by dramatically lit faces emerging from shadowy backgrounds, reflects the popularity in the artist's native Provence of Baroque painting, influenced by Caravaggio.[5] The latter appears as an actual quality of excess, of superfluity, in the movement of painterly description, as seen in works such as *Head of an Old Man*. This portrait, painted over but not quite obscuring a scene showing a procession of hooded worshippers, is a literal reminder of the artist's dark imaginative side, which lay beneath his early portrait practice.[6] Cézanne verges towards the grotesque in his imagined compositions, the closest to portraiture being the both fearful and ludicrous *Chained Woman* of 1862–4 (fig. 18).

His first self-portrait, a wild face that looms out of blackness, melds something of these two currents. The intensity of his gaze, and the pallid, almost morbid flesh with its blood-red accents, have been spoken of as, alternatively, reflecting crisis in Cézanne's life and evoking his emergence from the shadows of provincial anonymity onto the stage of the Parisian art world.[7] From the start, then, the expression conveyed by the face of the subject in Cézanne's portraits is open to different readings. In this case, a photographic source provided the gaze, although not its dour interpretation. He would continue to work from photographs from time to time; and always, a studio visitor reported close to the end of his career, 'in his case, it was necessary

to interpret this exact reproduction just as he would interpret nature itself.'[8]

This self-portrait adumbrates what will be the technique of most of Cézanne's early paintings before he took up the palette knife: simple modelling with brushstrokes that run horizontally across the brow, down the nose, and arch beneath the eyes. One notable exception is his profile portrait of his father of *c*.1865, where the face closely approaches the grotesque in its aggregate of individual, bulgingly modelled parts (fig. 19). However, this may have been the result of the fresco technique with which it was painted – it was made on a plaster wall in the salon of the Jas de Bouffan, the family home – that required each part to be set down separately. As such, it anticipates – perhaps prompted – the creation of portraits from separate strips of paint, and hence influenced Cézanne's adoption of the palette-knife technique, which also required the application of distinct patches of pigment.

Difficult to place is Cézanne's portrait of his child-hood friend Antoine-Fortuné Marion (cat. 1.2). Early scholars have dated it variously to the years from 1865 to 1868; more recent ones to 1870–1.[9] Here, we almost certainly see Cézanne at work after the palette-knife paintings, using strips and commas of juicy pigment to create black, ochre and dark blue zones set against a streaky white ground. In the autumn of 1866 he had depicted Marion, together with another friend from his youth, the poet Antony Valabrègue, setting out to paint a landscape (fig. 100); both were amateur artists. Marion would become a distinguished natural scientist, correspondent of Charles Darwin, and instructor in geology to Cézanne.[10] It may be pressing a point, though, to claim that the oblique, downward-looking pose that Cézanne gave him is a nod towards 'the scientist's materialist worldview and his fascination with things "below"'.[11] Cézanne had made other paintings with odd diagonal poses in 1867–8[12] and this painting may have been painted in that same period; we know that Marion and Cézanne saw each other frequently in the summer of 1867.[13] However, it may also be a later work; it does bear comparison in its handling and in the pose of the head with Cézanne's second portrait of Valabrègue (cat. 3.2) of 1869–70, also an extremely sympathetic portrait imbued with a quality of Romantic melancholy.

A more complex question of chronology is raised in the relationship between Cézanne's portrait of his sister Marie, and of his mother on the reverse side of the same canvas (cat. 1.3). The former is a palette-knife painting; therefore, painted in 1866 or possibly the following year. The latter is commonly dated to around 1870, but that is not certain: it does not yet have the assurance of the second portrait of Valabrègue.

However, there is convincing evidence that it was painted after the portrait of Cézanne's sister. The art historian Lawrence Gowing observed that the apparently random linear strips of colour, applied with a brush across the background and over the shoulder of Marie Cézanne, are the same as those in *The Artist's Mother* on the reverse. This suggests, he argued, that Cézanne swiped his brush over an abandoned, already dry canvas – partly in correction, partly in deletion – before rejecting the portrait of Marie in order to work on the reverse side in a later, more fluidly painted style.[14] The two sides of this canvas thereby document the change in Cézanne's portraiture from the palette-knife style of 1866–7 to the return to painting with the brush in 1867.

Additionally, the relationship of recto and verso has a final twist: *The Artist's Mother* was, like *Marie Cézanne, the Artist's Sister*, also abandoned unfinished; the final part of the work, his mother's white headscarf – a plain, peasant-like *fichu*[15] – was obviously added after the rest of the paint was dry. The headscarf is like the one worn by his sister, suggesting that Cézanne may have copied it from there.

FIG. 19
The Artist's Father, *c.*1865
National Gallery, London; FWN 398

CAT. 1.2
Antoine-Fortuné Marion, 1870–1
Kunstmuseum, Basel; FWN 424

But the scarf may have had another source. While the portrait of his mother uncannily evokes a much later painting, a figure from Vincent van Gogh's *The Potato Eaters* of 1885, his silvery portrait of his sister has something of the quality of an El Greco. Cézanne would later copy an El Greco portrait, *Lady in a Fur Wrap,* from an illustration published in 1860 (fig. 20), and his son identified that copy as being a likeness of his aunt, Marie.[16] We have to wonder whether, while painting his sister in 1886–7, Cézanne may have thought she resembled the elegant lady in the 1860 El Greco illustration, even as he painted her in the plainest of clothes.[17]

These two back-to-back portraits of mother and daughter probably accompanied the first (1866) and second (1867) versions of Cézanne's so-called *Overture to Tannhäuser*, completed in 1869–70 (fig. 21), whose young pianist and older seamstress have been said to represent them.[18] Whether or not that is the case, the figure composition was, along with *Paul Alexis Reading a Manuscript to Emile Zola* (cat. 3.3), the artist's first serious attempt to do what other Impressionists were doing, that is, blend portraiture and genre painting; not very successfully in Cézanne's case, until he painted his pictures of Card Players in the early 1890s.[19] JE

DEFIANT BEGINNINGS, 1862–72

FIG. 20
J.-B. Laurens, after an engraving of
El Greco, **Lady in a Fur Wrap**,
Le Magazin pittoresque, vol. 28, 1860

FIG. 21
Girl at the Piano, Overture to Tannhäuser, 1869–70
State Hermitage Museum, St Petersburg; FWN 600

1 See FWN 390, and the Chronology in this volume, where the self-portrait is dated 1862–4, along with three other works.

2 Emile Zola to Baptistin Baille, 10 June 1861; August 1861, reporting that Cézanne has told him he had destroyed the portrait. See Danchev 2013, pp.109, 110. However, Lawrence Gowing has suggested that Cézanne re-engaged that work in the summer of 1861, to produce 'an inconclusive, but forceful portrait of Zola' (London–Paris–Washington, D.C. 1988–9, p.7), a generous description of a work that he identifies with FWN 394 (where it is dated to 1862–4).

3 Gowing; ibid, p.80.

4 This painting has been said to be a portrait of Père Rouvel, the father of Madame Dumond, who was Cézanne's hostess at Bennecourt, where he spent the summer of 1866 (Rodolphe Walter, 'Cézanne à Bennecourt en 1866', *Gazette des Beaux-Arts*, February 1962 (new series), 6, 59, pp.103–18). This is disputed by Gowing; ibid, pp.9, 80, and Rewald, see R 97.

5 Lewis 1989, pp.11–22. Since vestiges of this approach persist in Cézanne's post-1866 portraits, the dating of such works is sometimes unclear. Notably, FWN 391 and 392 have both been dated to 1862–4. However, the rudimentary dense treatment of the former cannot be contemporaneous with the assured naturalism of the latter. Either Cézanne achieved a level of sophistication that he set aside on the path to more expressive painting, or, more likely, the latter belongs among his post-1866 canvases, dating possibly to as late as after 1870.

6 See Gowing in London–Paris–Washington D.C. 1988–9, pp.9, 80.

7 Ibid., p.72; Platzman 2011, p.29, in an extended study of the painting, including its indebtedness to photography. Cézanne's only other self-portrait known to have been made from a photograph is equally strange, but distanced rather than projective: see cat. 10.1.

8 Bernard 1907, p.609, reprinted in Doran 1978, p.129; Doran 2001, p.69.

9 FWN 424 gives three earlier and three later dates that have been proposed.

10 For Marion, see especially Dombrowski 2013, pp.46–52.

11 Ibid, p.46.

12 See FWN 416, 420.

13 See R 177. However, Rewald prefers a date of around 1871 for the painting.

14 Gowing in London–Paris–Washington, D.C. 1988–9, p.116; see also the discussion of this canvas in R 118. Both authors point out that in 1923, Georges Rivière, in the first serious art historical study of Cézanne's paintings, mentions a portrait of Cézanne's mother with a portrait of his sister on the reverse. However, it was for the portrait of his sister that the painting was acquired by the Saint Louis Art Museum; in fact, the portrait of his mother had by then been covered with a coat of black paint, which was removed in the 1960s.

15 Athanassoglou-Kallmyer 2003, p.40.

16 An association discovered by John Rewald in 1936: see R 568.

17 Cézanne's life-long, profound dialogue with the art of the past is the subject of Judit Geskó (ed.), *Cézanne and the Past. Tradition and Creativity* (Museum of Fine Arts, Budapest, 2012), where the association of the engraving and the painted copy (but without reference to the present work) is discussed in Anna Zsófia Kovácas, 'Cézanne's Use of Reproductive Prints', pp.136–8. I agree with Mary Tompkins Lewis, who, in an email dated 1 February 2017, points out it is significant that it was the engraving after El Greco – much rougher than the painting and therefore more compatible with his own early portraits – that sparked his imagination, already affecting his notion of what portraiture might be. Kovácas, p.139, says much the same of his general use of poor quality reproductions.

18 The development of the three versions is discussed by Rewald (R 149), who is not convinced by the identification. Extended discussions of the painting appear in Athanassoglou-Kallmyer 2003, pp.35–42, where the author asserts (p.36) that the two women are Cézanne's mother and his sister Marie; and in Dombrowski 2013, pp.138–74, where the author states (p.154) that they are 'either a mother-daughter configuration or a young woman with her governess'. Neither Henri Loyrette in Paris–London–Philadelphia 1995–6 (pp.110–12), nor Mary Tompkins Lewis in Lewis 1989 (pp.139–45) offer any identification.

19 See Introduction, pp.13, 15, for this and for Cézanne's parallel attempt to make portraits out of doors, as other Impressionists did.

CAT. 1.3 (recto)
Marie Cézanne, the Artist's Sister, 1866–7
Saint Louis Art Museum, Missouri; FWN 418

The Artist's Mother, 1867
Saint Louis Art Museum, Missouri; FWN 426

Portraits of Uncle Dominique

The 27-year-old Cézanne was living at the Jas de Bouffan, his father's estate near Aix-en-Provence, from mid-August 1866 to some time in February 1867. But there would soon be conflict. 'I'm here in the bosom of my family,' he wrote to his friend the painter Camille Pissarro, 'with the foulest people on earth who make up my family, excruciatingly annoying.'[1] So for subject matter he turned instead to his maternal uncle, the bailiff Dominique Aubert, of whom he made a set of arguably ten portraits.[2] This comprised two groups of canvases: six small portrait heads, three posed so similarly as to form a small series (cat. 2.3, cat. 2.4, fig. 23) and three facing in different directions (cat. 2.1, cat. 2.2, fig. 22); and four larger, half-length figures in varying costumes (cat. 2.5, cat. 2.6, fig. 24, fig. 25).[3] In November, the poet and art critic Antony Valabrègue, who saw Cézanne often at that time, wrote of this development to the budding writer Emile Zola, a childhood friend of Cézanne's: 'Fortunately, I only posed for one day. The uncle is more often the model. Every afternoon, there appears a portrait of him, which Guillemet belabours with terrible jokes.'[4] (Antoine Guillemet, a landscape painter from the Académie Suisse in Paris, had arrived in Aix in mid-October.)[5]

One painting a half-day speaks of an extraordinary energy and assurance, qualities that every one of these paintings conveys. However, Valabrègue's letter may well have been written while the smaller works were in progress, for it is hard to believe that each of the large canvases was painted in a single afternoon. And the fact that one of the small portraits was painted over another picture suggests that Cézanne was impatiently moving from one such work to the next, undeterred by having run out of canvas.[6] If this is so, it would confirm the otherwise undocumented consensus that the larger works were painted last; that is to say, after Valabrègue had written to Zola.[7]

In any event, common to both smaller and larger works is their palette-knife technique, aggressive to the point of truculence. Cézanne himself acknowledged the technique to be crude,[8] and the strong element of provocation in this 'ballsy' style was alone sufficient to have created the mischievous pleasure enjoyed by the artist and his friends.

The technique was indebted to Gustave Courbet, whose work Cézanne had known for some five years, and whose publicly nonconformist behaviour he emulated. However, Courbet's use of the palette knife was not for the painting of portraits; in fact he did not use it to structure the entirety of any painting. By contrast, Cézanne's great insight was, as the artist and curator Lawrence Gowing observed, 'to realise the necessity for the manner in which paint is handled to build up a homogeneous and consistent pictorial structure'.[9] That impulse lay 'underneath the rudeness of Cézanne's way with paint in 1866'.[10]

Recognition of the forcefulness and expressiveness of these paintings has sometimes led to the misunderstanding that they are works of a 'vehemence, even ferocity' rare in Cézanne's art.[11] However, heavy, wet patches of paint simply cannot be applied by knife to a picture surface in a violent or vehement manner without breaking the skin of previously applied patches.[12] What we see in these paintings has been built up step by step from flat, rarely blended slabs of pigment, laid onto a brown-grey ground,[13] with the deliberation of plastering a wall. 'A mason's painting' is how Valabrègue described the artist's method.[14]

The smaller paintings show this most powerfully for the simple reason that, compared to the larger ones, the size of the patches of paint are here proportionally bigger in relation to the size of the canvas. They bulge with a monumentality that is commensurate with their materiality. As Gowing observed of them, it was in these works that 'the massiveness and consistency of the palette-knife style were evolved. Body and background, light and dark alike are all trowelled out of the same substance.'[15]

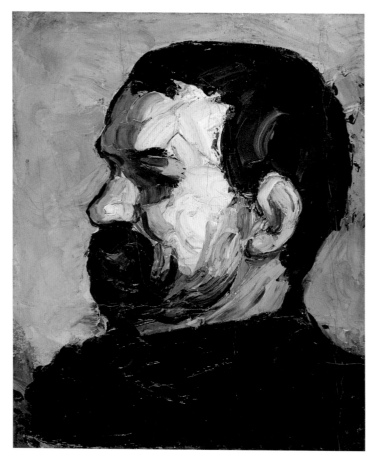

CAT. 2.1
Uncle Dominique in Profile, 1866–7
Fitzwilliam Museum, Cambridge; FWN 404

CAT. 2.2
Uncle Dominique, 1866–7 (W only)
Private collection, Boston; FWN 405

FIG. 22
Uncle Dominique in a Cap, 1866–7
Private collection; FWN 406

CAT. 2.3
Uncle Dominique in a Turban, 1866–7
Private collection; FWN 407

CAT. 2.4
Uncle Dominique, 1866–7
Private collection; FWN 409

FIG. 23
Uncle Dominique, 1866–7
Norton Simon Art Foundation, Pasadena; FWN 408

CAT. 2.1
Uncle Dominique in Profile, 1866–7
Fitzwilliam Museum, Cambridge; FWN 404

CAT. 2.2
Uncle Dominique, 1866–7 (w only)
Private collection, Boston; FWN 405

CAT. 2.3
Uncle Dominique in a Turban, 1866–7
Private collection; FWN 407

CAT. 2.4
Uncle Dominique, 1866–7
Private collection; FWN 409

FIG. 24
Uncle Dominique as a Monk, 1866–7
Metropolitan Museum of Art,
New York; FWN 411

Probably also in 1866, Cézanne painted a small, truly ferocious-looking self-portrait in the same manner, [16] inviting the interpretation that the small Uncle Dominique paintings, or at least this manner of working, carried a note of self-identification. The larger paintings did so in a different way: through Cézanne's choice of costume that his uncle wears. One shows him dressed as a lawyer (cat. 2.5), the profession intended for Cézanne that he had renounced; specifically, as a Daumier-like lawyer pleading a case, although inaccurately dressed in a toque and a collar of the same blue-grey colour.[17] Another, showing his uncle as an artisan, with a worker's smock over his bailiff's suit, may be thought to represent the artist Cézanne had become (cat. 2.6): just a few years earlier, Zola had urged Cézanne to adopt a more workmanlike approach.[18] In a third canvas, he successfully hides the suit underneath a monk's white habit (fig. 24), often said to comprise a visual pun, Uncle Dominique transformed into a Dominican.[19] However, others have argued that this, too, should be thought of as a personification of the artist as a celibate monk; in art historian Meyer Schapiro's words, 'a strong, fleshy person who strives to contain his passions ... [in] a kind of resignation, a death of the self'.[20] Ironically, the only one of these larger works in which Uncle Dominique wears what may be assumed to be bailiff's clothes is that thought by some to be a portrait of an unknown figure (fig. 25).[21]

Such fantasy costume pieces had long been a feature of historicist paintings and Cézanne later did make his own versions of such works.[22] They also, art historian Nina Athanassoglou-Kallmyer has convincingly argued, belong to the deep satirical strain of Provençal culture that revelled in mocking images of stock establishment figures, which in Aix meant most prominently figures in the legal and ecclesiastic professions.[23] As such, 'they offer,' she says, 'a witty panorama of Aix society reminiscent of the taxonomical-satirical spirit of contemporary popular *physiologies*, a genre midway between social ethnography and cartooning, in which varied costumes and headdresses served as symbolic indices'.[24] They also, by in fact abjuring the caricatural for matter-of-fact, mainly simple, face-on images, refer to *cartes-de-visite*, the hugely popular small portrait photographs, and belong to the growth of photographic documentation that would become ubiquitous in the French justice system. Cézanne's first self-portrait (cat.1.1) had been based on a photograph (p.44). The set of smaller portraits of Uncle Dominique in particular have the quality of photographs, but without the surface sheen and priority afforded to resemblance that photographs shared with Salon paintings. JE

CAT. 2.5
Uncle Dominique as a Lawyer, 1866–7
(see also detail, p.54) (P only)
Musée d'Orsay, Paris; FWN 410

CAT. 2.6

Uncle Dominique in Smock and Blue Cap, 1866–7

Metropolitan Museum of Art, New York; FWN 412

1 Cézanne to Camille Pissarro,
   23 October 1866.

2 Writing to Emile Zola c.19 October 1866,
   Cézanne tells of having 'just finished a
   little painting that I think is the best I've
   done: it shows my sister Rose reading to
   her doll' (a now-unknown work: FWN 401),
   and also refers to his 'Valabrègue'. Antoine
   Guillemet added a postscript to Cézanne's
   23 October letter to Pissarro, saying that
   'Cézanne has done some very beautiful
   paintings. He's lightened [the tone].' He then
   wrote to Zola on 2 November, mentioning
   Cézanne's *Overture to Tannhäuser* (an early
   version of fig. 21) and 'a portrait of his
   father in a big armchair … light [in tone]'.
   Danchev 2013, p.129. This suggests that the
   dark Uncle Dominique paintings were not
   begun any sooner than early November.

3 All these works were probably painted on
   standard size canvases, the smaller ones
   on the figure 6 (41 × 33 cm) or figure 8
   (46 × 38 cm) sizes. (The latter would become
   a favourite size for Cézanne's later small
   portraits.) The larger canvases approximate
   in size to the figure 15 (65 × 54 cm) or
   figure 25 (81 × 65 cm) sizes.

4 Aix-en-Provence 1984, p.120. The
   Valabrègue portrait (cat. 3.1) looks as
   if it took more than a day to paint, which
   raises the question: was Valabrègue
   exaggerating, or was Cézanne already

beginning his practice, discussed in the
Introduction, of working without, as well
as with, the sitter before him?

5 Cézanne to Zola, c.19 October 1866:
   'Guillemet arrived on Saturday evening.'

6 Cat. 2.2 is the work in question. I am
   grateful to Irene Konefal, Paintings
   Conservator, Museum of Fine Arts, Boston,
   who made digital x-rays of the painting, for
   sharing her research with me, and to the
   owners of the painting and the Museum
   of Fine Arts, Boston, for their consent. The
   painting beneath the portrait is occluded
   and does not lend itself to reproduction,
   but appears to be a still life with a vessel
   of some sort on a shelf or narrow table,
   possibly in front of a mirror. There are few
   extant works with which to compare it, but
   it would seem to date to the period 1862–4.

7 London–Paris–Washington D.C. 1988–9, cat.
   22, p.112. On the other hand, as these larger
   paintings show Uncle Dominique dressed
   in the costume of different professions,
   they could well have been the targets
   of Guillemet's 'terrible jokes' to which
   Valabrègue's letter refers.

8 See Introduction, p.15–18.

9 Lawrence Gowing, 'The Early Work
   of Paul Cezanne', in London–Paris–
   Washington, D.C. 1988–9, p.10.

10 Ibid.

11 Schapiro 1962, p.48.

12 Anthea Callen, *The Work of Art: Painting
    and Artistic Identity in Nineteenth-Century
    France* (Reaktion Books, London, 2015),
    pp.159–209, is an outstanding discussion
    of the palette-knife technique with respect
    mainly to later landscape paintings by
    Cézanne and Camille Pissarro.

13 I have not been able to inspect all ten
    paintings, but those I have seen show a grey
    to grey-brown ground. In one case (cat. 2.5),
    Cézanne scraped through the ground to
    expose the canvas in the top right corner.

14 Aix-en-Provence 1984, p.120.

15 London–Paris–Washington, D.C. 1988–9,
    cat. 22, p.112. One partial exception is
    cat. 2.5, whose white ground appears to
    have been brushed, as well as painted
    (and scored) with a knife.

16 FWN 403.

17 Observed by Henri Loyrette in London–
    Paris–Philadelphia 1995–6, cat. 7, p.89. Ibid.

18 Zola to Cézanne, 16 April 1860.

19 For example, by Gowing; see London–
    Paris–Washington, D.C. 1988–9, cat. 22, p.112,
    where he argues that this may be the first
    costume painting.

20 Schapiro 1962, p.48.

21 See FWN 413.

22 See, notably, FWN 561–4, 568–71.

23 Athanassoglou-Kallmyer 2003, pp.71–7.

24 Ibid., p.76.

Portraits of Valabrègue, Alexis and Zola

Submitted for consideration to the Paris Salon jury in 1866, Cézanne's portrait of his close friend and fellow *Aixois* Antony Valabrègue was his first ambitious, 'public' painting (cat. 3.1). A member of a local band of aspiring artists and writers that included Emile Zola, Baptistin Baille and Achille Emperaire, Valabrègue was from a well-respected Jewish family with roots in Provence dating back generations (Dramatis Personae, fig. 94). Encouraged by Zola, he sought a successful career in Paris as a writer and critic, and would manage a more secure life in the capital city than his comrade Cézanne.[1]

Both writer and painter were in Paris in the spring of 1866, the likely date of the Washington portrait. Valabrègue is portrayed in a three-quarter-length view, sitting stiffly with his hands clenched into fists against his thighs. His closed mouth is set tightly and his brow looks furrowed. Strokes of lurid red mark the lips and the tip of the nose, and flicker around the eyes, set off by a generous use of black in the central features of his face, in his hair and his jacket. The image projects a spirit of resistance and resolve.

Although the pose is conventional and Valabrègue wears a generic middle-class suit, his truculent tone and, most spectacularly, the thick paint with which he is rendered would have struck the intended audience, the Salon jury, like a slap in the face. Applied with heavily loaded brushes and with the palette knife, Cézanne signals Gustave Courbet's radically original manipulation of paint, particularly in his landscapes of the 1860s. Courbet defied the cool refinement of the academic *fini,* and invented new expressive possibilities through his physical engagement with paint on the picture surface. Cézanne's *manière couillarde*, or 'ballsy manner', was stylistically in line with a persona equally inspired by that of Courbet: the wild-haired, rough-hewn provincial, who descended upon Paris, cursing in a heavy

regional patois. The scruffy beard, working-class clothes and crude language established a bohemian position against urbane bourgeois propriety and the academic style it embodied.

The vigorously worked surface of the Washington painting moves well beyond what one finds in Courbet's landscapes, however, with areas in which Cézanne has smeared on pigment in thick slabs, leaving uneven edges with no representational function. Like Courbet, Cézanne used the knife to sculpt the paint once applied, but again, the effect here is coarser, more overtly gestural, and covers most of the canvas. Enhancing the filiation with Courbet, he signs his name in the Realist master's orange-red pigment.[2]

The undertone of aggression and even violence in the portrait was not out of step with other works painted by Cézanne at the time. His paintings of murder and rape during the 1860s combined with his *manière couillarde* to upset notions of civility, both pictorial and behavioural. In paintings like this portrait, Cézanne was both revealing his allegiance to and challenging the position of Courbet's most immediate Realist successor, Edouard Manet. As André Dombrowski has asserted, Cézanne's realism proposed an alternative to the controlled aloofness of Manet: something more personal, more physical, more passionate.[3]

Valabrègue had predicted a negative response from the Salon jury to this fierce picture, writing in a letter to Fortuné Marion, a mutual friend in Aix, 'Paul will without doubt be rejected at the exhibition. A philistine in the jury exclaimed on seeing my portrait that it was not only painted with a knife but with a pistol as well.'[4] According to Valabrègue's missive, the Barbizon artist Charles-François Daubigny had defended the picture, exclaiming that it was so much more daring than the 'nullities' accepted at every Salon. But in these final

Antony Valabrègue, 1866
National Gallery of Art, Washington, D.C.; FWN 399

years of the Second Empire, the arbiters of official art held fast and rejected the picture.

The outcome could not have surprised Cézanne; indeed, the artist may have planned the rejection in order to demand another Salon des Refusés like that held three years earlier, which had catapulted Manet into the avant-garde limelight. However, Cézanne's letter to the superintendent of fine arts, Comte de Nieuwerkerke, demanding a reprise of the sensational Refusés, was unsuccessful. The Comte refused to repeat an event that was such an affront to the 'dignity of art'.[5]

Cézanne painted Valabrègue again a couple of years later, between 1869 and 1870, at half the size, picturing just his head and shoulders (cat. 3.2).[6] In this less formal and more sympathetic format, the sitter is more relaxed, tilting his head to the side, hair tousled, jacket open, and the expression in his face is looser. Yet the thickness of the paint surface links the picture to the earlier version, the strokes applied with loaded brushes of various sizes as well as with the palette knife. Overlaid patches of flesh tones structure Valabrègue's face with highlights both brighter and thicker in facture. Blacks and dark tones have been applied in lower layers as well as in a final contour-defining phase, addressing features such as the nostrils and eyelids. Each individual stroke is visible, carefully placed, one imagines, with constant reference to the sitter. Applied more with brush than knife, the surface of the painting overall is more refined than that of the earlier version.

FIG. 26
Antony Valabrègue, 1874–5
Pola Museum of Art, Kanagawa; FWN 433

CAT. 3.2
Antony Valabrègue, 1869–70
J. Paul Getty Museum, Los Angeles; FWN 425

Unlike the portrait painted for the Salon in 1866, this picture is not signed, foregrounding the public address of the earlier work. Cézanne would paint Valabrègue at least once more in the mid-1870s, possibly when both returned home during the summer of 1874 (fig. 26).

Intellectual exchange and avant-garde camaraderie are also at the heart of Cézanne's double portrait of Zola and fellow *Aixois* Paul Alexis (cat. 3.3). Zola and Cézanne had been best boyhood friends, ideological comrades and artistic brothers in their mission to become leaders of the new movements in the arts and literature. Alexis knew Cézanne from their schooldays in Aix, and with his friend's encouragement, and that of Valabrègue, he arrived in Paris in 1869 to become a professional writer and poet. There he met Zola, and, seven years younger, would serve as a kind of literary acolyte to the Realist master. Both Cézanne and Alexis were witnesses at Zola's wedding in May 1870.

Made in the last year of the Second Empire, this painting, as well as another smaller work of around the same date, shows Alexis reading to Zola at the latter's home on the rue La Condamine in the Batignolles neighbourhood, the heart of the artistic counter-culture in Paris.[7] Henri Fantin-Latour was then painting his commemorative *Studio in Les Batignolles* (1870), which featured Manet as the Realist group's leader, and included Zola as well as several members of the soon-to-be-formed Impressionist movement. Cézanne is absent, not having yet found his place among the Parisian avant-garde.

In this double portrait, Cézanne may well have had in mind Manet's homage to Zola, presented at the Salon of 1868 (Introduction, fig. 12). Where Manet's painting is a kind of storyboard proclamation of avant-garde allegiance, Cézanne portrays Zola as an artistic colleague and mentor. Reclining like a pasha on a cushion at the centre, Zola appears to listen intently as Alexis reads aloud. Dombrowski has suggested that Alexis is reading one of his early experimental poems, perhaps the one dedicated to Zola in which he celebrates the sensuality and passion of Realism.[8] This relaxed communion was interrupted with the outbreak of the Franco-Prussian War in July 1870, however, and the painting was discontinued. MM

1 Rewald entry in *Essays in Honor of Paul Mellon: Collector and Benefactor*, ed. John Wilmerding (Schneidereith & Sons, Baltimore, 1986), p.292.

2 At some point Cézanne goes back over the signature in black. See National Gallery of Art, Washington, D.C., conservation report, 1 April 1992.

3 Dombrowski 2013.

4 Rewald 1948, p.49.

5 Correspondence between Cézanne and Nieuwerkerke, 19 April 1866. See Danchev 2013, pp.120–1.

6 Rewald dates the Los Angeles picture to 1869–70. Rewald 1996, p.50.

7 The other picture is 52 × 56 cm. FWN 601.

8 André Dombrowski, 'Cézanne, Manet and the Portraits of Zola', in *Interior Portraiture and Masculine Identity in France, 1789–1914*, ed. Temma Balducci, Heather Belnap Jensen and Pamela J. Warner (Ashgate, London, 2011), pp.101–23. On this double portrait, see also Henri Mitterand, 'Brothers in Art: Cézanne and Zola', in Paris 2011–12, pp.34–43; and John Rewald's seminal work, *Cézanne et Zola* (Sedrowski, Paris, 1936), published in English as *Paul Cézanne, A Biography* (Simon & Schuster, New York, 1948).

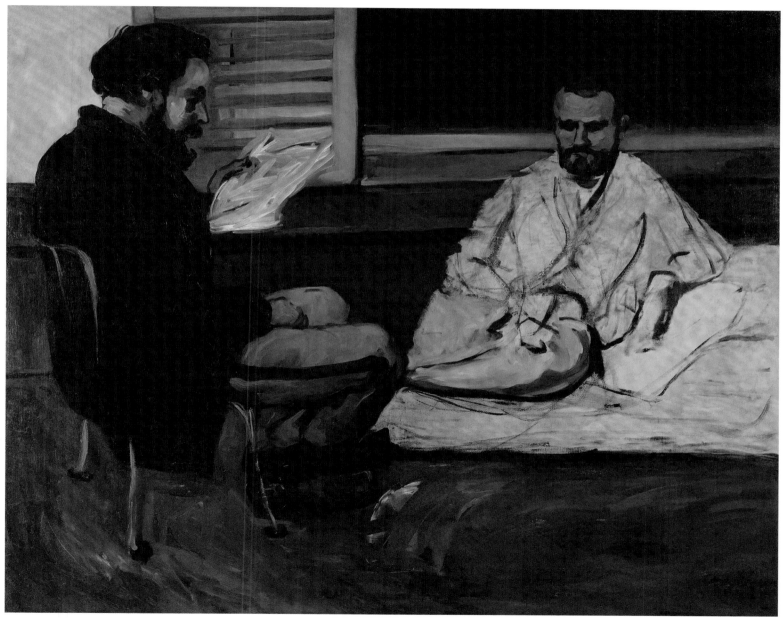

Paul Alexis Reading a Manuscript to Emile Zola, 1869–70 (see also detail, p.10)
Museu de Arte de São Paulo Assis Chateaubriand; FWN 602

Portraits of the Artist's Father and Achille Emperaire

The artist's father, Louis-Auguste Cézanne, was the only surviving son of Italian immigrants and grew up in the department of Var in Provence. He set up in business with a partner in Aix selling hats, then bought a bank in 1848, and became one of the richest men in town. Probably based on conversations with Paul Cézanne and his family, the artist's dealer Ambroise Vollard understood Louis-Auguste to have had a hard early life that forged an understandable attraction to money and an aversion to the precarious callings of a profession like art.[1] In this light, the efforts of Cézanne *père* to establish his only son in the family business, an obvious route to a stable, comfortable life, are entirely sympathetic.

This successful financier – decisive and by all accounts imposing – was the perfect counterpoint to his insecure and disorganised son. As a boy, Paul Cézanne was shy, dreamy and withdrawn, attracted to poetry and painting. He was evasive and deceptive in dealings with his father, vacillating professionally between the law and the family business in Aix and life as an artist in Paris. He must have been a source of great frustration. Various sketchbook drawings cast his father as psychologically and emotionally closed, looking down, his eyes shaded beneath the visor of his cap (fig. 27).

The agonistic narrative of the history of the avant-garde tempts one to read the Washington portrait (cat. 4.1) as a negative critique of the father, particularly given Emile Zola's condemnation of the man, *c*.1874, as 'mocking, republican, bourgeois, cold, meticulous, stingy … He is, moreover, garrulous and, sustained by his wealth, doesn't care a rap for anyone or anything.'[2] Of course, Louis-Auguste was Zola's adversary, not only with regard to his counter-cultural ideology but also in the struggle for the allegiance of Zola's best, beloved friend, Paul.

FIG. 27
Father of the Artist, 1865–70
National Gallery of Art, Washington, D.C.

Rather than an expression of filial frustration or anger, however, the portrait seems to involve the complicity of Louis-Auguste in a larger public battle. The tone is less one of contempt than homage to a frequently supportive paternal figure. Cézanne *fils* well understood that his life as a painter was enabled by his father's subvention.[3] Some years earlier, he had made a large-scale painting of his father, again seated and bent over a newspaper (fig. 19), for the central panel of the salon at the Jas de Bouffan, the eighteenth-century manor bought by Louis-Auguste in 1859. The portrait is flanked by female figures allegorising the four seasons, a familial decoration that suggests a more or less beneficent atmosphere.[4]

In the Washington picture, Louis-Auguste is portrayed on a monumental scale as an assured, informed man of business, relaxing at home in slippers and cap and reading the paper, 'like a pope on his throne in a big arm chair'.[5] The artist weaves himself into this iconic image of domestic masculinity by including on the wall behind his father one of his first still-life paintings, *Still Life with Sugar Bowl, Pears and Blue Cup*, done in his radical *manière couillarde* (fig. 28). The confident application of paint, with a palette knife and heavily loaded brushes, constitutes a kind of painterly swagger, in part, perhaps, to reassure his father of the strength and audacity of his vision. The portrait retains the vigour of the Uncle Dominique series (cats 2.1–2.6), but the artist has pulled back from his sitter to a respectful distance and averts a direct gaze. It is a powerful, compact painting, the figure wholly contained and securely anchored by the armchair and framed still life.

The public address of the painting is signified not only by its distinguished scale, aggressive facture and dramatic contrasts of light and dark, but also by a specific reference to contemporary culture. Louis-Auguste is absorbed in the pages of *L'Evénement*, the short-lived journal launched the previous year in which Zola published his famous defence of those artists refused by the recent Salon of 1866. Championing Edouard Manet in particular, Zola used the opportunity to indict official art policies and the academic painting they supported. The public backlash to Zola's strident article forced his resignation as literary critic, prompting him to republish it in a pamphlet titled 'Mon Salon'. Added to the journal text was a preface in the form of an affectionate letter to Cézanne in which

FIG. 28
Still Life with Sugar Bowl, Pears and Blue Cup, 1865–6
Musée Granet, Aix-en-Provence;
FWN 706

CAT. 4.1
**The Artist's Father,
Reading** *L'Evénement*, 1866
(see also detail, p.73)
National Gallery of Art,
Washington, D.C.; FWN 402

CAT. 4.2
Achille Emperaire, 1867–8
(P only)
Musée d'Orsay, Paris; FMW 423

FIG. 29
Jean-Auguste-Dominique Ingres,
Napoleon I on his Imperial Throne, 1806
Museé de l'Armée, Hôtel des Invalides, Paris

Zola evokes their shared origins and their dream for a new art.[6] The preface describes the difficulty with which these young men from the South of France navigated the Parisian art world: 'We felt ourselves lost in the midst of a complacent and frivolous crowd.' In this muscular picture, Cézanne offers a painting that is emphatically present, passionate and serious. It is both a personal and political manifesto: an homage to paternal and fraternal support, and to the 'new painting'.[7]

The portrait was accepted at the Salon of 1882, some sixteen years later, and listed rather cryptically, in typical Salon style, as 'Portrait of M.L.A.'. Cézanne identified himself as a student of one of the jury members, which allowed him to bypass the jury altogether, a devious back-door route that was formally discontinued the following year.

Achille Emperaire is a kind of pendant to Cézanne's portrait of his father. The two paintings share their monumental scale, heavy paint application and strongly contrasting light effects, as well as the combination of the personal and the political in subject matter (cat. 4.2). Emperaire was ten years older than Cézanne, and a member of the rebellious group of artists and poets of Aix. He was described as of 'small stature, a little hunchbacked, with a head of a musketeer of Louis XIII, a saffron-dyed moustache, who went through life with a cane or an umbrella placed under his overcoat, from behind, in the fashion of a sword'.[8] Like Cézanne, he was ambitious to succeed as an artist in Paris, and in the early 1860s they both worked in the Académie Suisse on the Ile de la Cité. Emperaire did not have the benefit of the younger artist's family support, however, and he remained largely in Aix. Cézanne helped him financially when he could, and Emperaire in return served as an intermediary in communications with his family when the younger artist was away from home.

Here, Emperaire sits in the same high-backed armchair as that used in the portrait of Louis-Auguste, but he is pulled closer to the picture plane and set against a black background. In gold stencilled lettering akin to that found in imperial portraiture, Cézanne wrote across the top of the picture, 'Achille Emperaire Peintre', playing on the royal cognate of Achille's last name. As Nina Athanassoglou-Kallmyer has argued, these august trappings for this small figure, wrapped in a blue robe, his tiny legs pulled up onto a footstool, can only be understood as a provocation to institutional French painting and its poster-boy, Ingres, who along with his followers still dominated the academic field.[9] It certainly brings to mind Ingres's portrait of Emperor Napoleon I (fig. 29). Yet, like the portrait of his father, the painting must also be understood in personal terms. The affection expressed in the sensitively rendered graphite studies of Emperaire (figs 30, 31) reinforces what is known of their friendship. The painting stands as an homage to a misunderstood and ignored contemporary artist, deformed but dignified by his passion, intelligence and commitment to the art of the future.

These two extraordinary early portraits are striking in their public intent.[10] They targeted an artistic arena vilified by critics as increasingly debased and commercialised, that of Salon portraiture. The proliferation of academic portraits recording the ascendance of bourgeois supremacy, and the complicity of the market in this enterprise, disgusted avant-garde artists and provides the context for Cézanne's provocation. Certainly these aggressive pictures answered Zola's call for a rebellious, militant, even violent art to reclaim French painting from the effete 'perfumed hands' of the academics. With his father's support and that of his artistic brotherhood, Cézanne publicly takes a stand, which is duly rejected by the Salon – *Achille Emperaire* was declined by the jury in 1870 – and caricatured in the press (fig. 95).[11] Later portraits would be less direct in their transgressions, concerned not so much with public art-world issues but more with private perception and personal sensibility and philosophy. MM

1 Vollard 1923, pp.11–12.

2 From notes for Zola's *La Conquête de Plassans*, 1874. Quoted in Rewald 1971, p.39. For Zola's reference to Louis-Auguste's antipathy towards him, see letter from Zola to Baptistin Baille, 22 April 1861, Danchev 2013, p.106.

3 Perhaps encouraging his reluctant but meaningful support was the nature of Louis-Auguste's own unconventional life. He seems to have made his own rules, had two children out of wedlock and married their mother when son Paul was five.

4 National Gallery, London (FWN 398). There is also a smaller portrait of Louis-Auguste, again reading the paper (FWN 430-TA), as well as several sketchbook drawings devoted to the father, mostly reading.

5 Antoine Guillemet in his letter to Emile Zola, 2 November 1866, Rewald 1976, p.117.

6 Emile Zola, 'Mon Salon' [1866], *Mon Salon: Manet, Ecrits sur l'art*, ed. Antoinette Ehrard (Flammarion, Paris, 1970).

7 See Rewald 1971, pp.49–50 and Nina M. Athanassoglou-Kallmyer, 'An Artistic and Political Manifesto for Cézanne', *Art Bulletin*, vol.72, no.3, September 1990, pp.482–92. In a letter from Guillemet to Zola in November 1866 reporting on the well-being of Cézanne, he describes Louis-Auguste as reading *Le Siècle* in Cézanne's portrait, not *L'Evénement*. This is more likely, for, as the most widely read of the French daily newspapers, it was opposed to the Second Empire without provoking trouble from censors. Cézanne may have changed the masthead in the painting to make a more aggressive statement. Furthermore, *L'Evénement* expired in November 1866, inflecting its inclusion, perhaps, with a commemorative spirit. (Suggested by Margaret Doyle in conversation with the author, March 2016.)

8 Quotation from *Encyclopédie Departementale des Bouches-du-Rhone*, in John Rewald, 'Achille Emperaire and Cézanne', *Studies in Impressionism*, ed. Irene Gordon and Frances Weitzenhoffer (Thames & Hudson, London, 1985), pp.57–68.

9 Athanassoglou-Kallmyer 1990, see note 7, p.487.

10 See Athanassoglou-Kallmyer's suggestion that these paintings could be seen as pendants, united in their 'militant proclamations of radical political and aesthetic ideals'. Athanassoglou-Kallmyer 1990, see note 7, p.482.

11 For the development of the modern portrait in nineteenth-century France, see Heather McPherson, *The Modern Portrait in Nineteenth-Century France* (Cambridge University Press, Cambridge, 2001).

FIG. 30
Head of Achille Emperaire, *c.1867–70*
Kunstmuseum, Basel

FIG. 31
Head of Achille Emperaire, *1867–70*
Musée d'Orsay, Paris, on loan to Musée du Louvre, Paris

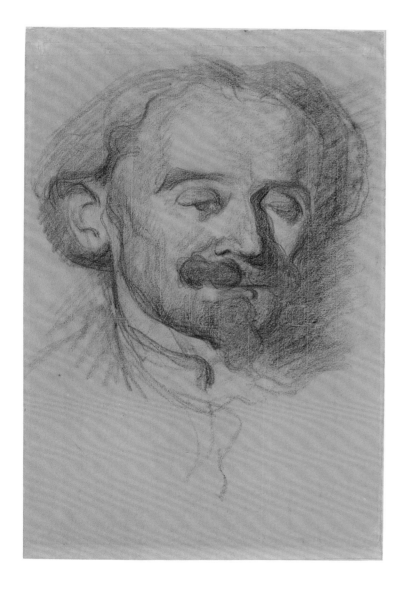

2 Impressionism and After

1872–85

Paul Cézanne, photographer unknown, *c.*1875
Photograph found amongst the papers of artist Achille Emperaire

TWO CRITICAL EVENTS in Cézanne's life occurred in 1872. In January, his affiliation with Hortense Fiquet, with whom he had been living since 1869, was cemented by his formal acknowledgement of the paternity of their newly born son, Paul. Cézanne would paint more portraits of Hortense than of anyone else. Then, in August, he began working alongside the Impressionist Camille Pissarro, learning how to record methodically the effects of light and shade on landscape. This approach being less applicable to indoor subjects, Cézanne's portrait production, which had slowed after 1870, remained low until mid decade.

It revived in 1875 in a group of impassive self-portraits whose most prominent feature was the artist's prematurely bald head, which became almost as much an admired volume in his paintings as that of the apples in his still lifes. These portraits are as close as Cézanne came to making what can be called Impressionist portraits. But, in 1876–7, in portraits of Hortense and the art collector Victor Chocquet, he broke through, beyond Impressionism, to something

new for him: the use of heightened colour. Particularly in the portrait of Hortense in a red armchair, he began recreating the homogeneous materiality of his early monochrome palette-knife portraits by constructing areas of prismatic colour that shape a vivid human presence.

Cézanne consolidated this achievement over the next seven or eight years, creating portraits of extraordinary sculptural gravity. These included, around the end of the 1870s, paintings of Hortense, their young son and his friend Louis Guillaume; and in the early years of the following decade, new bald-headed self-portraits. Both sets maintain the passivity of earlier canvases, supporting the common conclusion that, while the Impressionists painted effects, Cézanne painted things. However, two early 1880s self-portraits show the artist with his head covered – in one by a wide-brimmed hat, in the other by a stubby pyramid of white cloth – casting suspicious-looking glances at the viewer. They speak of a new interest in affect that characterised Cézanne's portraiture in the second half of the decade. JE

CAT. 5.1
Self-Portrait, *c*.1875 (see also detail, p.87)

Musée d'Orsay, Paris; FWN 434

'Impressionist' Self-Portraits

'He builds up the paints, which he mixes and grinds with extraordinary ardour, going back over the thicknesses to nuance the tone; sometimes his touch follows the sense of the form, sometimes it is a long slash, but it always carries with it sombre, plentiful pigment, sculpted with an energetic lightness.'[1] The great French art historian of the interwar period, Henri Focillon, used these words to describe the evolution of Cézanne's painting in the early 1870s.

This process of working characterised his self-portraits made around 1870, as with his portraits of Antoine-Fortuné Marion and Antony Valabrègue (cats 1.2, 3.2), where Cézanne sculpted the relief of the face with broad strokes of rich paint. It is also evident in the thick, overlapping strokes of what may well be the earliest of his self-portraits of the mid-1870s (cat. 5.1).

Cézanne's very first self-portrait (cat. 1.1) had been painted from a photograph; in the mid-1880s he would repeat the process (cat. 10.1). He painted the present

canvas and the remainder of his self-portraits by looking in a mirror, thereby making face-to-face contact also with the viewer. We must wonder whether he deliberately included in this first mirror self-portrait a clue as to how he painted it: the landscape in the background, Armand Guillaumin's *View of the Seine, Paris* of 1871 (fig. 32), is reversed as it would have appeared in the mirror.[2] This self-portrait is thought to have been made in Guillaumin's studio at the quai d'Anjou on the Ile Saint-Louis in Paris.[3] It also recalls a self-portrait by another painter friend, Camille Pissarro, of 1873 (fig. 33). Cézanne, with his bushy beard and clothes somewhere between those of a bourgeois and a peasant, exhibits a rejection of staging similar to that in Pissarro's self-portrait: both artists offer a truthful image of themselves that is serious and profoundly human.[4] It is an image that is also pointedly professional; in Cézanne's case, he gives testimony to his close friendship with both Guillaumin and Pissarro. (He participated

FIG. 32
Armand Guillaumin,
View of the Seine, Paris, 1871
Museum of Fine Arts, Houston

CAT. 5.2
Self-Portrait, Rose Ground, *c.*1875 (see also detail, p.8)

Musée d'Orsay, Paris; FWN 436

FIG. 33
Camille Pissarro, **Self-Portrait**, 1873
Musée d'Orsay, Paris

with them, outside the confines of the official Paris Salon, in the 1874 and 1877 exhibitions of the group that came to be called the Impressionists.) And it is tempting to imagine, outside the frame of this self-portrait, his dirty hands holding a brush.

After Cézanne's initial foray into self-portraiture in the 1860s, which produced only three canvases,[5] and leaving aside his appearance in the same number of imaginary scenes, which he painted around 1870,[6] this work and its accompanying canvas *Self-Portrait, Rose Ground* (cat. 5.2) represent his return to painting self-portraits. He would continue to make them with some regularity until within six or seven years of his death. As such, they assume an autobiographical function all the more significant since interpersonal communication was often difficult for him. However, while they have been said to 'record the evolution of Cézanne's mien and state of mind', from the 'uncouth wild man' of *Self-Portrait* (cat. 5.1) to increasingly

milder representations,[7] beginning with *Self-Portrait, Rose Ground* – and broadly do so – his mien and his mind are often very hard to read.

Cézanne looks less wild in the latter painting, probably painted soon after its predecessor, not only because he has had his hair cut and beard trimmed, but also because he has placed himself before a lush and beautiful rose-coloured background, probably but not certainly wallpaper. However, its thick paint looks tormented, and both its paler and darker elements intrude upon his features. It is the first instance of Cézanne exploring the relationship between figure and patterned background, a practice that he pursued intermittently until the completion of *Seated Peasant* of c.1900–4 (cat. 24.2). *Self-Portrait, Rose Ground* was among the paintings at the memorial exhibition of Cézanne's work at the Salon d'Automne of 1907, the year following his death. The Austrian poet Rainer Maria Rilke saw it on that occasion, but rather than comment

FIG. 35
Self-Portrait, *c.*1877
Musée d'Orsay, Paris; FWN 444

FIG. 34
Self-Portrait, *c.*1877
Phillips Collection, Washington, D.C.;
FWN 449

on the background, he wrote eloquently of Cézanne's head, notably of 'the powerful structure of this skull, formed as though by hammering from within'.[8]

In a third self-portrait (fig. 34), showing Cézanne posed as he is in these two canvases, Cézanne's skull looks softer, the bony structure less visible beneath a continuous, seemingly malleable envelope of skin stretched tight around the eyes. Made probably later, in about 1877, this effect is due to it having been painted with much shorter, more delicate strokes, thus beginning a process of experimentation that would lead to the so-called 'constructive brushstrokes' of his canvases of the early 1880s (see p.98). (The clothing and background are barely sketched in, suggesting that this was an experiment that he duly gave up.) The same is true of a related, much smaller self-portrait (fig. 35), where the hatching of the constructive brushstrokes, but not their arrangement in parallel, is starting to appear.[9] JE/XR

1 Henri Focillon, *La Peinture au XIXe siècle* [1928]: *du réalisme à nos jours,* vol. 2 (Flammarion, Paris, 1991), p.272.

2 The reversal is pointed out by Lawrence Gowing in London–Paris–Washington, D.C. 1988–9, p.194.

3 See Henri Loyrette's fine discussion of these two self-portraits together with that in the Phillips Collection (fig. 34), in Paris–London–Philadelphia 1995–6, pp.145–50, to which the present discussion is indebted.

4 'Remember that I am of rustic temperament, melancholic, rough-looking and wild; it will take time for people to learn to like me,' wrote Pissarro to his son on 20 November 1883. *Correspondance de Camille Pissarro,* ed. Janine Bailly-Herzberg (P.U.F. et Valhermeil, Paris, 1980), vol. I, letter 190, p.252. Cézanne could well have said the same of himself. The paintings in the background of Pissarro's picture, which are deliberately hard to identify, evoke his studio in Pontoise, which

Cézanne used on occasion, for example to paint FWN 726.

5 FWN 390, 397, 403.

6 See FWN 609, 610, 614.

7 Lorette in Paris–London–Philadelphia 1995–6, p.146.

8 Rilke 2002, pp.74–5.

9 The process may be followed from this work, through FWN 445 and 450, to the three canvases discussed in 'Self-Portraits of the Early 1880s' in this volume.

CAT. 6.1
Victor Chocquet, 1876–7 (w only)
Private collection; FWN 437

Portraits of Victor Chocquet

Victor Chocquet holds a singular position in Cézanne's artistic biography as his most avid collector, consistently close friend and aesthetic soulmate. They shared a particular love for the works of both the Realist master Gustave Courbet and the leader of Romanticism Eugène Delacroix. The writer Georges Rivière recounts an afternoon spent at Chocquet's apartment, with the painter and collector kneeling side by side before an array of Delacroix's works on paper, handling them like precious relics with tears in their eyes.[1]

Chocquet discovered the work of Pierre-Auguste Renoir at the spring 1875 auction of Impressionist paintings at the Hôtel Drouot, Paris, met the artist soon after, and was then introduced by Renoir to Cézanne.[2] Chocquet bought his first Cézanne, a small scene of three bathers, in October that year from Julien 'Père' Tanguy, a colour merchant who sold art supplies in Paris, often accepting paintings as payment from artists he favoured.[3] A customs official by profession, Chocquet was not a man of great means, but he was able to satisfy his collecting habit through a careful selection of drawings and paintings, as well as furniture, silver, porcelain and other objets d'art. Described at the time by critic Théodore Duret as 'of a perfect politesse and a great modesty', he was fully convinced by 'the new painting', and offered financial and moral support in the difficult early years of the movement.[4] In the catalogue of the 1876 Impressionist exhibition, he was listed as the owner of works by Claude Monet and Camille Pissarro, and some six by Renoir.[5]

At the 1877 Impressionist exhibition, Cézanne displayed a portrait of his new friend (cat. 6.1). A head study, with the sitter looking to his left, his collar open and his thick mane of grey-streaked hair brushed off his high forehead, the painting drew a vicious critical response. The sitter was deemed a maniac, or sick, or a criminal. Louis Leroy, well-known ridiculer of the Impressionists, warned potential visitors to the exhibition to steer pregnant women clear of 'this head, the colour of the underside of boots, so strange', lest it incite premature birth.[6]

While the overtly casual presentation of a somewhat unkempt-looking Chocquet may have been a little startling, it was most probably the paint surface that so strongly offended viewers. Thick strokes of barely mixed pigment are layered densely across the surface, creating a rough-hewn effect. To the contemporary eye, used to refined modulations of volume and delicate evocations of dignified sitters, the portrait must have been quite jarring. Cézanne almost certainly worked on the picture over time, as he was travelling back and forth from Aix to Paris during these years. The 'crumbled, granular surface' noted by the English critic Roger Fry suggests incessant revision and continual painting.[7]

Although made around the same time, the Columbus portrait (cat. 6.2) is quite different, perhaps even a response to the criticism of the head study. The sitter has been pushed back from the picture plane so that the frame fully encapsulates his compact, seated body. In his apartment on the rue de Rivoli, Chocquet sits in a Louis XIV armchair, having turned away from an antique desk to gaze steadily at the painter. He is anchored by the gilded frames of the paintings hanging behind him. The sitter's interlaced fingers, crossed legs and frontally posed torso and head underline the coherent balance of the picture, while the glowing red of the lozenges in the wallpaper, in the upholstery and in the patterns of the rug maintain the painting's vibrancy.

Here Cézanne advances a new idea of pictorial unity, akin to that of the Boston *Madame Cézanne* (cat. 7.1) of the same period, in which the surface is carefully built up into a pattern of 'constructive' strokes. Comparing the work to Renoir's portrait of Chocquet (fig. 36), art critic Julius Meier-Graefe likened it to a stonemason's construction. 'Cézanne would get to the bottom of the truth while painting him,' he wrote.[8] Attributing the

FIG. 36
Pierre-Auguste Renoir, **Victor Chocquet**, *c*.1875
Harvard Art Museums, Cambridge, Massachusetts

FIG. 37
Victor Chocquet, *c*.1877
Virginia Museum of Fine Arts, Richmond, Virginia; FWN 438

meditative intensity of the process to the unusual communion between painter and collector, he continued, 'The mental atmosphere of the sitter, who was a peculiar individual, became plastically intelligible in Cézanne's portrait.'

Indeed, the painting exudes the kind of lively equanimity that Cézanne ascribed to Chocquet's character. Years after the completion of the portrait, in a letter to his friend, Cézanne praised the 'great equilibrium of vital faculties' that allowed Chocquet, in the painter's mind, to achieve his goals. 'I am struck by this serenity ... Fate has not endowed me with an equal stability, which is the only regret I have about the things on this earth.'[9] One can imagine Cézanne fully absorbed, in the presence of his patient friend during

multiple painting sessions, in a productive process that was simultaneously profoundly reassuring.

Cézanne would paint Chocquet several more times, including a smaller version of the head in the Columbus painting, which Degas acquired from Parisian art dealer Ambroise Vollard in 1896 (fig. 37), two head studies from around 1880 (figs 8, 9), and a large, late portrait of the collector in a white jacket.[10] Chocquet held by far the largest single cache of paintings by Cézanne, some thirty-five in total, from small sketches to fully realised, masterful canvases, such as *House of the Hanged Man* (FWN 81), *Bridge at Maincy* (FWN 143) and *Mardi Gras* (FWN 668). The two men remained close friends, socialising with their wives (rare for the Cézannes), until Chocquet's death in 1891. MM

1   Rewald 1969, p.56. Georges Rivière, *Renoir et ses amis* (Floury, Paris, 1921), pp.39–40.

2   Vollard 1914, chapter VIII.

3   On buying the picture (*Three Bathers*, FWN 918), Chocquet reportedly commented, 'How well this will look between a Delacroix and a Courbet.' Rewald 1969, p.39.

4   Théodore Duret reported Chocquet at the 1877 exhibition approaching visitors to proselytise on behalf of the 'New Painting'. See John Rewald, 'Cézanne and Victor Chocquet', *Bulletin of the Columbus Gallery of Fine Arts* 20, nos 3–4 (Summer 1950), pp.3–6. Reprinted in *Art Quarterly* (Summer 1950), pp.251–4.

5   Rewald's groundbreaking article, 'Chocquet and Cézanne', quotes Monet, Renoir and Duret on the subject of Chocquet's support. See Rewald 1969, pp.33, 42, an expanded and republished version of the essay quoted in note 4. For an excellent account of Chocquet as a collector, see Mariantonia Reinhard-Felice, *Victor Chocquet: Ami et collectionneur des impressionnistes Renoir, Cézanne, Monet, Manet* (Hirmer, Munich, 2015), with exhaustive essays by Anne Distel and, on Chocquet and Cézanne's relationship, Jayne S. Warman.

6   Louis Leroy, quoted in Rewald 1969, p.51.

7   Rewald quotes Fry's account in Rewald 1969, p.49.

8   Meier-Graefe 1927, p.40.

9   Cézanne to Chocquet, Gardanne, 11 May 1886.

10 Respectively, FWN 438, 453, 454 and 498.

CAT. 6.2
Victor Chocquet, 1877
Columbus Museum of Art, Ohio; FWN 439

CAT. 7.1

Madame Cézanne in a Red Armchair, *c.*1877

Museum of Fine Arts, Boston; FWN 443

Early Portraits of Hortense Fiquet, later Madame Cézanne

Ambroise Vollard recounts that Cézanne hated being watched at his easel, a fact that obviously complicated the artist's portrait practice.[1] Additionally challenging was the artist's prerequisite of extreme patience from his sitters during repeated and prolonged sittings throughout which they were urged not to move or speak. As the practice was so important to him – he once told Vollard, 'The goal of all art is the human face'[2] – he forged ahead, mostly painting people with whom he felt comfortable and who, out of love, respect, loyalty or remuneration, would perform the kind of patience required: a handful of very close friends, household servants, himself, and of course his lover and eventual wife, Hortense Fiquet, whom he painted twenty-eight or twenty-nine times.[3]

The Boston and Stockholm portraits of Hortense are among the earliest. They were made in Paris in the apartment Cézanne shared with her and their son Paul, who would have been around five years old, on the rue de l'Ouest from mid-April 1875 until early 1880.[4] Crucially for Cézanne, Hortense was not Parisian, but like himself from the provinces, and was brought to the city by her parents who were in search of employment. She succumbed to the Parisian fashion craze, and, perhaps transferring her skills as a bookbinder to personal dressmaking, presumably made some of the sartorial confections shown in the painted portraits.[5] In the Boston painting (cat. 7.1), she wears a *robe de promenade* in blue, festooned with ribbons and a shimmering striped skirt.[6] The dress so stimulated Cézanne that, in describing its forms, textures and colours, he surpassed not only his own previous work but also created a milestone in the history of painting.

How to account for this stunning work, a 'breakthrough picture', as one art historian has put it?[7] The artist was clearly entranced as he realised the figure

on canvas. For Cézanne, such an achievement required a purity and intensity of presence on the part of the sitter, and a powerful rapport between sitter and artist, a condition seemingly fulfilled by Hortense.

She sits in a high-backed, red armchair at a comfortable distance from the picture plane, gazing steadily at the artist. Her face is modelled by flat planes of colour that sculpt her brow, the bridge of her nose and her cheekbones. Cézanne employs a sumptuous array of liquid blue and green, purple and mauve, turquoise, grey and taupe patches, amplified by the glowing red upholstery. Her right side is firmly frontal in its presentation, while her left relaxes into the agreeable contours of the armchair, the brushstrokes in the skirt loosening as it falls. There is a dignity and extraordinary monumentality to the figure; she is a 'regal presence on her great red throne', such that the painting in memory seems much larger than it actually is.[8] There is also a softness to the portrait, in the gentle compositional curves of the chair back, the way Hortense leans to the right with her elbow resting on the arm of the chair, that marks out this sympathetic portrait from many of the later works.[9] Cézanne conveys a sense of intimacy, not through eye contact where one expects it, but through impossibly lush colour and intensely responsive brushstrokes. The poet Rainer Maria Rilke, having seen the painting at the Salon d'Automne in 1907, suggests the emotional power of the picture: 'the consciousness of her presence has grown into an exaltation which I perceive even in my sleep; my blood describes her to me'.[10]

The Boston portrait of Hortense disrupts a genre of painting that was already under critical fire during these years.[11] Both the over-proliferation of portraiture crowding the walls of the Paris Salon and the burgeoning business of portrait photography put

CAT. 7.2
Madame Cézanne Sewing, 1877
Nationalmuseum, Stockholm; FWN 442

pressure on the aesthetic claims of the genre. Cézanne displaced the expressive power of the portrait from traditional notions of likeness and identity to the overall design of the picture and, above all, to the abstract pleasures of colour.

The Stockholm painting (cat. 7.2) is smaller and squarer in format, and the effect of the interior is more staid. The palette is more subdued, the blue-red juxtaposition of Hortense's dress against the armchair uncomplicated by the prismatic patches of the Boston version. She focuses downward on her stitching, her neatly coiffed bun and angular facial features suggesting domestic precision. Cézanne has shifted the location of the broad-backed chair so that it spans, or blocks, the doorway, the brown knob and lock hovering beside her head. The sense of her complete absorption, enhanced by interior elements, appears also in a slightly later drawing where, as in the Stockholm painting, the geometric forms of the enclosing furniture contain, order and protect her (fig. 38).

The paintings emit a peaceful radiance, and indeed the life of Cézanne's family during these years was relatively easy. They lived off Cézanne's allowance from his father, which would be secure until the spring of 1878, when a letter from Victor Chocquet posted to Cézanne in Aix was opened by his father. The reference to 'Madame Cézanne et petit Paul' exposed the son's deceit, for their existence had been kept a secret from the patriarch. Henceforth, family life would become more transient and turbulent, the strain captured in later portraits. MM

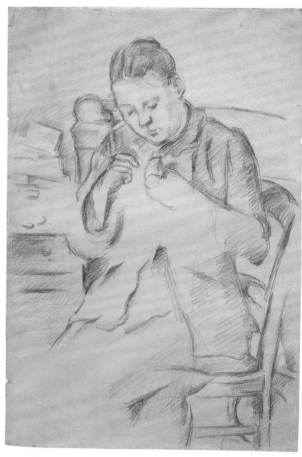

FIG. 38
Madame Cézanne Sewing, *c*.1880
Samuel Courtauld Trust, Courtauld Gallery, London

1   Vollard 1923, p.126.

2   Ibid., p.133. See also Introduction to this volume, note 86.

3   For the most focused treatment of Cézanne's portraits of Hortense Fiquet, see Sidlauskas 2009 and New York 2014–15.

4   See Françoise Cachin's entry in Paris–London–Philadelphia 1995–6, p.170. The wallpaper, yellow-green with blue medallions, is that of the apartment at 67 rue de l'Ouest, in the 14th arrondissement.

5   Butler 2008, p.41.

6   See Anne Van Buren, 'Madame Cézanne in Oil and Pencil', MA Thesis, University of Texas at Austin, 1964, on the dresses in the portraits of Madame Cézanne.

7   Cachin in Paris–London–Philadelphia 1995–6, pp.170–2. Cachin downplays the emotional expressiveness of the picture in favour of focusing on Cézanne's staggering formal achievement.

8   Butler 2008, p.44.

9   Lewis 2000, p.177.

10 This is quoted from a letter that Rilke wrote to his wife from Paris on returning to his hotel room from the exhibition. Rilke 2002.

11 See Zola's complaints about the genre in his Salon review of 1875. See Heather McPherson, *The Modern Portrait in Nineteenth-Century France* (Cambridge University Press, Cambridge, 2001) for an account of the critical milieu for portraiture, pp.7–8.

CAT. 8.1
Self-Portrait, 1880–1 (see also detail, p.101)
National Gallery, London; FWN 462

Self-Portraits of the Early 1880s

Despite the hint of concern in the look cast by a some-what closed face, the *Self-Portrait in a Wide-Brimmed Hat* (fig. 39) testifies to Cézanne's new, calmer attitude in the early 1880s. His attire is becoming increasingly reminiscent of a middle-class *bon bourgeois*, albeit by no means as elegant as that of Edouard Manet or Edgar Degas. However, as the art historian Joseph Rishel observed, 'the addition of the felt hat – from his father's first successful business venture in Aix? – and the sharply cropped beard result in an image that is positively rabbinical'.[1] The choice of an interior – clearly identified by a red, glass-panelled door that structures the composition in a surprisingly rigid and severe fashion – also serves to further distance the scene from the working atmosphere of a studio. In fact, Cézanne was entering a new phase in his career, refusing, from 1879, to participate in the exhibitions held by the Impressionist group, hoping – but succeeding only once – to be accepted at the official Paris Salon.[2] Moreover, after a period of great tension, his father, who suspected – quite rightly – that Cézanne now had a wife, and probably a child, concealed from him, began to look more kindly on his son's artistic ambitions, and by the mid-1880s he had built a studio for him in the manor house at the Jas de Bouffan.

The rigour displayed in *Self-Portrait in a Wide-Brimmed Hat* is even more apparent in the smaller *Self-Portrait* (cat. 8.1). Although the contrast between figure and ground is less strong, the contrast is greater between the living, organic volume of the head and the flat, geometric plane of the olive wallpaper behind it.[3] However, that counterpoint is complicated by the compromised contrast of the very geometric curve of the shoulder meeting a vertical that would form a straight line but for being broken by the curls of the artist's hair. Conversely, the zig-zag of the coat's lapel and the angular lines of the wallpaper mutually relate, while the little star-crossed lozenges on the wallpaper look out of the composition like the artist's eyes.[4]

FIG. 39
Self-Portrait in a Wide-Brimmed Hat, 1879–80
Kunstmuseum, Bern; FWN 451

As in his trio of great mid-1870s self-portraits (cats 5.1, 5.2; fig. 34), Cézanne makes great use of the volume of the dome of his skull. Here, it is the creation (more fully than in any previous portrait) of his so-called 'constructive brushstrokes', a technique that he developed in the 1880s in which patches of paint of a similar size are applied in a parallel, usually diagonal, direction. Here, they run more or less continuously across the facial features, and in a more generalised form across the coat and the background. In a some- what later *Self-Portrait* (cat. 8.3), a work with a very similar pose but much tighter framing, the brush- strokes are more prominent, linking face and figure together against a neutral, dark grey, undefined space. The artist's eyes, at once piercing and oddly unfocused; the strong contrast of light and dark, leaving part of his face in shadow; and the translucent light, emerging through the brush strokes, all serve to dramatise the monumentality of Cézanne's self-image.

The painter covered his bald head once again when making his *Self-Portrait in a White Bonnet* (cat. 8.2), a work that has often been compared to Chardin's *Self-Portrait with Eyeshade and Spectacles* of 1775 in the Louvre (fig. 40), to which the artist made reference many years later in a letter to the painter-critic Emile Bernard of 1904:[5]

> You remember the fine pastel by Chardin, equipped with a pair of spectacles and a visor providing a shade. He's an artful fellow, this painter. Haven't you noticed how [a visor], by letting a light plane carry across the bridge of the nose, allows the eyes to better see tonal values.[6]

Cézanne's interest in Chardin is not surprising: the two artists shared a humility, a rejection of the hierarchy of genre, and an investment in the art of still life. This clearly stated lineage is represented in their eccentric appearance – in both cases, an impromptu head covering, certainly reserved for private use, ever so slightly contradicting the elegance of the knotted scarf or the cravat. This helps to give Cézanne a look of indifference towards the viewer and with it a greater confidence than we find in his earlier self-portraits.

Additionally, his headgear may be a plasterer's hat made from a napkin or small towel;[7] therefore, possibly a deliberate artisanal reference, even a reminder that his childhood friend Antony Valabrègue had called his early portraits 'mason's painting'.[8]

Here, the constructive brushstrokes are short, narrow, lighter in feel and more lively than in the preceding two self-portraits; perhaps a response to the pastel medium of Chardin's composition. Observing how Cézanne's painting, 'for all its textural and coloristic variety, seems remarkably unified,' Rishel concluded, 'it is the reconciliation of surface animation with a settled psychological aura that most distinguishes this self-portrait from others by Cézanne.'[9] JE/XR

FIG. 40
Jean-Baptiste-Simeon Chardin,
Self-Portrait with Eyeshade and Spectacles, 1775
Musée du Louvre, Paris

1 Paris–London–Philadelphia 1995–6, p.210.
2 His single acceptance, in 1882, made use of a subterfuge that allowed him to bypass the jury – he submitted his entry as 'a student of Guillemet'.
3 The same wallpaper appears in varying forms in Cézanne's 1877 portraits of Hortense Fiquet (cats 7.1, 7.2) and in a number of other canvases that may be found by a search in FWN under the keywords 'wallpaper, lozenge'.

4 Fine analyses of this painting that make these points appear in Schapiro [1952] 1962, p.64, and Stokes 1947, p.22.
5 This is referred to by Joseph R. Rishel in Paris–London–Philadelphia 1995–6, p.232.
6 Cézanne to Emile Bernard, 27 June 1904. This passage has been misunderstood, and therefore incorrectly translated, in all the published English-language versions. See John Elderfield, 'Chardin's Visor', *The Brooklyn Rail*, 3 September 2012, p.39.

7 Rishel, as note 5.
8 Aix-en-Provence 1984, p.120. See Introduction, p.17.
9 Rishel, as note 5.

CAT. 8.2
Self-Portrait in a White Bonnet, 1881–2 (P, L only)
Neue Pinakothek, Munich; FWN 464

CAT. 8.3
Self-Portrait, *c.*1882 (P only)
Pushkin State Museum of Fine Arts, Moscow; FWN 463

CAT. 9.1
Louis Guillaume, 1879–80 (w only)
National Gallery of Art, Washington, D.C; FWN 448

Sculptural Portraits

In the years around 1880, Cézanne produced a group of still lifes against a blue-grey wallpaper with a delicate floral pattern that have been celebrated for their purity and serenity, their deceptive simplicity, their 'perfect coherence' as one art historian put it.[1] Joseph Rishel describes the dignity and restraint of these still lifes as an 'Aristotelian resolution', particularly in the consummate *Apples and Biscuits* of 1879–80 (fig. 41).

Cézanne achieved similar effects in the genre of portraiture, approaching these three smaller-scaled, single figures as discrete architectural problems to solve (cats 9.1–9.3). Against the same wallpaper as that in the group of still lifes, Cézanne poses Louis Guillaume squarely in the centre of the frame,

bolstered by the arc of the chair back coming in from the left edge of the picture. His oval-shaped head is slightly tilted, setting off a gently dynamic motion of interlocking arcs and ellipses tied together neatly by the cravat, its plump, soft fabric echoed in the decorative shapes on the wall seen over the boy's shoulder. Guillaume's crisply defined features – the neat hairline of his closely cropped crown, the clean shapes of his ears, eyes, nose and mouth – are uncorrupted by the deformations of age. The portrayal is a counterpoint to the group of self-portraits of the same period, in which the contour of the artist's head is broken by his bushy beard and unkempt hair, his lips and chin obscured, his eyes wary (cats 8.1–8.3).

FIG. 41
Apples and Biscuits,
1879–80
Musée de l'Orangerie, Paris;
FWN 773

CAT. 9.2

The Artist's Son, 1881–2 (see also detail, pp.40–1)

Musée de l'Orangerie, Paris; FWN 465

The effect is one of perfected abstraction. Competing arcs curve towards one another in a rhythmic swinging action, revolving back and forth, holding the figure in tensile equilibrium. Meyer Schapiro described the 'accented closure of forms within an atmosphere of reverie' as achieving a level of abstraction unparalleled in the art of the time.[2] This portrait would have a significant impact on the development of early twentieth-century modernism. It was shown in 1895 at Cézanne's first monographic exhibition at Ambroise Vollard's gallery at rue Lafitte, Paris, and at the Salon d'Automne in 1906, where one critic noted its simultaneous evocation of infinity and eternity.[3] Later, both Juan Gris and Arshile Gorky copied it in the process of digesting the lessons of 'Papa Cézanne'.[4]

Despite the pearly lustre of the boy's face, Schapiro found no inner life in the sitter, no 'spiritual light'. The portrait is not, however, without emotional affect. Louis was the son of Cézanne's friend and neighbour, Antoine Guillaume, a shoemaker by trade who lived in the same Parisian building as Cézanne and was the original owner of the picture.[5] The smooth, rhythmic forms of the boy's features and the evenness of the paint surface suggest an untroubled innocence. There is a similar youthful freshness, a delicate beauty, in the face of Michelangelo de Rosa in *Boy in a Red Waistcoat* (cat. 15.1). Both pictures were at one time owned by the same collector, Egisto Fabbri.

These paintings of young men were probably informed by Cézanne's relationship with his son, Paul *fils*. Born in 1872, Paul would have been nine years old in 1881, the approximate date of *The Artist's Son* (cat. 9.2). Although Cézanne did not always live with Paul and his mother, he doted on his son, filling his sketchbooks with life studies, and in the period in which he produced this portrait, painting numerous oil sketches.[6] These intimate visual records chart Paul's growth from infancy through pubescence. Cézanne remained close to Paul, his only heir, depending on him practically and emotionally to the end of his life. 'As a go-between he will ease the difficulty I have in coping with life,' he wrote in a letter of 1903.[7]

As in the portrait of Louis Guillaume, Cézanne describes the neat features of the boy's young face, his perfectly shaped eyes and eyebrows, nose, mouth and ears. The minimal composition focuses on anatomical geometry, the oval head placed on the pedestal of the neck, firmly secured by the black collar into the arc of his shoulders.[8] A strangely amorphous shape – we recognise it as the back of the family's red upholstered armchair – hovers to the boy's left. He turns and leans slightly towards it. Its curving shape and the open facture of its surface convey a benign presence.

For art historian John Rewald this picture marks the shift in Cézanne's technique in the early 1880s from heavy oblique brushstrokes to paint diluted with turpentine and more precise and linear compositional designs.[9] The surface of this picture is so thin and smooth that one wonders if Cézanne had left it in an early, iterative stage. More likely it is an experimental picture, taken as far as the artist felt it needed to go.

Cézanne enacts a similar experiment with a portrait of his wife Hortense in the early to mid-1880s, *Madame Cézanne in a Striped Dress* (cat. 9.3). Like the portrait of his son, the paint is applied thinly and loosely, defining clear contours. A heavy use of black enhances the schematic character of her features, giving her face a mask-like effect. Transparent dark washes are brushed over deep red pigment in the chair back and in the thin-skinned parts of her eyes, mouth and ears. Although she is pulled up to the picture plane, she is psychologically distant, impenetrable. The canvas was probably painted at the same time as (at least the early stages of) the larger and more ambitious Bührle Collection portrait, *Madame Cézanne with a Fan* (fig. 42), in which Hortense maintains her reserve but addresses the viewer with a disturbingly direct gaze through mostly blacked-out eyes.[10] The wallpaper is the same as that in the portrait of Louis Guillaume, and the red armchair and her hair style – pulled back with a small tufted fringe in the centre of her low forehead – are familiar from the Yokohama picture, but here she wears an impressive blue dress with ribboned sleeves.

Both the Bührle and the Yokohama portraits have a radical, proto-Cubist quality underlined by their provenance. The art collector Gertrude Stein hung the Bührle portrait in her salon in Paris, profoundly affecting the avant-garde artists who gathered there in the early decades of the twentieth century. The Yokohama picture was exhibited by patron John Quinn in the revolutionary Armory Show of 1913; it was then owned by co-founder of the Museum of Modern Art in New York, Mary Q. Sullivan, and later by the benefactor Walter Chrysler, who also held some ninety works by Picasso in his collection.[11]   MM

FIG. 42
Madame Cézanne with a Fan, *c.*1879; reworked 1886–8
Foundation E.G. Bührle Collection, Zurich; FWN 447

1 Michael Hoog, *Catalogue de la collection Jean Walter et Paul Guillaume* (Editions de la Réunion des Musées Nationaux, Paris, 1984), p.10: quoted in Paris–London–Philadelphia 1995–6, p.234. The still lifes are: FWN 765–71, 773–5, 777–82. See Jayne S. Warman's chronology in *The Paintings of Paul Cézanne: An Online Catalogue Raisonné*. Warman places these paintings in Melun, near Paris, where Cézanne rented an apartment in 1879–80.

2 Meyer Schapiro 1952, p.56.

3 L. Fulep, 'Salon d'Automne', *Szerda*, 31 October 1906. Quoted in Rewald 1996, p.283.

4 Juan Gris made a copy in graphite in 1916, and Arshile Gorky painted *Self-Portrait at the Age of Nine* (Metropolitan Museum of

Art, New York) after seeing Cézanne's *Portrait of Louis Guillaume* at Wildenstein's gallery in Paris in 1928. See Michael Taylor's discussion of Gorky's copy in Joseph J. Rishel and Katherine Sachs (eds), *Cézanne and Beyond* (Yale University Press in association with Philadelphia Museum of Art, Newhaven, 2009), pp.420–1.

5 Louis Guillaume would later pose, alongside Cézanne's son, for one of the artist's most accomplished figural paintings, *Mardi Gras* (1888, State Hermitage Museum, St Petersburg; FWN 668). See also the preparatory drawing of Guillaume's head for *Mardi Gras* (c.1888, Kunstmuseum, Basel).

6 See, for instance, FWN 456–60, 469 and 470.

7 Paul Cézanne to Charles Camoin, 22 February 1903. Danchev 2013, p.326.

8 For an excellent account of this unusual portrait, see also Richard Shiff, 'Mark, Motif, Materiality: The Cézanne Effect in the Twentieth Century', in Vienna–Zurich 2000, pp.108–9.

9 Rewald 1996, p.313.

10 For more on the Bührle portrait of Madame Cézanne, and her comparison of the picture with Pablo Picasso's *Gertrude Stein*, see Sidlauskas 2009, pp.4–5.

11 Lukas Gloor, 'Art History in the Making: The Reception of Cézanne between 1920 and 1950', in Judit Geskó (ed.), *Cézanne and the Past: Tradition and Creativity* (Museum of Fine Arts, Budapest, 2012), p.20.

CAT. 9.3
Madame Cézanne in a Striped Dress, 1883–5 (W only)
Yokohama Museum of Art; FWN 466

3 Comparative Portraiture

1885–90

Paul Cézanne, photographer unknown, c.1890
Photograph used for an exhibition card at the Salon of 1900

IN THE SECOND HALF of the 1880s, Cézanne painted some thirty-four portraits, a number equalled only in the second half of the 1860s when his portraiture practice was just beginning. However, two principal factors distinguish these periods: Cézanne was a much slower, more methodical artist in the 1880s than the impetuous young painter of the 1860s; and fully one half of the later portraits are of one person, Hortense Fiquet.

Cézanne produced twenty-eight or twenty-nine portraits of Hortense over the two decades from 1872 to 1892. The seventeen he painted in the second half of the 1880s represent the most condensed, continuous examination of the features of any one person that he ever made – and, in such a short period, of any single motif except Mont Sainte-Victoire.

The portraits form distinct groups. The first, a set of small, lightly painted canvases, was made just prior to or shortly after Hortense and Cézanne married in the spring of 1886. Although elusive in characterisation, these are the most expressive images of her he had yet made, and mark a major shift in his portraiture practice, which broadens its affective range from this moment. The second group, probably made a year or two later and comprising mostly larger, more heavily painted works, is more explicit in its description of emotion: showing Hortense as sulky and mournful, these have provoked startlingly misogynist interpretations of her character and connubial influence. So has, in a different way, the third group, of four portraits, showing a remote Hortense wearing a red dress. However, in all three instances, Cézanne matches affect with materiality, requiring us to engage with subtle and complex painterly constructions as much as with the illustrational.

The same is true of other portraits that he made in these years: newly expressive self-portraits made contemporaneously with the first set of images of Hortense; an exceptional painting of his young son made at the time of the second group; a further portrait of male adolescence, that of a boy wearing a red waistcoat, made along with the third; and, at some time during these years, his only self-portrait of himself at work, as monumental and forbidding an image of an artist as has ever been made. JE

CAT. 10.1
Self-Portrait, *c.*1885 (see also detail, p.42)
Carnegie Museum of Art, Pittsburgh; FWN 480

Self-Portraits of the Mid-1880s

The first of three self-portraits painted in 1885–6 (cat. 10.1) was based on a photograph taken in 1872 (fig. 43). It is, together with Cézanne's earliest self-portrait, which was painted two decades before (cat. 1.1), the only painted self-portrait to be composed in this way. The year in which this work was most probably made, 1885, was so extraordinarily unsettled for the artist that it may reasonably be described as one of crisis and personal transformation. Acute attacks of neuralgia in the early spring were succeeded by a disastrous love affair that led to two months of restless travel until, in August, Cézanne reached Gardanne, a hill town near Aix. Finally conceding to himself that he had no personal future except with Hortense Fiquet and their son Paul, he arranged for them to join him there in the autumn. The couple would marry the following spring legalising an almost seventeen-year-long relationship.[1] Whether or not this portrait was painted at Gardanne, we are right to wonder why Cézanne based it upon a photograph of 1872, the year when he legally recognised Paul as his son. And, whether or not we choose to associate it with that particular event, we must acknowledge that it was a retrospective production.

It is a strange image: the featureless turquoise background is similar to that of small, contemporaneous portraits of Hortense (cats 11.1, 11.2) and, more strikingly, to a large painting of her wearing a red dress painted a few years later (cat. 14.3). Here, the spectral, gaseous, undifferentiated space in which Cézanne stands reinforces the suggestion provided by his face that he is suspended in introspection. As with one of the small portraits of Hortense (cat. 11.1), one eye offers a frontal gaze while the other is occluded, but even the gazing eye here is unfocused, seeming to look but not see.

It has often been observed that the head seems too small for, or not securely attached to, the body.[2] This discontinuity becomes increasingly apparent when, scanning down the figure, we see that Cézanne has laid out the painting in three zones: head, torso and (not in the photograph) hands, resting on the back of

FIG. 43
Paul Cézanne, photographer unknown, 1872
Photograph on which cat. 10.1 was based

an upholstered chair. And he looks thinner, and his beard more carefully trimmed, than we have come to expect. Putting together the pieces, we see the artist, dressed as he looked thirteen years earlier, but now lost in thought, standing – may we say, waiting – in a featureless space behind an unoccupied chair.

By contrast, the two self-portraits that Cézanne probably made later, in 1885–6 (cats 10.2, 10.3), show a figure more forthcoming yet no more sociable. Almost identical in pose, they depict the artist wearing a bowler hat and looking back over his shoulder. Many earlier, and all later, self-portraits show him turned to look back in this direction, as may be expected from a right-handed painter looking at a mirror placed at his left. The only such portraits that show him turned still

further, actually looking behind himself, were those that he made twenty years earlier, in 1865–6, following his first self-portrait made after a photograph.[3] This succession of photograph-based and backward-looking self-portraits in both Cézanne's early and fully mature practice may be merely fortuitous. Or it may tell us something about his sense of identity in a way that invites comparison between these two periods of his work, twenty or more years apart.

They are the only painted self-portraits to show Cézanne wearing a bowler hat, although, judging from photographs, it would become his favourite headgear in his later years. Unsurprisingly, its appearance here has been associated with his father's hat-making profession prior to becoming a banker, and with his own entrance into 'the ranks of the bourgeoisie through his marriage'.[4]

In these interpretations, it is a symbol of a respectable Cézanne in his late forties – therefore, the polar opposite of how he had presented himself in the self-portraits of his early twenties with their backward-looking pose. Curator Lawrence Gowing spoke of the 'ferocity' displayed in one of the earlier works.[5] Neither of the later self-portraits are like that; yet they show not a confidently bourgeois figure but a dyspeptic one, wary and distrustful, with more than a hint of irritability in the tight-lipped, glaring face.

The portraits are more or less identical in size, and the thinly painted Copenhagen canvas appears to have functioned as an *esquisse* (painted sketch) for the other, more densely worked image. However, the former painting was not quickly sketched. True, the background is loosely hatched with multi-directional

CAT. 10.3
Self-Portrait with Bowler Hat, 1885–6
(P, L only)
Private collection; FWN 479

strokes, built up over a dense grid of pencil strokes, and the hat and jacket are left with multiple small, and a few large, patches of uncovered canvas. When painting the head, though, Cézanne carefully modelled the large volume in the diagonal, constructive brush-strokes of the 1880s. Moreover, he returned later to the image to outline in pencil the internal and external contours of the face and neck, paying particular atten-tion to the ear and nose, and to add a few strokes of the turquoise used in the background to the side of the beard; these arrest our focus even as we are conscious that the artist's eyes are glaring at us.

The second painting is not only more heavily painted than the first, it is also heavily painted in thick, dark pigment that gives it a material density akin to that of Cézanne's early portraits. The contraction of the image into one unit, from the curve of the shoulder to the crown of the bowler, adds mass to the density; and the painting of the beard – grey and dark ochre hinting at green, and reading as paint before it reads as facial hair – cements the portrait to its similarly toned ground. The tenebrous result has something of the unreal quality of an image in a dark mirror, as well as recalling a photograph. JE

1 Danchev 2012, pp.228–34.

2 R 587, in an extensive entry on this canvas.

3 FWN 397-TA, 403.

4 Platzman 2001, pp.161–7, 170.

5 Lawrence Gowing, 'The Early Work of Paul Cézanne', in London–Paris–Washington, D.C. 1988–9, p.5.

Small Format Portraits of Madame Cézanne

Hortense Fiquet became Madame Cézanne in spring 1886, shortly before or just after certainly three, and probably all four, of these portraits were painted. Compared to the stately, reserved figure in the preceding, densely painted portraits of her (see cats 7.1, 7.2), we see a far more delicate and vulnerable young woman. In fact, we may be forgiven for thinking her actually much younger, especially in the Berlin portrait (cat. 11.1), than the figure enthroned on the red chair in the work that so impressed the poet Rainer Maria Rilke (cat. 7.1), painted eight or nine years earlier.

Younger, and also more human. Despite – or perhaps aided by – their modest size, these four canvases mark a major change in Cézanne's portraiture. They comprise two pairs: delicately painted canvases (cats 11.1, 11.2) and the weightier portraits (cats 11.3, 11.4).[1] As a series, they demonstrate four very different representations of Hortense; and with them, more definitively than in any portraits that precede them, the fiction that Cézanne painted figures without affect finally has to break down.

This is not to say, though, that the emotion that Hortense displays is unequivocal, transparently one-dimensional.[2] On the contrary, it is extremely hard to particularise, especially in the Berlin painting. Critics seem agreed that, while she is almost pretty and vividly present, the frontal gaze of her right eye is opposed by the occlusion of her left; and that this division may be thought to speak of inner power projected versus a sad, unfathomable introspection, which means that she is at once open and closed to the viewer.[3] At the same time, the sculpted, almost perfect oval of her head approaches idealisation.

However, affect presents itself not solely in facial expression: it also does so in terms of bodily position, as much when Hortense is shown as all but immobile, as she is here, when her posture *implies* movement, as in two of the other three of these paintings. And affect may also be recorded in other areas of the painting, through markings that, while not illustrative of perceived emotion, may embody it in their touch, speed, scale and, of course, colour.

The painting of the brocade dress in the Berlin and Philadelphia paintings (cats 11.1, 11.2) is a case in point. Its lively patterning was produced by light, diagonal brushstrokes that run on top and beneath the curling linear patterns that decorate the front and collar. Cézanne would speak to the poet Joachim Gasquet of wanting to capture the effect of 'brightness, gently rocking to and fro, moist and shimmering'.[4] In the Berlin painting, the tempo of the shimmer slows as it rises, the pattern gradually disappearing and the light within the colour darkening until both are extinguished in the solid black that drapes Hortense's shoulders. Although Cézanne's paint handling includes passages of quick, spontaneous application, these sit within an impression of patient and methodical composition that accrues to our understanding of the sitter even as we recognise that it speaks of the painter.

The delicate washes of cool blue-green, applied in overlapping vertical strokes, which fall gently around Hortense's neck and head, speak of carefulness and caring alike. However, they also reinforce a sense of vitreous fragility, especially when they meet a range of warmer tones that lighten to pink highlights, again delicately applied, where the very solicitude of the painter's brushwork disinvites touch.

In the Philadelphia painting (cat. 11.2), by contrast, the surface of the dress, its pattern shimmering at the left side of its fastening, darkens abruptly, the linear pattern disappearing with it, at the right side, which seems hurriedly filled. Moreover, this dissonant jump in value across the dress, together with the sharp thirty-degree leftward tilt of its fastening (continued by the angle of her head), combine to give to a conventional three-quarter pose the implication of decidedly turning away from contact with the viewer, including the painter, of course.

CAT. 11.2
Madame Cézanne, 1885–6
Philadelphia Museum of Art; FWN 476

FIG. 44
Madame Cézanne, a study, 1885–6
Solomon R. Guggenheim Museum,
New York; FWN 481

Art historian Ruth Butler describes the facial expression as 'rigid, pinched, angry'.[5] This may be too strong. But a face composed of distinctly unblended diagonal patches, with the hair even more summarily treated, conveys an impatience akin to that shown by the treatment of the dress. It is reinforced by the background, where the gentle rain of colour in the Berlin painting is replaced by storm clouds dropping vertically and buffeting the left side of Hortense's face. Whether the disquietude came from sitter to painter, or vice versa, hardly matters; what is significant is the way that what presents itself as barely contained displeasure so bristles with pictorial energy. And perhaps Cézanne had asked his wife to pose like this.

Compared to these, the second pair of paintings show figures from which their own energy seems drained. The portrait in Aix-en-Provence (cat. 11.3) has been said to convey a look of 'baleful reproach' and 'accusatory annoyance',[6] but could also be said to show sheer tiredness. The one in Philadelphia (cat. 11.4) has been thought to suggest melancholy, almost mournfulness,[7] but also 'weakness, submission, and self-concern, such as we find in old images of praying and penitent saints'.[8] It has also been pointed out that a woman awaiting the arrival of a lover was often shown letting down her hair.[9] The ambiguity of these paintings does not extend to incorporating all such readings. In fact, the last of these suggestions presumes that Cézanne would have fallen so low as to deliver the kind of narrative we might expect from a Pre-Raphaelite. Nonetheless, the very fact that they have all been proposed does point, at once, to the danger of being too specific about such works, and to the artist's passivity about meaning that opens them up to such ambiguity.

Like the first pair of portraits considered here, one of this pair is all but immobile and the other expressive of movement. The former, the Aix-en-Provence painting, is also akin to the one in Berlin in having one staring and one unfocused eye, the figure being settled in place with frontal matter-of-factness to reach almost to the top of the pictorial rectangle. It is the greater tilt of the head that makes all the difference, pressing the pose into a more questioning position. And while the dappled, lightly touched, watercolour-like treatment of the background to the right gives it a quality of tenderness like that of the Berlin painting,[10] the opaque banding at the left side, perhaps derived from the meeting of two walls, is a brake to it. Set between these very opposite zones, Hortense's head floats mysteriously, the glimpse of bright red, carmine lake pigment above her collar associating with the wispy strands of sienna brown that weave through the upper part of her hair. What may well be a study for this painting (fig. 44) shows Cézanne already planning something special for this part of the picture.

The vertical division at the upper left of the second Philadelphia portrait, more certainly describing the corner of two walls, irrationally does not carry on

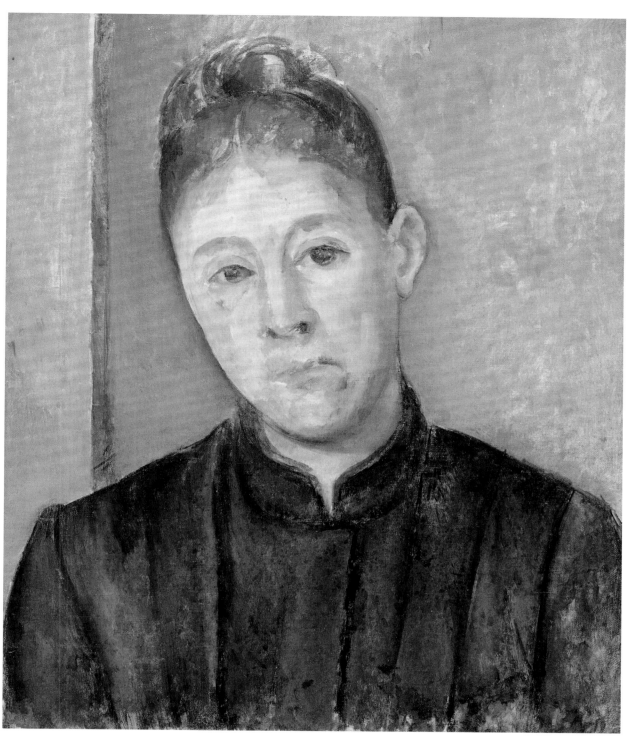

CAT. 11.3
Madame Cézanne, 1885–6
Musée d'Orsay, Paris, on loan to Musée Granet,
Aix-en-Provence; FWN 482

FIG. 45
Lady in a Fur Wrap, after El Greco,
1885–6
Private collection; FWN 472

below the side of Hortense's head.[11] Cézanne nearly always used some device to link a portrait figure to the picture shape.[12] This one, however, serves the additional functions of stopping a movement of the head that is propelled by vigorous brushmarks on its opposite side, at the right of the painting; of measuring the tilt this movement has produced; and of calling out the stripes on the bodice of Hortense's dress, stripes that, as Meyer Schapiro observed, 'contribute a soft, wavering current of feeling channelled to the head and prolonged in the silhouette of the hair,'[13] where it carries through this one vertical to the top edge of the painting.

This 'soft, wavering current of feeling', carried by ribbons of shimmering grey and black that stream over and shape the figure, and flow on to surround her face,

is no less important to setting the mood of the portrait than the depiction of withdrawal in the face itself. Cézanne had noticed something similar in a portrait by El Greco that he had copied from an engraving (fig. 45), namely that what reads as a protective mantle invokes a quality of wilful self-isolation. However, Schapiro asks us to see this portrait of Hortense not only as an image of 'the passive and frail in this feminine nature … a tender image of ascetic feeling', but also one in which 'it is as if [Cézanne] transferred to his wife his own repression and shyness'.

It may reasonably be said that all four of these paintings speak of these qualities, whether transferring them to, or discovering them in, his wife. JE

1 The second Philadelphia painting (FWN 500) was dated 1890–2 by John Rewald without explanation of why it should be thus separated from the other three paintings discussed here, which he dates to 1885–7. Venturi conversely dated this work to 1885–7 and the three other works to 1883–6. (See R 475, 476, 482, 685.)

2 Sidlauskas 2009, p.780 ff., argues this point eloquently.

3 Butler 2008, p.63; Sidlauskas 2009, pp.10, 96.
4 Gasquet 1921, p.118; Gasquet 1991, p.153.
5 Butler 2008, p.66.
6 Sidlauskas 2009, p.74.
7 Ibid., p.70.
8 Schapiro 1962, p.70.
9 Sidlauskas 2009, p.71.
10 See Charlotte Hale, 'A Template for Experimentation', in New York 2014–15, p.58, for the watercolour-like treatment of this work.

11 Hale, ibid., p.59, points out that technical examination shows Cézanne did not paint out the lower part of the vertical division but rather never intended it to continue in the lower part of the composition.
12 Ibid.
13 Schapiro 1962, p.70.

CAT. 11.4

Madame Cézanne in a Striped Dress, 1885–6 (see also detail, p.115)

Philadelphia Museum of Art; FWN 500

CAT. 12.1
Paul Cézanne, the Artist's Son, 1886–7 (w only)
National Gallery of Art, Washington, D.C.; FWN 486

Portraits of Father and Son

Cézanne's previous half-dozen or so paintings of his son, Paul, born in 1872, had pictured him as a young boy aged from three to ten, or a little older. This portrait (cat. 12.1) was probably painted between October 1886 and January 1888 at the Jas de Bouffan, where Cézanne was living while Hortense and young Paul had been settled elsewhere in Aix. If so, it shows him aged fourteen to sixteen, but looking grown-up, dressed-up and proud of it.[1] Art historian Jayne S. Warman has conjectured whether he could be wearing the outfit he wore on 28 April 1886 for his parents' wedding.

The young Paul Cézanne wears a bowler hat similar to, and possibly even the same as, the one that his father wore in two self-portraits made a year or two earlier (cats 10.2, 10.3). But it seems a little too small for him, and his jacket a bit tight, so as well as suggesting a teenager wearing adult clothing, it also suggests one who is growing out of his clothes. And he looks a trifle smug. Compared to the impassive or sullenly disconnected appearance of his mother in contemporaneous portraits (see cats 11.3–11.4), he also appears to be far more self-aware. But it is impossible to know whether this is because he was a less seasoned model than his mother, or because he was a less familiar model for his father. Either way, Cézanne paints him as a fascinating specimen of humanity new to his scrutiny, a surprising image recording a surprised painterly confrontation.

The painting has the additional resonance of placing the teenager in a space that speaks of both his parents. The tear-drop wallpaper against which he is posed is clearly the same as that behind his mother in the two large, contemporaneous portraits of her now in Houston and Detroit (cats 13.2, 13.3), and possibly a smaller one in Paris (cat. 13.1);[2] and he seems embedded in its warm pattern, just as she is, especially so in the Detroit painting. Both are rich, painterly constructions. But, whereas she faces out to us, her son looks to his left, offering the right side of his head to us just as his father does in virtually all his self-portraits. And this implication that he is a surrogate for his father (against the background of his mother) is emphasised by the edge of what is probably the painted frame of a mirror in front of him. The association of a painter beside his canvas is inescapable – especially because Cézanne also painted a portrait of himself beside his canvas, *Self-Portrait with Palette* (cat. 12.2), in which he wears a very similar jacket and open-necked shirt.

Although often said to be a later canvas, there is good reason to believe that *Self-Portrait with Palette* may have been painted in the same timespan as the portrait of his son.[3] If so, art historian Mary Tompkins Lewis's description of the painting – 'a poignantly personal construction' conveying 'a sense of isolation or protective refuge that he finds in his art' – gains a specific context, that of Cézanne living apart from his family and painting at the Jas de Bouffan.[4] In 1865, he had painted an interior view of his studio, focusing on an unframed canvas positioned behind the stovepipe, its 'face' turned away from the viewer, a traditional image of the mystery of creation in the privacy of the workplace.[5] More than twenty years later, he reprises the theme with his own presence behind the easel, thereby tying this self-portrait to its great, seventeenth-century prototypes by Velázquez and Rembrandt.[6] But, in addition to mystery and privacy, the elements of the composition of Cézanne's canvas invoke a fortification – critics have used the terms 'barrier' and 'barricade' – constructed to exclude the outside world.[7]

Meyer Schapiro has written eloquently of how, in this painting, 'the most human element is bound to the non-human and both are stable and constrained', this bond requiring that 'the normal, irregular overlapping of things' be surrendered.[8] The almost vertical left edge of the shield-like palette is, therefore, made precisely continuous with the sleeve above it; and the tips of the brushes stop abruptly, just short of the far edge of the jacket, their bristles overpainted by the black strokes of the adjacent sleeve. That sleeve, in turn, appears to be

CAT. 12.2
Self-Portrait with Palette, 1886–7 (P only)
Foundation E.G. Bührle Collection, Zurich; FWN 499

in plane with the side of the canvas, and sleeve, canvas and palette share the actual picture plane – except that the diagonal strut of the easel is the most proximate part of the composition. The materials of painting, the canvas on the easel and the palette and brushes, make a rectangular frame for the artist at work. Schapiro aptly compares the strict, closing pattern to the diagram of a building plan, yet the painting is all façade with no sense of a ground plan at all, everything compressed into the shallowest of depth. Even so, the body seems massive and barrel-chested, the head sculpturally carved, and the palette and canvas oversized; all to a monumental effect.

This is the only painted self-portrait to show him with the tools of his trade.[9] Although his shirt and jacket are not dissimilar to those worn by his son and have been said to speak of a properly dressed artist,[10] other writers have seen his attire to be more akin to workers' clothes, and this painting Cézanne's self-presentation as an artist-labourer.[11] If so, he presents himself hardly as plebeian. Even more than usual in his portraits, the tone is hard to fix. He is at once in self-protective custody within the fortress of the geometry, and an aggressive, virile presence contained.

The motif of the exposed thumb next to the brushes would perhaps seem less phallic had not Picasso and Matisse both restated it as such in their own self-portraits,[12] but it is placed to be noticed. So are the mismatched eyes (often to be found in his portraits), his right one perhaps looking at his canvas while his left glances surreptitiously at us; that is also to say, at his own image in a mirror. However, owing to their unfinish, both eyes seem to be almost sightless within a face that may appear utterly impersonal or entirely absorbed – or even, given the glints of reflected light in the eyes, radiant with the artist's vision. And the stony, hewed power of the image is pulled back from sternness or harshness by the delicate landscape colouration of the background and of the patches of paint that completely fill the palette, making it seem like a fragment of a landscape painting itself.

This delicacy notwithstanding, it is a forbidding image of a disquieted artist; and, knowing that its composition is echoed in the portrait of his son, the note of complacency that he observed in Paul *fils* becomes the more evident by contrast. We hardly ever think of Cézanne as an ironical artist, but this may be a rare exception. JE

---

1 The dressed-up appearance of Paul *fils* associates this portrait with his appearance as the model for Harlequin in the three later paintings of this subject, as well as *Mardi Gras*, a work in which he is accompanied by Pierrot, modelled by his friend Louis Guillaume. See FWN 668–71.

2 I owe to Jayne S. Warman the suggestion that these works – therefore, by extension, this painting of Paul *fils* – were made at Aix during this period. They have been placed later, and in Paris; however, features of the background of the Detroit and Houston paintings resemble those known to have been painted at the Jas, including FWN 522.

3 It has been argued that *Self-Portrait with Palette* could have been seen by Vincent van Gogh in the Paris shop of the colour merchant Julien 'Père' Tanguy, prompting the Dutchman to paint his own *Self-Portrait in Front of an Easel*, a painting dated between December 1887 and February 1888. See Françoise Cachin and Bogomila Welsh-Ovcharov in *Van Gogh à Paris*, exh. cat.,

Musée d'Orsay, Paris, 1988, cat. 68, p.174. If Cézanne's self-portrait was indeed painted prior to Van Gogh's, the latest it could have been painted was within the year or so beginning October 1886; and the low wainscot behind Cézanne in the self-portrait was a feature of the Jas de Bouffan that appears in paintings known to have been painted there, including the later portraits with arms crossed (see p.184, note 4). Although dated *c*.1890 by Rewald, *Self-Portrait with Palette* was dated by Venturi to 1885–7; then revised to 1883–5 (which does seem too early); and by Ratcliffe possibly to 1886–8. In this work, Cézanne looks closer in age to his 1885–6 portraits (cats 10.1–10.3) than the aged figure in those of the mid-1890s (FWN 511, 517). He resembles his image in drawings customarily dated to the early 1880s, for example Andersen 1970, no.19, which shows a similar treatment of the nose with the side and front planes schematically divided.

4 Lewis 2000, p.244.

5 FWN 703; see John Elderfield, 'Studio Visits', in *In the Studio. Paintings*, exh. cat., Gagosian Gallery, New York, 2015, pp.21–2.

6 Rembrandt, *Portrait of the Artist at His Easel*, 1660, Musée du Louvre, and Velázquez, *Las Meninas* or *La Familia de Felipe IV*, *c*.1656, Museo Nacional del Prado, Madrid.

7 Schapiro 1962, p.34; Lewis 2000, p.244.

8 Schapiro, ibid.

9 He also appears behind a canvas in a lithograph of *c*.1899 (fig. 75).

10 Lewis 2000, p.246.

11 Platzman 2001, pp.177–9, in a fine description of this painting; Athanassoglou-Kallmyer 2003, pp.229–31, referring to accounts of Cézanne leading the life of a peasant; however, her suggestion that this painting defines him as a 'plebeian worker-artist' (p.229) hardly gels with the majesty of his self-representation.

12 Pablo Picasso, *Self-Portrait with Palette*, 1906, Philadelphia Museum of Art, and Henri Matisse, *Self-Portrait*, 1918, Musée Matisse, Le Cateau-Cambrésis.

Portraits of Madame Cézanne in a Blue Dress

After some fifteen years spent living off Cézanne's allowance and occasional loans from his friends, and constantly moving between apartments in Paris and back and forth to the South of France, in the later 1880s Hortense Fiquet experienced some domestic stability. Although he had been referring to her as his 'wife' and 'Madame Cézanne' for over a decade, Cézanne finally acknowledged their union publicly, marrying her in Aix in 1886. His father passed away several months later, leaving Cézanne an inheritance, and Hortense's father then died in 1889, presumably leaving her a little money of her own. However, years of living in the shadows with their son, left in Marseille while Cézanne visited his father and sister at the Jas de Bouffan or his mother at L'Estaque, or alone in Paris while he visited friends and painted in various locations in northern France *sur le motif* ('before nature'), had surely taken their toll.[1] Even after they were made a legal couple, Cézanne rented accommodation for Hortense and Paul in Aix, to which he moved their furniture from Paris, while remaining himself with his mother and sister at the Jas de Bouffan. While he would take care of her and seemed to want her nearby, he could not bring himself to live with her.[2]

The Paris, Houston and Detroit portraits of Cézanne's wife exude an emotional character that corresponds to what we know about the sitter and her life. She seems sullen, dislocated and melancholic. We sense the expression not only of Hortense's emotional self-presentation to the painter, but also Cézanne's own profound comprehension of her plight. His complicity in, and identity with, her latent anguish underlies the effect of these images.

Cézanne's refusal to make the gestures traditional to the genre of female portraiture unleashed one of the more startling strains of misogyny in art history. Writers regret that she was not more beautiful, the historical arbiter of a female sitter's worthiness of artistic attention, and her refusal to ingratiate, her failure to smile, damned her in critics' eyes.[3] One

writer inferred from her impassivity a 'stunned stupidity',[4] another blamed 'that sour-looking bitch' for what he perceived as the artist's repression.[5] Dumb, mean, unsupportive and irrelevant – the dehumanisation and vilification of Hortense is generic to the Cézanne literature.

Indeed, these three portraits of her in a blue dress are among the 'toughest'. Her hair is pulled back severely, which de-feminises her in a way that most of the other portraits, which at least allow a glimpse of her topknot, or more movingly her loose tresses in the Philadelphia work (cat. 11.4), do not. The most austere is the Paris head study (cat. 13.1). Owned during the first half of the twentieth century by Henri Matisse, it is the most abstract, with the elegant understatement and polish of a Brancusi sculpture.[6] Her sparse head is simplified to include only one ear, which serves to balance the composition the way her right ear does in the New York painting, *Madame Cézanne in a Red Dress* (cat. 14.4).[7] The artist turns the sitter's head slightly off a frontal axis, misaligning her sharp hair-parting from the seam in the wall behind, and echoing her profile in the suggestion of faint lozenges in the wallpaper to her right. Against this subtle torsion, the strong contours of her head, face and neck ground her in the composition. The soft, open collar and fluttering seam descending her jacket enliven the geometry. The thinness of the paint surface, with evidence of graphite under-drawing across her face, and the smaller dimensions mark this as a study for the Houston and/or Detroit paintings (cats 13.2, 13.3).

In the Houston painting, her face is turned wholly towards the painter, whom she engages with a direct gaze in a pose of 'obdurate frontality'.[8] Her left ear is seen in profile, however, and her head breaks free from alignment with the wall seam behind her and with the strongly sculpted pedestal of her neck. The decorative shapes of the brown sideboard and wallpaper to her right animate the background, advancing menacingly towards the sitter until the composition opens up

CAT. 13.1
Madame Cézanne, 1886–7
Musée d'Orsay, Paris; FWN 488

Madame Cézanne in Blue, 1886–7 (see also detail, p.127)
Museum of Fine Arts, Houston; FWN 489

CAT. 13.3
Madame Cézanne, 1886–7 (L, W only)
Detroit Institute of Arts; FWN 487

again into luminous cool tones, lightly brushed into the verticals and horizontals of the wall moulding. The painting succeeds in offering a convincing presence, even as the image dissolves into illegibility and abstract marks on the canvas.

Larger but less resolved, the Detroit *Madame Cézanne* has Hortense posed against the same wallpaper, but backed by a curtain. Cézanne has pulled further back to include her lap and clasped hands. The entangled thumbs and index fingers feel tentative, as if their reach is not quite afforded by her short arms. Her nose is more hooked and her mouth is pulled into something of a pout. While the scattered glimpses of naked canvas in the Houston painting enhance the luminosity of her coat, in the Detroit painting there is more a sense of unfinish.

With these three paintings, Cézanne has thoroughly deconstructed the conventions of female portraiture. Rather than present an ideal of beauty or morality, or a seductive muse, the paintings record his sensations and emotions experienced visually over time, sharing her space, allowing the perceptual moment to guide his brush. His challenge is to remain open to the constant flux of visual input, not only from sitting to sitting but also from moment to moment, while adhering to more 'decorative', abstract impulses. In a period in which identity, and more emphatically gender identity, was overtly rigid in construction and definition, this slipping away from conventional terrain was, and remains, quite radical.[9] MM

1 See Butler 2008, p.46.

2 Cézanne seems to have had a close relationship with his mother, who was a constant source of support and affection throughout his life. See Danchev 2013, with a specific account of this fact in a letter to the artist Charles Camoin, 3 February 1902. There is a mysterious letter, perhaps never sent, written by Cézanne to an unknown lover in the late 1880s, as well as at least one reference (August 1885) to his use of brothels (Danchev 2012, p.239).

3 Susan Sidlauskas, 'Emotion, Color, Cézanne (The Portraits of Hortense)', *Nineteenth-Century Art Worldwide*, 3, no.2, autumn 2004, p.1.

4 Jack Lindsay, *Cézanne: His Life and Art*, 1969, p.131, quoted in Sidlauskas 2004, see note 3, p.2.

5 Roger Fry to Helen Anrep, 1 May 1925, in *The Letters of Roger Fry*, ed. Denys Sutton (Chatto & Windus, London, 1972), p.568.

6 Paris–London–Philadelphia 1995–6, p.320.

7 Tamar Garb, 'Touching Sexual Difference: *Madame Cézanne in a Red Dress*', in Garb, *The Painted Face: Portraits of Women in France 1814–1914* (Yale University Press, New Haven, 2007), p.169.

8 Linda Nochlin, 'Cézanne's Portraits', Geske Lectures (College of Fine and Performing Arts, University of Nebraska, Lincoln), 1996, p.11. See also Charlotte Hale's study

of infra-red and x-ray images of several of the Fiquet portraits, in which she finds earlier, more emotionally expressive iterations of the sitter, which had been overlain with paint marks as Cézanne abstracted her form to serve the painting as a whole. Charlotte Hale, 'A Template for Experimentation: Cézanne's Process and the Paintings of Hortense Fiquet', in Amory 2014, pp.45–71.

9 See Sidlauskas 2009, p.147, and Garb 2007, see note 7, p.171.

Portraits of Madame Cézanne in a Red Dress

Having inherited a considerable estate on the death of his father, early in 1888 Cézanne rented an upper-middle-class apartment on the fifth floor of a building at 15, quai d'Anjou in Paris, on the north side of the Ile Saint-Louis; and then, or later that year, he also established a studio on the rue du Val-de-Grâce, a half-hour's walk away on the Left Bank, not far from the Jardin du Luxembourg.

Cézanne retained the apartment for two years, before moving his family in January 1890 to the avenue d'Orléans. His wife and son appear to have lived there more or less continuously, but recent research suggests that Cézanne did not, spending five months over the summer of 1888 at the Hôtel Delacourt in Chantilly, visiting and painting in Paris from time to time, and another five months at the Jas de Bouffan in Aix from July through to November 1889.[1] Nonetheless, the quai d'Anjou proved to be an extremely fertile venue for the artist, the two sets of portraits he made there, or in the nearby studio, comprising sequential examinations of a sitter executed in extremely systematic ways. Four were of a young Italian man, shown in different poses (cat. 15.1, figs 50–2). The other four were portraits of his wife, shown in an identical pose, paintings that all but complete his long series of portraits of her, which began almost twenty years before. After leaving the quai d'Anjou, he made only one or two more.

After Cézanne and Hortense Fiquet began their relationship in 1869, they were rarely apart for the next nine years. Subsequently, though, there were more periods of separation than of cohabitation, until an interval before and after their marriage in April 1886, when they spent a year together in Gardanne. But then came another, roughly similar period of separation, during which Cézanne was living at the Jas de Bouffan, and Hortense and their son were ensconced elsewhere in Aix. Therefore, even allowing for Cézanne's two spells of absence, he and Hortense spent what was for them a considerable time together at the quai d'Anjou; and, moreover, in a superior apartment with the implication, presumably, of a more settled family life.

An important question posed by this extended period of cohabitation, coming after their unsettled existence, is what effect did it have on the creation of these paintings? One answer is straightforward: it afforded continuity and familiarity. Another, however, is counter-intuitive: it induced the representation of distance.

In three of the four paintings, Hortense posed in a red dress, seated on a yellow, floral-patterned, seventeenth-century-style chair in the quai d'Anjou apartment. Cézanne clearly enjoyed the pattern created by the shawl collar leading into heavy folds down the centre of the bodice, with tight vertical pleats to each side. It allowed him to renew the 'persistent parallelism' that had entered his work with the portrait of Achille Emperaire (cat. 4.2) twenty years earlier.[2] And he once bragged to Camille Pissarro, 'I, only I, know how to paint a real red.'[3] Art historian Susan Sidlauskas has explained that this is a house dress of the kind that most nineteenth-century bourgeois women would not have worn outside.[4] But if this places Hortense in the uniform of a *femme au foyer*, a housewife, the vividness of the red, together with the formal immobility of her pose, dispels any thought of domestic activity on her part – an immobility reinforced by the repetition of the same pose, one pair of these works showing Hortense half-turned to the left (cats 14.1, 14.2), the other pair in full face (cats 14.3, 14.4).

Cézanne typically worked by laying down sketchy lines and loosely brushed areas in turpentine-thinned paint. Charlotte Hale, Senior Paintings Conservator at the Metropolitan Museum of Art, New York, who has studied these four canvases the most closely,[5] observes that in the Basel canvas (cat. 14.1) much of this lay-in is still visible, together with areas of unpainted, white canvas that run throughout the composition, most noticeably in the face and hands, in the lower part of the dress and chair, and in the chair-rail running across the background.[6] However, it seems clear that some details were added after the paint had dried or almost

CAT. 14.1

Madame Cézanne in a Red Dress, 1888–90 (P, W only)

Fondation Beyeler, Basel; FWN 490

CAT. 14.2
Madame Cézanne in a Red Dress, 1888–90
Art Institute of Chicago; FWN 492

FIG. 46
Basel portrait (CAT. 14.1) and Chicago portrait (CAT. 14.2) superimposed

Both these works are on standard canvas size with external contours of dress and chair, and internal contours of dress, almost identical in both, suggesting that the second may have been traced from the first.

dried,[7] suggesting more than one session of work on the painting; perhaps it had been taken back from the apartment to the studio and worked on there without the presence of the model.

It is also more than possible that the Chicago painting (cat. 14.2) was worked on entirely in the studio, without the presence of the model, so evidently is it a development of the Basel portrait. Both are on a standard figure 25 canvas (81 × 65 cm), and the external contours of the dress and chair, and critical internal contours of the dress, are almost identical in both works, suggesting that the second may actually have been traced from the first, and then fine adjustments made (fig. 46). Technical examination has, in fact, revealed that the under-drawing and initial painting of the Chicago canvas were close to those of the preceding work, and then, as Cézanne worked, he tightened and simplified the composition. Most noticeable is the powerful volumetric inflation of both face and costume, Hortense's cheeks puffed out as if she were holding her breath. The warm colour causes the red dress to both expand and advance, the cool grey-blue wall falling back behind her. Cézanne has pulled her head to the left to align it better with the line of folds running down the bodice, and added

paint around the eyes and mouth to reduce them to narrow slits in her bloated mask of a face – with, as usual, only one ear visible. As Ruth Butler has observed, 'Never before, when working with Hortense, had he created anything that was at once so monumental and so remote. Hortense is barely Hortense.'[8]

Images of Hortense in a blue dress, made before the red-dress paintings, have similarly slit-like eyes and mouths (cats 13.1–13.3).[9] Cézanne may well have referred to one of these, the canvas in Detroit (cat. 13.3), when reshaping the arms from the Basel painting into more continuous tubular volumes and repositioning the hands for the Chicago painting. In the Detroit portrait, the hands comprise a lumpy conglomerate. In the Chicago picture, they resemble something 'half octopus, half tropical flower', as art historian Kenneth Clark described the hands of Thetis in Ingres's great painting that Cézanne knew from the Musée d'Aix-en-Provence (today the Musée Granet).[10]

The entwined hands also invoke a celebrated remark that he made later to Joachim Gasquet. Spreading his hands apart, then bringing them together and intertwining his fingers, he said, 'That's what one needs to achieve ... I advance all of my canvas at one time, if you

FIG. 47
São Paulo portrait (CAT. 14.3) and New York portrait (CAT. 14.4) superimposed

Despite their dissimilar sizes, the contours of the dress in both paintings are almost identical, suggesting that the figure in the second may have been traced from the first.

know what I mean.'[11] The mutual touching of the hands and interlocking of the fingers may therefore be thought to be at once an analogy for the process of pictorial composition and a reminder of the painter's joined brushstrokes that shape the composition.[12]

In the second pair of portraits, the São Paulo and New York paintings (cats 14.3, 14.4), the hands with their sinuous fingers are untwined, and one of them holds a flower. The canvases are similar to the first pair in that, despite their dissimilar sizes – the former on an 89 × 70cm canvas (not a standard size), the latter on a figure 50 canvas (116 × 89cm) – the contours of the dress in both paintings are almost identical (fig. 47).[13] The former has been said to be a study for the latter, comprising an examination of the motif on a smaller canvas, and without a setting, before embarking on the larger, more developed and more complex composition.[14] Whether or not this is so, the São Paulo work is unique among Cézanne's larger portraits in abjuring any background incident whatsoever.[15] He spread a bright, atmospheric green around the red dress, itself brighter than in the other three paintings, but made to seem brighter still by virtue of the complementary contrast. Nothing quite like this would be painted by any artist for

twenty years; it is Cézanne's most 'Matissean' painting.[16]

It is, in one respect, the most casual and straight-forward of all four,[17] but in another it is also hieratic and sculptural. It may be inferred that Hortense is sitting on a short bench, which is covered by the skirt of her dress. However, she seems almost to float on the picture surface, the red dress, now placed in a frontal position, displaying an almost vertical drop of folds from neck to hands so as to divide the figure. Cézanne has described the volume of the dress as being like the pleats of a pair of bellows that describe the air they contain – and the dress may be perceived as hollow, vacant of internal substance; viewed thus, its buoyancy increases, and Hortense looms into proximity. However, Cézanne has opposed the clarity of the face to the uncertainty of the flower, so distant beneath it that face and flower can only be taken in as two discrete events in successive perceptions of the painting. As attention competes with distraction,[18] Hortense's presence becomes less close than it had seemed.

The companion New York painting more explicitly sets attention against distraction, showing a more absorbingly detailed figure built from what extended viewing shows to be competing as well as collaborating

FIG. 48
The Curtain, 1888–90
Abegg Foundation, Riggisberg,
Switzerland; FWN 817

parts. Moreover, this vividly human presence also competes and collaborates with the world of objects that surround it in a domestic interior. It is the earliest of a trio of late paintings where Cézanne untypically placed a portrait subject within the reach of, yet able to dominate, extremely distracting surroundings.[19] Here, he unleashes environmental disequilibrium, while giving the image of Hortense the power to rein it in; and the painting, again in extended viewing, quivers with these contradictory messages.

Hortense, full-face, impassive and aloof, stares at the viewer with her right eye, but looks past into space with her left. She is seated, as she is in the Basel and Chicago paintings, on the familiar yellow chair against the familiar wall, again divided into blue and grey by a dark stripe and the chair-rail below it, both of which now tip down giddily to the right, threatening to tip her off balance. They also appear to push forward the lower part of the wall; and once this is recognised, Hortense on her chair moves forward towards us. Then, the edge of a gold-framed mirror in the upper left corner appears to float impossibly even further forward. Cézanne made a separate study, set against an undifferentiated space, of the opulent swag of drapery patterned with fruit and flowers that we see above (fig. 48). In the New York painting, it casts beautiful, grey shadows, but these do not rest on Hortense's head, and it is neither ahead, adjacent, nor behind where Hortense sits, motionless, as the pieces of her surroundings, seemingly freed from gravity, move around her. Beside the edge of the fireplace at the left, the long arms of fire irons are shown in a repetitive blur, as if the eye is not focusing on them properly. And yet, for all this movement, she commands the space, her tilt to the right of the painting seeming to be as much the cause, as the result, of the tilting of the room itself.

Her dress is divided more firmly down the centre than in the preceding painting, and the enclosure of its tapered vertical pleating by the arms the more strongly asserted – to such a definitive extent that she appears to have risen up to assume a solid form, from hands to head, from the translucent veil of the skirt beneath. And the division of the body is echoed in the bifurcation of the face, the side in shadow – the side that looks at the viewer – seemingly that of an older person compared to that represented by its doll-like illuminated counterpart.[20] But both sides are equally, explicitly, made of paint; patches, strokes and smears of it (fig. 49). These features imbue her image with a slower temporal quality, suggestive of becoming, in contrast to the more detached, piecemeal shifts in the space around her. The rose is less clearly defined here than the flower in the preceding painting: it would otherwise have become too arresting a prop, prompting restless up-and-down viewing, inimical to the quiet movement within Hortense's body that distinguishes it from the staccato world of objects that hem her in from both sides. JE

1   See Chronology, p.240.

2   The term is Lawrence Gowing's: see 'The Early Work of Paul Cézanne', in London–Paris–Washington D.C. 1988–9, p.15.

3   Pissarro to his son Lucien, 20 January 1896. Butler 2008, p.74.

4   Sidlauskas 2009, pp.178–9.

5   Charlotte Hale, 'A Template for Experimentation', in New York 2014–15, pp.67–71.

6   Further evidence of the spontaneity of composition is the fact that the face reveals a 'wet-in-wet' painting process – new paint added to areas still wet – unlike the more deliberate layering of Cézanne's more developed canvases. Ibid., p.68; through to p.71 for the later canvases.

7   Ibid., pp.55, 68.

8   Butler 2008, p.74.

9   Cézanne may also have repainted the face of a much earlier, 1879 painting (FWN 447) in this manner at around this time.

10   Kenneth Clark, *The Nude. A Study of Ideal Art* (John Murray, London, and Pantheon Books, New York, 1960), p.143.

11   Gasquet 1921, p.80; Gasquet 1991, p.148.

12   Tamar Garb, *The Painted Face. Portraits of Women in France, 1814–1914* (Yale University Press, New Haven and London, 2007), pp.139–79, which is based on this painting, is mainly a wide-ranging examination of touch and its critical discussion.

13   I owe this observation to Jayne S. Warman, who prompted me to look for correspondence between the Basel and Chicago paintings.

14   See Hale in New York 2014–15, pp.68–9, 150.

15   Cézanne had previously used such open backgrounds for paintings of Hortense only in small, close-up heads, similarly placing the figural image against an atmospherically washed blue-green background. Almost, but not quite falling into the category of this larger painting, and also with a turquoise background, is a *c*.1885 self-portrait (see cat.10.1).

16   Matisse could conceivably have seen it when it was in the art dealer Ambroise Vollard's possession.

17   See Hale in New York 2014–15, p.68.

18   Jonathan Crary, *Suspension of Perception* (MIT Press, Cambridge MA, 1999) is invaluable on this theme.

19   (The other two paintings are the *Woman with a Cafetière*, cat. 17.2 and *Gustave Geffroy*, cat. 17.1.) The association of this painting and *Woman with a Cafetière* has led to the suggestion by Joseph J. Rishel that it, too, should be dated to *c*.1890–5: see Paris–London–Philadelphia 1995–6, cat. 167, p.400.

20   Sidlauskas 2009, pp.178–9, discusses the bifurcation of the face in different terms.

CAT. 14.3
Madame Cézanne in Red, 1888–90
Museu de Arte de São Paulo Assis Chateaubriand; FWN 491

Madame Cézanne in a Red Dress, 1888–90 (see also details, pp.132, 139)

Metropolitan Museum of Art, New York; FWN 493

CAT. 15.1
Boy in a Red Waistcoat, 1888–90
National Gallery of Art, Washington, D.C.; FWN 497

Portraits of a Boy
in a Red Waistcoat

The series of paintings of a young man in Italian garb was made in the apartment rented on the quai d'Anjou between 1888 and 1890. Identified as a model named Michelangelo de Rosa, the sitter appears in four oil paintings, three of similar dimensions with the figure seated, and a fourth slightly larger of him standing in magnificent *contrapposto*.[1]

The Zurich, Philadelphia and New York works (figs 50–2) all include a painted red band above the wainscot to ground the composition horizontally. Although the sitter's features – crisply parted long hair, small round eyes, aquiline nose, small mouth and large ears – are consistent across the portraits, each conveys a different character. There is a childish insecurity to the Philadelphia painting, with de Rosa posing frontally but looking askance, his head sunken into his shoulders, his facial features noted with abrupt, emphatic marks. Both ears bow out from his head, holding back the sweep of his hair. He appears more adolescent in the New York painting, hunched in profile, his oversized hands collected limply in his lap. There is a faint shadow of hair on his upper lip, and the point of view is more elevated. One of two watercolours of de Rosa casts a similar character, with the teenager sitting on a stool, legs spread wide, his oversized hands hanging limply from his lap.[2]

The Zurich painting, in which he sits at a table propping up his head with his forearm, rehearses a pose that reappears in the early 1890s in the series of portraits of the gardener, Paulin Paulet (cat. 16.2, figs 56–7), and a decade later in the Los Angeles work, *Young Italian Woman* (fig. 65). Cézanne has elongated de Rosa's arms and torso, and his right ear is enlarged, particularly in comparison to the small, delicate features of his face. In each painting, one senses a boy who has not entirely grown into his body, not yet having arrived at full physical and psychological maturity. As art historian Joseph Rishel put it, the pictures convey 'a profound sympathy for the psychological vicissitudes of youth'.[3]

FIG. 50
Boy in a Red Waistcoat, 1888–90
Foundation E.G. Bürhle Collection, Zurich; FWN 496

143

FIG. 51
Boy in a Red Waistcoat, 1888–90
Barnes Foundation, Philadelphia; FWN 494

FIG. 52
Boy in a Red Waistcoat, 1888–90
Museum of Modern Art, New York; FWN 495

Cézanne was clearly captivated by the state of
male adolescence. By all biographical accounts, his own
early adulthood was marked by affectionate fraternity,
freedom, and a spiritual and physical immersion in
the spectacular countryside of Provence, all enhanced
by the aesthetic pleasures of classical poetry. It was a
golden age, before women, professional duty, familial
obligations and urban modernity disrupted the
enchantment. At the time of the de Rosa portraits,
Cézanne's beloved son Paul was also an adolescent
(he would have been sixteen years old in 1888) (fig. 53).
Cézanne was working on images of him cast as a
harlequin, employing the same vibrant hues of red
and blue found in this series (fig. 54).[4] Having worked
through various personal 'looks' of his own in Aix and
Paris, Cézanne was sensitive to costume and identity,
and in these works he effectively keyed clothing to
the identity formation of puberty.

As the largest and the most resolved of these works,
Washington's *Boy in a Red Waistcoat* (cat. 15.1) can be
taken as the series *summa*. The paint surface is thin
and unlaboured, with flickering patches of exposed
canvas throughout the composition. Cézanne has

abandoned the device of the red band and back wall
and placed de Rosa fully before the curtain. The image
suggests the influence of the Old Masters, and specifically the paintings Cézanne studied in the Louvre by
sixteenth-century Florentine Mannerists such as
Bronzino and Pontormo, who painted such iconic
images of urban, male adolescents. Here, de Rosa wears
a crisp, oval hat and strikes a classical pose in which
the cocked hips enliven the symmetry of the body by
tilting the head, shoulders, hips and knees at slight
counter-angles to each other. The swag of the curtain
behind him mimics the tilt of his hips, while the chair
back at his right reinforces the solid stability of the
painting's left register. The serpentine contour of the
waistcoat lapel and button seam establishes the rhythm
that carries on through de Rosa's body. The confidence
suggested by his right hand, resting on his hip, is
belied by his impossibly long left arm, which plunges
towards the lower edge of the frame, and by the rather
uncertain look on his pretty facial features. He has the
head of a child with short locks of hair brushed back,
and the body of man, dressed in a man's waistcoat
and leather chaps. He is simultaneously elegant and

COMPARATIVE PORTRAITURE, 1885–90

awkward, vital and relaxed, physically imposing and contemplative, even melancholic.

When the painting was exhibited at Cézanne's solo 1895 show at Ambroise Vollard's gallery in Paris, it was singularly celebrated.[5] Amedeo Modigliani, whose development of Modernist painting focused almost exclusively on the genre of portraiture, was said to carry a reproduction of *Boy in a Red Waistcoat* in his coat pocket as a source of constant reference and reverie.[6] MM

1 Venturi 1936 gives the model the name of Michelangelo de Rosa 'according to tradition'. There are also two watercolours of de Rosa, RW 375 and RW 376.

2 In the second, very similar watercolour, he sits in a more contained pose, his legs brought parallel and his hands neatly clasped, RW 376.

3 See Paris–London–Philadelphia 1995–6, p.322.

4 Ibid., pp.313, 322.

5 See Gustave Geffroy, *La Vie artistique* (Floury, Paris, 1900), p.218.

6 Meryle Secrest, *Modigliani: A Life* (Knopf, New York, 2011).

4 The Working Class and the Art World

1890–1900

Paul Cézanne in his Paris studio,
working on *The Apotheosis of Delacroix*, 1894
Photograph by Emile Bernard

As the 1890s began, Cézanne and Hortense drifted apart. Either she and their son were unavailable to be painted, or Cézanne had lost interest in painting them. Instead, he turned for subjects to local people in and around Aix-en-Provence: mainly agricultural labourers, referred to as *paysans* or peasants in the titles of paintings; women, who were primarily domestic servants; and, perhaps surprisingly, children.

The first category included the subjects of Cézanne's celebrated series of Card Player compositions, begun probably in 1891, which were accompanied by independent portraits of some of the players. As by now common with Cézanne, he painted both single portraits and related canvases showing a figure in the same or a similar pose. Either way, they record his admiration for people who had grown old without changing their ways, abandoning themselves to the laws of time. As such, the workers he painted resemble each other sufficiently so as to seem like members of the same family.

The paintings of women, by contrast, show different characters: a stately housekeeper sitting next to a coffee pot (painted either in Aix or Paris); a stooped old woman holding a rosary; another sitting quietly and contentedly. The paintings of children, perhaps, form a counterpoint to Cézanne's increasing preoccupation with old age.

In the second half of the decade, however, he also painted a very different kind of subject. His first solo exhibition, at art dealer Ambroise Vollard's Paris gallery in 1895, brought with it a swift recognition of the importance of his work, and Cézanne found himself making portraits of his art-world admirers, among them the writers Gustave Geffroy and Joachim Gasquet, Vollard himself, and a young Norwegian painter, Alfred Hauge. These portraits caused him difficulty, though, perhaps because he was less comfortable painting people who were interested in him than those who were not. Hence, he set aside even those portraits that were within a few strokes of being finished. By contrast, he did complete – albeit with the usual revisions and second thoughts – portraits of people he appears to have found, rather than those who sought him out, returning to the type of sitter with whom he began the decade: one subject looks like an artisan; another like a shopkeeper. JE

Portraits of Peasants

The sitters in these works of the 1890s were attractive to Cézanne not only because they were local and at hand as 'motifs', willingly available to him as he continued to work in the genre of portraiture, but also because they embodied aspects of Aix that he revered. We know very little about the sitters themselves, but the paintings project a uniform aura of dignified self-assurance. Their dress is simple in the extreme: earth-toned, shapeless jackets and creaseless trousers, paired with unremarkable hats.[1] Their poses and gestures are unperformative, utterly undramatic, as they sit alone, quietly smoking. In the meditated solidity of their construction, the pictures have an epic quality that heroises the sitters, contrary to more conventional images of peasants that romanticised or sentimentalised them at best and at worst caricatured, mocked, and/or demeaned them. As in his still lifes and landscapes, here Cézanne applies his seriously sophisticated artistic consideration to subjects generically ranked as beneath such ambitious attention.

Cézanne's affinity with these men has been likened to his emotional attachment to the Provençal landscape. Forged during his youth in Aix, by his own account a golden age of spiritual harmony and sundrenched nature, Cézanne's love for the region and its inhabitants seemed to intensify through constant comparison with Paris and Parisians. The artist grew sensitised to cultural difference as he shuttled back and forth between the capital and Provence, and his fierce, contrary temperament polarised the peasant and the city dweller, placing them in opposing camps. As the artist Emile Bernard recalled in 1904, Cézanne celebrated the grounded 'goodness' of the former, and derided the latter as 'dandies and socially polished types whose corrupt taste and worldly insincerity he loathed'.[2]

One of Cézanne's favourite writers, the popular intellectual Hippolyte Taine, provided in his theory of *milieu* a compelling conceptual framework for what the painter perceived as the *Aixois* character of his local sitters. These men were moulded by the warm, bright climate and rugged topography of Provence, by the region's classical history, a myth of timelessness and grounded authenticity. Like Mont Sainte-Victoire, they were sculpted in earthy colours, eternally reassuring in their stability and sincerity. They have little to do with the machinations of urban modernity that Cézanne essentially renounced in the last decades of his life in favour of his native region, 'that old native soil, so vibrant, so harsh', and its inhabitants.[3]

That these men were not public figures was key to the more or less successful resolution of the artist's work with them. As they were not notable, Cézanne could avoid the public pressures of producing a recognisable likeness, thereby preserving the privacy of his painting enterprise. They stand apart, then, from his later and more fraught portrait projects with Gustave Geffroy and Ambroise Vollard.

In *Man with Pipe* (cat. 16.1, overleaf), Cézanne places the figure squarely at the centre of his canvas in a frontal view, his head turned slightly to the left. His broad, sloping shoulders span the width of the picture, with reinforced contours that define them against the sketchily painted background. His large right ear and the rim of his hat open up the right side of his face, while his left eye feels more circumspect in its gaze. His mouth closes tight over the stem of his white clay pipe, his jaw slightly shifting beneath a bushy moustache. The tall crown of his hat emphasises the authority of this sitter, whose assured stature is also present in the two-figure Card Players series (see fig. 55).[4]

CAT. 16.1

Man with Pipe, 1891–6 (L, W only)

Samuel Courtauld Trust, Courtauld Gallery, London; FWN 504

Cézanne painted another local *Aixois*, identified as Paulin Paulet, a gardener at the family estate of Jas de Bouffan, in three portraits of equal dimensions (cat. 16.2, figs 56, 57). Shown smoking, while seated at a table with his elbow supporting his head, he too makes a further appearance as one of the protagonists in the more ambitious Card Players series.[5] In the St Petersburg picture, Paulet is placed before a similarly scaled but horizontally formatted painting, *Still Life with Pots, Bottle, Cup and Fruit* (fig. 58) and, barely visible above his head, *Bathers* (1890–1).[6] Tacked to the wall, alongside a corner of a third painting, these canvases signal the location as the artist's studio. The still life is from the late 1860s, when Cézanne painted thick surfaces with

brush and knife. Paulet seems to stand in for the ceramic cup and plate-shaped napkin, echoing the half-circular curve that energises the right side of the painting in both compositions. The diagonal of the fabric that slants down from the upper right corner (perhaps a curtain, or a large, unprimed canvas) synchronises with Paulet's right arm and left forearm and crosses with the diagonals of the table and his left hand, a cruciform mediated by the horizontals of the tacked pictures and the oval shape of his hat rim. Thus, Cézanne's earlier still lifes and outdoor figure paintings merge with studio props and a live subject to form a complex, compact image, challenging its construct as a 'portrait'.

A similar geometric design underpins the Mannheim painting, but in this version Paulet's eyes connect with the viewer in a direct gaze and his posture is more alert and forward-leaning. As in a preparatory work on paper, the figure's presence is less mediated by the background (fig. 59). In the Pushkin painting, Cézanne pulls back to include the legs of the sitter and of the table, and as in the St Petersburg work, he involves an earlier picture, a sliver of the Detroit *Madame Cézanne* (cat. 13.3) tacked to the wall at the right. The arch of her right arm is echoed in

his leaning torso, initiating a series of curves, counter-curves, horizontals and verticals that maintain a lively rhythm despite the sedentary pose of the sitter.[7]

Although many of Cézanne's images of local peasants in the 1890s, on both paper and canvas, might have functioned as preparatory works for the great series of five-figure Card Players compositions, the pictures discussed here stand apart, particularly the portraits of Paulet.[8] Rather than studies for genre compositions, these works address the discrete personalities of two men local to the artist's beloved Jas de Bouffan. MM

1 Nina Athanassoglou-Kallmyer marks this provincial outmodishness as a form of rejection and resistance to the centralised hegemony of Paris/France. See Athanassoglou-Kallmyer 2003, pp.28–9.
2 See Paris–London–Philadelphia 1995–6, p.38. See also Gasquet on Cézanne and his relationship with Aix, Gasquet 1991, p.141.
3 Danchev 2013, p.276.
4 In the two-figure series, see also examples from the Musée d'Orsay, Paris (FWN 684)

and a private collection, Qatar (FWN 685), in addition to the work from the Courtauld Gallery, London (FWN 686) illustrated here. See also a related study from the National Gallery of Art, Washington, D.C. (FWN 683), a watercolour (RW 378) and a drawing (C 1095).
5 He sits to the right in FWN 684, 685 and 686, and to the left in FWN 680 and 681. There is also a single-figure study for the two-figure Card Players (FWN 682) and another single-figure study of him sitting in the studio,

facing forward with his hands folded in his lap (FWN 523). There are several studies of him in graphite and watercolour: RW 380, RW 381, RW 377, C 1093, C 1094.
6 FWN 710 and 949.
7 For a recent account of this fascinating painting, see Charlotte Hale, New York 2014–15, pp.45–86.
8 See London–New York 2010–11, for an excellent account of the Card Players series.

FIG. 59
Leaning Smoker, 1890–1
Barnes Foundation, Philadelphia

CAT. 16.2
The Smoker, 1893–6 (see also detail, p.148) (L only)
Pushkin State Museum of Fine Arts, Moscow; FWN 507

Portraits of Gustave Geffroy and a Woman with a Cafetière

The critic Gustave Geffroy was just short of his fortieth birthday when Cézanne began his portrait in April 1895 (we also know what he looked like from a photograph by Nadar, fig. 60). Geffroy had known Claude Monet since 1886, and it was he who had probably prompted Geffroy to write what would be the first profile of Cézanne by a well-known critic to be published in a prestigious publication, *Le Journal,* where it appeared on 25 March 1894.[1] Cézanne, extremely moved, wrote to Geffroy to express his gratitude;[2] and the two met that November at a luncheon arranged by Monet, at which Cézanne offered to paint the critic's portrait. On 4 April 1895, he wrote to Geffroy to say he had a plan,[3] which was to show the critic in his library surrounded by his books, and he was soon travelling almost daily to Geffroy's house in the Belleville suburb of Paris to work on the portrait. All seemed to be going well, but after some three months had passed, Cézanne wrote to Geffroy on 12 June to tell him that he was 'unable to bring to a satisfactory conclusion the work that is beyond my powers', and asked him to give to the messenger who delivered his letter the painting equipment he had left in Geffroy's library.[4] At the critic's pleading, he relented:

> He came back, and, for a week or so, he seemed to work, building up, as only he could do, those slender films of colour, always maintaining the fresh and brilliant appearance of his canvas. But his heart was no longer in it.

Cézanne then left for Aix, having promised to return to the portrait when he came back to Paris.[5] However, Geffroy reports, 'a year later, on 3 April 1896, [he] sent again for his painting equipment. He never came again, leaving the portrait as he left so many other paintings which are no less admirable in conception or realization for being unfinished'. For Geffroy, his portrait, 'in spite of its unfinished state, is one of [Cézanne's] most beautiful works':

FIG. 60
Portrait photograph of Gustave Geffroy
by Nadar (Félix Tournachon), date unknown

> The library, the papers on the table, Rodin's little plaster model,[6] the artificial rose which he brought at the beginning of our sittings, everything is first rate. There is also a person in the scene, painted with meticulous care and richness of tone, and with incomparable harmony. He had only sketched in the face. And he would always say, 'We'll leave that for the end.' Sadly, there was no end.

Especially worthy of note in these warm reminiscences are four things, two technical and two conceptual. First is the reference to 'slender films of colour'. They are

FIG. 61
Edgar Degas, **Portrait of Edmond Duranty**, 1879
Burrell Collection, Glasgow

CAT. 17.1
Gustave Geffroy, 1895–6
(see also detail, p.156)
Musée d'Orsay, Paris; FWN 516

fully in evidence, each seeming to have been allowed to dry before another was applied.[7] Additionally, though, some more heavily applied brushstrokes are present, including dark blue lines to reinforce contours, a practice that Cézanne would continue throughout his later portraits. Second is that the face, though incomplete, is more than sketched; it is the hands that are visibly unfinished. Third is that Geffroy equates himself with the objects around him, effectively acknowledging that the portrait would become, as Meyer Schapiro observed, 'a gigantic still life', adding, 'the world of objects absorbs the man and lessens the intensity of his person; but it also enlarges him through the rich and multiple surroundings'.[8] And fourth, Geffroy's reference to 'the artificial rose that he [Cézanne] brought at the beginning of the sessions' associates this painting with the last two of four portraits of Madame Cézanne in a red dress (cats 14.3, 14.4), where his wife holds such a rose in her hands. And Schapiro's observations on Cézanne's depiction of Geffroy also apply to the artist's presentation of his wife in the fourth of these works.

Some scholars have dated that fourth portrait not to its more probable date of 1888–90 but to 1893–5 for its similarity to *Woman with a Cafetière* (cat. 17.2).[9] There is certainly an affinity. However, a broader conclusion may be drawn here: the fourth *Madame Cézanne in a Red Dress*, *Gustave Geffroy* and *Woman with a Cafetière* reveal a sequential development that Cézanne had not really attempted before and would not attempt again.

Cézanne's basically traditional conception of what comprised a portrait (as opposed to what he made within that traditional form) distinguishes him from painters of his Impressionist generation in that he rarely made portraits out of doors in natural light, or group portraits, or portraits in the context of the sitter's familiar environment, preferring more or less neutral backgrounds. However, the trio of paintings just mentioned comprise by far the most prominent examples of those works that do show people situated within the world in which they lived. He may well have been influenced by the critic Edmond Duranty, either from reading his *La Nouvelle peinture* of 1876, which had urged painters to do just that, or by taking Edgar Degas's portrait of Duranty, which shows him in his library (fig. 61), as the model for his own portrait of Geffroy (he could have seen the Degas work at the Fourth Impressionist Exhibition in 1879).[10]

With the exception of most of his 1860s portraits, Cézanne had generally provided a nominal background feature of some kind to anchor his subjects; as many were head only or half-length pictures, their modest size as well as their format precluded including much more than that. In fact, almost half of all his portraits are fairly small, not exceeding in their dimensions the French standard canvas size 10 (55cm in height). It is telling, then, that nearly all his later portraits are larger than that size. And almost half of the portraits painted from around 1890 onwards were canvas size 30 (92 cm in height) or larger. The increase in size of his

CAT. 17.2
Woman with a Cafetière, *c.*1895 (see also detail, p.162)
Musée d'Orsay, Paris; FWN 514

later portraits was occasioned by the increasing number of half- and three-quarter-length examples that he made, a move motivated by his desire to paint different kinds as well as types of portraits. This thinking lay behind the fourth *Madame Cézanne in a Red Dress* and *Gustave Geffroy*, both painted on large size 50 canvases (116cm in height), while *Woman with a Cafetière*, along with *Boy with Skull* (fig. 62), were painted on still larger, size 60 canvases (130cm in height), the biggest of all Cézanne's late portraits.

Early in his career, in the mid-1860s, he had made four portraits whose extremely large size was commensurate with the singular, elemental presence of their subjects, and the provocation that these canvases were intended to elicit (see cats 3.1, 4.1, 4.2). Late in his career, Cézanne, long uninterested in public protest, simply needed more space on the canvas. He was taking portraiture into unknown territory, where his subjects would retain their presence but surrender their singularity, participating in their surroundings. This would not last, but while it did, it produced some of the most admired and certainly most complex portraits of Cézanne's career.

As discussed on page 138, the fourth *Madame Cézanne in a Red Dress* shows a figure that bends with, and against, an apparently moving world of objects in environmental disequilibrium. With *Gustave Geffroy*, the environment is also in movement: the tiers of books rise and bend until they press against the subject's head; the open volumes seem to float over the table; the fireplace at the left tips dangerously. But this is not the frenetic, virtual movement of the portrait of his wife; rather, a continuum of movement in staccato, quivering rhythms of repeated, constantly varied linear accents that appear to ebb and flow around the rigid figure of the critic. He is not painted as if frozen in time, nor as permanently static. Instead, motion is momentarily suspended, his right hand (resembling a bundle of the spines of the books behind him) poised above the book that he is reading.

D. H. Lawrence wrote of the fourth *Madame Cézanne in a Red Dress* that, by making her still, the artist 'starts making the universe slip uneasily about her. It was part of his desire: to make the human form, the *life* form, come to rest. Not static – on the contrary. Mobile but come to rest. And at the same time, he set the unmoving material world into motion.'[11] This applies also to the

Geffroy portrait, except that the motion of the material world is slower. In *Woman with a Cafetière*, it slows to a halt, as the effect of a life form that has come to rest overtakes the entire painting.

The model in this portrait is unknown: the artist's son said it was the mother of the sitter in the identically-sized *Boy with Skull*,[12] which was painted at the Jas de Bouffan, and is most often dated to 1896–8. Whether or not this is true, she was presumably painted in the kitchen at the Jas, with the panelled doors of the room or of an armoire behind her,[13] and a sturdy oilcloth (*toile cirée*) covering the table on which sits the *cafetière* (or *cafetière à piston*, a coffee press rather than coffee pot, as it is commonly described), and beside it a cup and saucer with a spoon, improbably standing to attention above.[14]

This majestic painting has frequently been cited as illustrative of Cézanne's celebrated advice, to the painter- critic Emile Bernard in 1904, that one should 'treat nature by means of the cylinder, the sphere, the cone'.[15] It certainly provides sufficient support for that suggestion: the massive pyramidal body set against the

FIG. 63
Woman with a Cafetière, a study, c.1895
Private collection, New England; FWN 513

geometry of the panelling; the cylindrical forms of the *cafetière* and the cup; the upright spoon almost parallel to the vertical axis of the pleated dress; the orderly fanning of the pleats themselves. But nothing is rigid or mechanical, and the geometry is tempered by softer forms that flow from left to right across the painting: from the irregular and irregularly spaced flowers of the wallpaper, to the scatter of snowy dashes on the upper part of the blue dress, and the malleable, organic folds of the oilcloth on the table. Moreover, the subject of the portrait is very far from being an excuse for the display of Phileban solids.[16] We see from her roughened hands and face, and her severe, no-nonsense costume, that she is a working-class woman, and Cézanne paints her with an empathetic respect for her dignity and grandeur.

Cézanne painted a small study of her head (fig. 63), which raises the question of whether the painting was entirely made in the presence of the model,[17] as do signs of reworking, especially of the contours, something that was by now becoming increasingly common in his work.

The final puzzle is this. If *Woman with a Cafetière* and the same-sized *Boy with Skull* do show a mother and her son, then this pairing is far more droll than we might expect from Cézanne: the mother in the kitchen beside a sturdy working table with a *cafetière* on it; the son seated in the salon at a decoratively carved table with books and a skull resting on it.[18] But it is hard to imagine Cézanne conceiving of such an upstairs-downstairs production. JE

1   This background information, including Geffroy's account of Cézanne working on his portrait, is drawn from Doran 1978, pp.21–6; Doran 2001, pp.3–6. An extended study of the work by John Rewald can be found in R 791, and an excellent, broader account of the Cézanne-Geffroy relationship, in the context of some other sitters, is given in Danchev 2012, pp.279–91.

2   Cézanne to Geffroy, 26 March 1894.

3   Cézanne to Geffroy, 4 April 1895.

4   Cézanne to Geffroy, 12 June 1895.

5   Recounted in Cézanne to Monet, 6 July 1895.

6   Although Geffroy does not explicitly say so, the implication is that the Rodin plaster cast was his; but if so, whether or not he placed it there for his portrait must be a matter of conjecture. The question is raised, however, by the circumstances under which Cézanne and Geffroy met – for luncheon at Monet's house at Giverny, where Rodin was also a guest, and where, in Geffroy's account, Cézanne 'knelt before Rodin, in the middle of the path, to thank him again for shaking his hand'. See Doran 1978, p.22; Doran 2001, p.4. Danchev 2012, pp.281–2, reasonably concludes that Cézanne was hamming, but Geffroy saw this as evidence of 'the primitive soul of Cézanne'. Did that have

anything to do with the plaster cast getting put on the table?

7   As Rewald observes (R 791), Ambroise Vollard also reported that Cézanne worked in this way when painting his portrait (p.174).

8   Schapiro [1952] 1962, p.100, in an extraordinary, beautiful appreciation of this work.

9   See Paris–London–Philadelphia 1995–6, p.400.

10 See Introduction, p.127. Degas's portrait of Duranty, and Cézanne's portrait of Geffroy, look back to Edouard Manet's 1868 portrait of Zola (p.27).

11 D.H. Lawrence, 'Introduction to these Paintings', *The Paintings of D. H. Lawrence* (Mandrake Press, London, 1929), excerpted in Wechsler 1975, pp.91–2. See also Introduction, note 96. The equation is reversed in Cézanne's *Still Life with Plaster Cupid* (FWN 692), also painted around 1895, where the figural subject is an unmoving entity, a sculpture, surrounded by the living forms of fruit and vegetables, which are coaxed into motion through their painting.

12 Paris–London–Philadelphia 1995–6, p.403.

13 The panelling behind the figure in *Woman with a Cafetière* seems to be the same as that seen behind Henri Gasquet (fig. 69) in his portrait, known to have been painted at the Jas de Bouffan.

14 The oil cloth resembles that in a number of contemporaneous Card Players compositions (FWN 684, 685, fig. 55), painted in the farmhouse at the Jas de Bouffan, rather than in the main house, but such a cloth also appears in a portrait (FWN 506) painted in Cézanne's studio in the main house (as evidenced by unstretched canvases tacked to the wall), as well as in three still lifes (FWN 836, 842, 869). It is entirely reasonable to suppose that it was also used on the kitchen table of the main house.

15 Cézanne to Emile Bernard, 15 April 1904.

16 Deriving from classical aesthetics, the Phileban solids comprise the sphere, cube, cone, pyramid, cylinder and prism.

17 A watercolour (RW 543) is associated with the painting in Paris–London–Philadelphia 1995–6, p.404, but seems to belong more closely to the two much later *Seated Woman in Blue* paintings (cats 23.1, 23.2).

18 The only pair like this one comprises the strange juxtaposition of *Self-Portrait with Palette* of 1886–8, which shows Cézanne looking fierce, with that of his son, looking smug, in his contemporaneous portrait (cats 12.1, 12.2).

Portraits of Women

Although not as numerous as Cézanne's late paintings of male Provençal peasants, those of local women are notable for their more sombre and serious presence. Of these, the most famous is *Old Woman with a Rosary* (cat. 18.1). John Rewald associated this work with the slightly earlier *Girl with a Doll* (cat. 19.1), observing that 'the brooding face of the girl and the humble expression of the old woman in these canvases share a barely perceptible, and for Cézanne highly unusual "sentimental" aspect.'[1] Hard-hearted critics have, in fact, found it to be explicitly sentimental, too much an image of a character and a conventionally touching one at that.[2] This is, in part, a reaction against the highly emotional valorisation of the painting since its inclusion in important early twentieth-century exhibitions,[3] no doubt fuelled by the improbable, maudlin story attached to it by its first owner, the poet Joachim Gasquet. The sitter, he said, was a nun who, having lost her faith at the age of seventy, had leapt over the wall of her convent to be found, destitute and hallucinating, by the solitary artist, who had taken her in as an act of charity.[4] She was actually a former servant of a lawyer, Marie-Joseph Demolins, who was one of Gasquet's friends.[5]

It should be acknowledged, though, that the need to avoid cliché characterisations, central to Cézanne's portraiture practice, is not the same thing as avoiding the characteristic types of subjects he found around him in Aix. Character studies, especially of country people, were integral to his work from around 1890. Hence, this painting, together with the quietly contemplative portrait of a woman in a simple brown dress (cat. 18.2) and that of a brusque working-class woman in a red-striped dress (fig. 64), form a trio of different rural types, of older local Provençal women whose features reflect lives of labour. In the case of the *Old Woman with a Rosary,* the image of piety is also emblematic of female Provençal peasants with whom Cézanne would have come in contact after joining the

FIG. 64
Portrait of a Woman, *c.*1898
Barnes Foundation, Philadelphia; FWN 533

THE WORKING CLASS AND THE ART WORLD, 1890–1900

CAT. 18.1
Old Woman with a Rosary, 1895–6
National Gallery, London; FWN 515

CAT. 18.2
Portrait of a Woman, c.1900
Private collection; FWN 536

FIG. 65
Young Italian Woman, *c*.1900
J. Paul Getty Museum, Los Angeles; FWN 534

Catholic Church in 1891; her costume of blue frock, black shawl and frilled cap was typical of such older women.[6] As such, the counterpart of this painting is Cézanne's other specifically ethnographic female portrait of this period, known as the *Young Italian Woman* (fig. 65) but in fact a young woman in traditional Provençal costume.[7] Both paintings show types that were quickly vanishing in the face of modernisation; and if Cézanne's paintings of this kind have, as John Rewald put it, a 'sentimental' aspect, it lies in the sense of nostalgia for and approbation of what the artist perceived as an authentic vernacular existence that was slipping away. The paintings themselves are far from pathetic, and not overacted but psychologically astute. Close inspection of the face of the old woman

in the London painting shows a figure not so much absorbed in the comfort of prayer as caught with an unseeing, troublingly disconnected, and almost feral expression.

This painting was the first, or among the first, of the dark-toned, heavily manipulated and reworked portraits that grew in number over the final decade of the artist's life. Gasquet, again straining belief, claims that he found it under a coal scuttle on Cézanne's studio floor, the artist having worked on it furiously for eighteen months and then abandoned it.[8] However, the canvas does show the results of labour in the subject's features, especially in the face and the hands; and the shawl and frock reveal the obsessive overdrawing in thin lines of dark paint that continued to characterise the dark-toned portraits, such as those of Vollard (cat. 20.2) and the *Man with Crossed Arms* (cat. 21.1).

In contrast to the *Old Woman with a Rosary*, the *Portrait of a Woman* (cat. 18.2) has rarely been exhibited or discussed in the literature on Cézanne.[9] It comes without a story: we do not know who the woman is, or precisely when the work was painted. The artist had long been interested in painting pleated costumes, initially in portraits of Hortense Fiquet. In the 1890s, the motif found its most extravagant expression in the right-hand figure of two of his Card Player compositions;[10] then, in softer form, in portraits of domestic servants and country workers, into which category this woman must belong. If this canvas was painted around 1900, it forms a fascinating counterpoint to the contemporaneous *Young Italian Woman*. The latter work contains a virtuoso display of sumptuous pleating with something of the voluptuousness of a Venetian painting, albeit tempered by the fact that the figure assumes the traditional pose of melancholy. The *Portrait of a Woman* reveals an equally virtuoso display, but in a subdued, Dutch manner; an image of rectitude, quiet and dignified in its brown and grey tonalities, as well as a sympathetic study of the pinched features of old age. JE

1   R 806.
2   E.g., David Sylvester, *About Modern Art, Critical Essays 1948–96* (Chatto & Windus, London, 1996), p.433, broadly following the complaint of 'cliché' in *The Paintings of D. H. Lawrence* (Mandrake Press, London, 1929). See Introduction, p.35.
3   These exhibitions included the 1907 first posthumous retrospective at the Grand

Palais, Paris; Roger Fry's 1910 *Manet and the Post-Impressionists* at the Grafton Galleries, London; and the 1913 Armory show in Boston, Chicago and New York. See FWN 515.
4   Gasquet 1921, p.67; Gasquet 1991, p.132. Versions of his account continue to appear in both the specialised and popular accounts of this work.
5   See Cézanne to Gasquet, 12 May 1902.

6   Athanassoglou-Kallmyer 2003, pp.221–2.
7   Ibid., pp.140–7, on this type in Van Gogh's and Gauguin's work as well.
8   Gasquet 1921, p.67; Gasquet 1991, p.132 (see note 4).
9   See FWN 536.
10 See FWN 680, 681.

CAT. 19.1

Girl with a Doll, *c.*1895

Private collection, New York; FWN 518

Portraits of Children

The greatest surprise of Cézanne's few late portraits of children is that he painted any at all. Apart from a lost early portrait of his young sister Rose, and a half-dozen very modest portraits of his son and two highly ambitious ones (cats 9.2, 12.1; Introduction, figs 6, 7), children did not feature at all in his earlier painting, as they did prominently in the work of a number of his former Impressionist colleagues. Nonetheless, the appearance of five portraits of children in the years after 1895 would seem to have a simple explanation: they formed the counterpoint to his increasing preoccupation with old age.

In fact, the first two of these paintings show a child on whose face the shadow of time has fallen. The lost early portrait, known only through a sketch in an October 1866 letter from Cézanne to Emile Zola, showed his sister reading to her doll.[1] Thirty years later, a somewhat boyish-looking girl of indeterminate age holds an extremely rudimentary doll on her lap, but ignoring it, stares into the distance (cat. 19.1). If Ambroise Vollard is correct in remembering that this canvas was included in his 1895 exhibition of Cézanne's work, his suggestion that it was painted c.1894 will take precedence over the date of c.1896 commonly given to it, on the basis that the quality of personal reverie Cézanne found in the girl's pose approaches the intense inwardness of the 1895–6 *Old Woman with a Rosary* (cat. 18.1).[2] Indeed, although by no means as heavily worked as the latter painting, its *grisaille* tonality conveys a similarly grave, almost penitential character. And the feel of a figure constrained is reinforced by the narrow brown line of the chair-rail, if that is what it is, visible to each side of the girl; completed by the similar line of her belt, it seems to strap her in place.

Cézanne made a companion painting to this one showing the same girl facing frontally to the viewer (fig. 66). Here, the huge, densely painted forms make it difficult to imagine the size and age of the figure, while the blank facial expression leaves the gender uncertain. And because of, not despite, the vividly

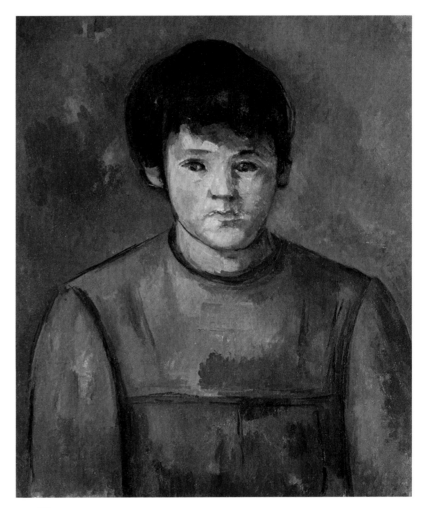

FIG. 66
Portrait of a Young Girl, *c.*1896
National Museum of Art, Bucharest; FWN 519

169

FIG. 67
Lac d'Annecy, 1896
Samuel Courtauld Trust,
Courtauld Gallery, London; FWN 311

material presence of the work, the figure, frozen in time and space, supports the suggestion that some of Cézanne's portraits look like people from another planet.

A portrait that is far more humanly present, *Child in a Straw Hat* (cat. 19.2) is commonly thought to have been painted in 1896, when Cézanne was staying at the Hôtel de l'Abbaye, a former monastery, in Talloires on Lac d'Annecy in July and August of that year. It may have been painted (or completed) at the Jas de Bouffan, for the panelling behind the child resembles that in an 1896 painting known to have been painted there.[3] However, a watercolour study for the portrait has a view of the lake on the verso.[4] And its subject has traditionally been regarded as that of the son of a Monsieur Vallet, one of the gardeners at the hotel.[5]

It was the artist's second summer vacation in French Switzerland. The first, in 1890, had been forced on him and was not a success (see p.240). This time, he had again been induced into going, writing to Joachim Gasquet from Talloires on 21 July that 'after much toing and froing, my family, in whose hands I find myself at the moment, has persuaded me to stay for the time being in this spot'.[6] And two days later he was already unhappy, writing to the *Aixois* sculptor Philippe Solari, 'When I was at Aix, I had the feeling I'd be better off

somewhere else; now that I am here, I miss Aix. For me, life is becoming deathly monotonous...To relieve my boredom, I'm painting.'[7]

The principal result of his painting was the celebrated *Lac d'Annecy* (fig. 67), the 'persistent parallelism' of whose reflections in the water mirror the more sparsely painted, vertical banding of the portrait. From the panelling of the wall to the left, through the child's pleated smock, to the door or curtain at the right, carefully spaced, parallel verticals gently hold the figure in place against the plane of the surface, while the odd perspective of the panelling swings out to open space behind the child. Within this drawn framework, the colour is at once simple and subtle: a pinkish-grey for the panelling, repeated in the child's heart-shaped face and intensified in his large and extraordinary ear; a bluish-grey above the panelling; and, next to it, the cool grey-green of the child's smock. Then, complementary to the smock and abutting it, the warm orange of the right side of the painting, carried with thinner and a trifle cooler paint over the straw hat. The decisive simplicity of design and colour formalises a subject that could have decorated a *bibelot* or trinket, creating something as gravely beautiful as the *grisaille* portrait that preceded it.[8] JE

1 Cézanne to Zola, c.19 October 1866.

2 See FWN 518 for dates suggested for this painting; and R 806 for Rewald's association of it with *Old Woman with a Rosary*. It could, in fact, be contemporaneous with an early state of that painting, which, while completed in 1896, was probably begun in 1895 or even earlier.

3 FWN 522.

4 See RW 482, 468; also, for additional studies, ibid., 480, 481, 483.

5 Philippe Cézanne, 'My Great-Grandmother Marie-Hortense Fiquet', in New York 2014–15, p.43.

6 Cézanne to Joachim Gasquet, 21 July 1896.

7 Cézanne to Solari, 23 July 1896.

8 Cézanne made two more paintings of a child in a straw hat, both seated out of doors (FWN 537, 538). Both are commonly dated to 1902–4, but have also been said to have been made at Annecy. The former may, in fact, be a study for the present work. The latter, however, is a girl with a doll and was most likely painted on the terrace of the studio at Les Lauves.

CAT. 19.2
Child in a Straw Hat, 1896
Los Angeles County Museum of Art; FWN 520

Portraits of Men

Cézanne's first solo exhibition, at the age of fifty-six, at Ambroise Vollard's gallery in Paris in 1895 marked the beginning of increasing recognition of his work, and, with it, increased contact with his admirers. His portrait of the critic Gustave Geffroy (cat. 17.1), painted in 1895–6, was thus followed by a small series of such portraits. Cézanne met the subject of the first of them, an *Aixois* poet and critic named Joachim Gasquet (fig. 68), in April 1896, at precisely the moment that the artist's warm relationship with Geffroy had suddenly soured.[1]

Gasquet was an ideal replacement, the 23-year-old brilliant son of one of Cézanne's schoolmates, Henri Gasquet, who had become a prosperous citizen of Aix;

and Joachim was an even more right-wing, regionalist patriot than Cézanne. The two therefore got along wonderfully, despite the thirty-four years that separated them. They took long walks together and were reciprocally influential in their Arcadian, Virgilian understanding of their native Provence.[2] Cézanne, for reasons unknown, painted the father first at the Jas de Bouffan, producing the only portrait of him that could be called jovial (fig. 69). The son, to his surprise, sat for his own portrait (cat. 20.1) only five or six times: 'I thought that he had given up the picture. Later, I discovered that he has spent roughly sixty sessions on it ... he worked on it after I had left.' He had been painting from memory.[3]

FIG. 68
Joachim Gasquet, photographer and date unknown

FIG. 69
Henri Gasquet, 1896
Marion Koogler McNay Art Museum, San Antonio, Texas;
FWN 522

Most of the work appears to have been done in May 1896.[4] The young man was posed at the Jas de Bouffan in front of a folding screen that Cézanne had augmented in 1859–60 (fig. 82), when he was just a few years younger than Gasquet was then. (More of the screen can be seen in Cézanne's c.1897 *Man in a Blue Smock*, cat. 24.1.)[5] The figure is pitched to his right in an exaggerated way and his right shoulder is unnaturally larger than his left. Perhaps the treatment of the yet-unfinished left border has tempered this somewhat, but Cézanne clearly was interested in using again the prominent diagonal posture that we find in some of his very early portraits.[6] In this case, it adds contemplative gravity to the pose. The face comprises a patchwork of thin, transparent areas of pink, yellow, grey and blue – watercolour-like in their delicacy, and awaiting more definition. Cézanne has made progress with the eyes, nose and mouth, starting to define their contours with darker marks; but a lot remained to be done. While he followed Gasquet's appearance in giving him a blond beard, he was starting to carry a large mop of dark hair up to the top edge of the canvas, dividing it into circular forms that mimic the adjacent decorations on the painted screen. And he had yet to begin painting one of the collars of Gasquet's shirt when, in early June, Cézanne must have set aside the canvas on his departure from Aix, not returning until the following spring.[7]

Some two years later, either in the spring or autumn of 1899,[8] Vollard (fig. 70) began sitting for his portrait in Cézanne's Paris studio on the fourth floor of the Villa des Arts at 15, rue Hégésippe-Moreau (cat. 20.2).

According to Vollard's famous account, he sat for 115 sessions, each beginning at 8am and lasting until 11.30pm.[9] This was probably an exaggeration, but it was certainly a long, arduous process; after talking to the dealer, the Symbolist painter Maurice Denis wrote in his journal that 'Vollard has been posing every morning at Cézanne's for what seems like for ever'.[10] He continued: 'As soon as he moves, Cézanne complains that he has made him lose the *line of concentration*.'

And Vollard's recollection of Cézanne's outburst when he *did* move has been one of the artist's most frequently quoted remarks: 'You wretch! You've spoiled the pose! Do I have to tell you again you must sit like an apple? Does an apple move?'[11]

Gasquet claimed that, as with his own portrait and that of his father, 'during many sessions, Cézanne seemed to make only a few brushstrokes', but 'the next day, M. Vollard found that the canvas had been advanced by three or four hours of intense work'. Again, Cézanne had been painting from memory.[12] And Vollard himself noted similarities in the early stages with Cézanne's portrait of Gasquet: 'He did not paint with thick impasto, but put one layer of paint as thin as watercolour over another; the paint dried instantly.'[13] However, Vollard's portrait is far more developed. While there are some colour patches that seem imperfectly attached to their surroundings – notably the greens across the forehead and oranges around the subject's right sleeve – they are in the main more closely adjusted to each other than in Gasquet's portrait, so settling into place.

Denis learned from Vollard how, 'in order to prepare himself for his morning painting sessions, [Cézanne] strolls through the Louvre or the Trocadéro in the afternoons and draws statues, antiquities, or the Pugets, or he makes watercolours *en plein air*; he maintains this predisposes him to *see* well the next day.'[14] The studies made in the museums were pencil drawings of sculptures that emphasised rhythmic sequences of forms; and while these had no direct relationship to what he painted in the mornings, they were exercising his faculty of building sequences for the placing of patches of colour.[15] Hence, when Vollard had the temerity to mention two patches of bare canvas in the hands, Cézanne replied, 'If my study in the Louvre presently goes well, perhaps tomorrow I shall find the right colour to fill the white spaces', adding the conversation stopper, 'Just understand, if I put something there at random, I should have to go over the whole picture

CAT. 20.1
Joachim Gasquet, 1896 (see also detail, p.172) (P only)
National Gallery, Prague; FWN 521

Ambroise Vollard, 1899

Musée des Beaux-Arts de la Ville de Paris, Petit Palais, Paris; FWN 531

FIG. 70
Ambroise Vollard, photographer
and date unknown

FIG. 71
Ambroise Vollard, 1899
Harvard Art Museums, Cambridge, Massachusetts

again starting from that spot.' Vollard remembers, 'the prospect made me tremble'.[16]

The watercolours *en plein air*, conversely, were directly related to the mornings' activity of setting down layers of transparent colour in the studio. 'If it is sunny,' Denis added, 'he complains and does little work: what he needs are *grey days*.'[17] He needed grey days in order to see the small gradations of colour and tone that would be bleached out by overly bright light.

Cézanne also made at least one drawing of Vollard (fig. 71), but his interest in the rippling curve down the front of the jacket evaporated as he advanced the painting along the path of geometric clarity. It is shaped by big tent-like diagonals that fall from around Vollard's neck, overlapped by his matching bent arms and opposed by

the twin lapels of his jacket, before coming to rest around the rising peak of his bent knee. In a year or two, Cézanne would develop this pyramidal structure in a more schematic form in his *Seated Peasant* (cat. 24.2). Here, it quietly controls the painting, which gives the impression of naturalness, although it was clearly the result of long labour. The crustiness in the repeated, dark contours are but one obvious example of this; another is the carefully contrived analogy between the bow tie on the shirt front and the highly abstracted motif of the window in the background. According to Vollard, Cézanne said that he was 'not discontent with the front of the shirt' when he abandoned work on the portrait after the 115 sessions.[18]

That summer, Cézanne left Paris to work in Marlotte, near Fontainebleau. There, at the Hôtel Mallet where he was staying, he met, probably at the beginning of July, a 23-year-old Norwegian painter named Alfred Hauge.[19] Hauge was well aware of Cézanne's fame, but had thought he was dead; and, in fact, described him as looking as if he did not have many years left. Nonetheless – in what sounds like a reprise of Cézanne's attraction to the young Gasquet – the two regularly dined together in the hotel garden, and Cézanne offered to paint the Norwegian's portrait.

The painting (cat. 20.3) shows a carefully dressed, elegant and refined young man, as seen in a contemporary photograph (fig. 72). Cézanne used a similarly subdued tonality, here of blue and brown, to that of the Gasquet and Vollard portraits, and repeated the triangularity of the latter in an exaggerated form that dominates the slighter figure. Hauge's face, though, is less fully developed than Vollard's, but more so than Gasquet's. The three works together offer a fascinating primer as to how the artist set down and adjusted patches of contrasted and adjacent colours to modulate form. Here, blue meets orange within larger areas of cream and ochre; patches of the reddish ground of the background appear in the blue-black hair; and the cravat is given that same colour within the thinnish blues of the jacket. It is a painting with great presence, and therefore surprising that Cézanne became so frustrated with it that, Hauge reports, 'he suddenly cut it to pieces with a knife in anger'.[20] Cézanne's son, who visited him every Sunday with his mother, arranged to have the canvas taken to Paris and remounted. This he did, although signs of damage are still evident on the surface. He also said that he would give it to Hauge. But he did not.

The identity of the figure shown in the final portrait of this group (cat. 20.4) is unknown. Judging from his appearance, he was not an *Aixois* worker; more likely, a Parisian shopkeeper or innkeeper, either in Aix or in Paris. The drapery seen in the background of this

FIG. 72
Alfred Hauge, photographer unknown *c*.1899

painting seems to have been among the few items that travelled back and forth with the artist between the two cities during 1896–8, appearing also in several Paris still lifes and in *Boy with Skull* (fig. 62), painted in Aix.[21]

This portrait has the grandeur of *Seated Peasant* (cat. 24.2), without so overtly schematic a presentation. Nonetheless, the figure comprises a huge pyramidal mass that would have seemed perched in mid-air had not Cézanne provided the bare hint of a chair seat between the subject's splayed legs. Like the Gasquet and Hauge portraits, it is a study in blue; like the latter, specifically, a blue jacket modified by dark reds from the background. But the background itself is afforded much more prominence than in any painting since that of Geffroy; and we have to look to the contemporaneous

CAT. 20.3
Alfred Hauge, 1899
Norton Museum of Art, West Palm Beach, Florida; FWN 532

Young Italian Woman (fig. 65) for something similar: the juxtaposition of a weighty, weary figure with sumptuous patterned fabric. Our reading of the fabric is complicated by the fact that the top right corner of the canvas has been cut off and replaced by a triangle of new canvas, when and by whom we do not know.[22] However, this does not interfere with the almost Matissean way in which the organic forms that decorate the fabric seem animated as they curl over and around the sitter's head. Below, his right hand holds a book showing a fragment of typography. The edges of the white pages are coloured grey, orange and blue, reprising in a lighter tonality the dominant contrasts of the painting. JE

1 See Cézanne to Gasquet, 30 April 1896.

2 On Gasquet; Athanassoglou-Kallmyer 2003, pp.215–23. Paris–London–Philadelphia 1995–6, pp.413–14.

3 Gasquet 1921, p.56; Gasquet 1991, p.113. Adriani 1993, pp.209–10. This account of portraiture continued from memory is discussed in the Introduction, pp.30–1.

4 Cézanne to Gasquet, 21 May 1896, appears to refer to rescheduling a sitting.

5 Gasquet would see this work in Cézanne's studio: correspondence between Cézanne and Gasquet, March–April 1898, cited in Rewald 1959, p.34.

6 E.g. FWN 416, 420, 424.

7 Cézanne left for Vichy, where he spent the following month; and from there travelled in July to Switzerland; then in August continued to Paris, where he spent the winter.

8 The precise period in which this portrait was painted is uncertain. A letter from Cézanne to Emile Solari, dated 25 February, Paris, and thought by Rewald and others to have been written in 1899, refers to the subject of this portrait. It begins: 'Two sittings a day with the model are more than enough to wear me out. And that is how it has been for several weeks.' According to Vollard, however, he sat for one not two sessions a day (Vollard 1914, p.92; Vollard 1937, p.77). Additionally, though, a letter from Cézanne to his niece Marthe Conil, dated 16 May 1899, Paris, includes the statement, also thought to refer to this portrait, 'At present I am detained in Paris by a fairly lengthy piece of work, but I hope to come down to the Midi sometime next month.' However, at this period Cézanne was also working extensively on one of his large, late Bathers compositions (probably FWN 980), as Vollard attests (Vollard 1914, p.96; Vollard 1937, p.79). And it is possible that these February and May letters refer to that work. A later, autumn date for the work is suggested by Maurice Denis having apparently written in his journal on 21 October 1899 that 'Vollard has been posing every morning at Cezanne's for what seems like forever' (*Journal*, vol. 1 [1905–20], La Colombe, éditions du Vieux Colombier, Paris, 1957, p.157). However, since this and Denis's account, quoted below, of how Cézanne spent his mornings doubtless were based on a conversation with the dealer, it cannot be assumed that he is referring to contemporaneous events. Jayne S. Warman has pointed out to me first, that a spring date is suggested by Vollard's recollection of a discussion with Cézanne – while the portrait was in progress – about the forthcoming auction of the Chocquet collection, which took place in early July (Vollard 1914, p.104); and second, that it is possible that Cézanne checked in at his studio in October, after leaving Marlotte and before going to Aix, and that Denis visited him then.

9 Vollard 1914, p.105; Vollard 1937, p.86.

10 Denis 1957, vol. 1, p.157. See note 8.

11 Vollard 1914, p.92; Vollard 1937, p.77.

12 Gasquet 1921, p.57; Gasquet 1991, p.114. See note 3.

13 Vollard 1914, p.99; Vollard 1937, p.81.

14 Denis 1957, vol. 1, p.157. See note 8.

15 See Lawrence Gowing, 'Cézanne: The Logic of Organized Sensations', in New York–Houston 1977–8, p.61.

16 Vollard 1914, pp.95–6; Vollard 1937, p.79.

17 Denis 1957, vol. 1, p.157. See note 8.

18 Vollard 1914, p.105; Vollard 1937, p.86. See note 16. Vollard says that Cézanne asked him to leave the clothes in which he had been posing, so he could rework parts of the figure, as well as deal with the two spots of white canvas on the hands. But apparently he never did return to work on it.

19 Hauge wrote to Edvard Munch on 7 July 1899 telling him that he had met Cézanne; and later elaborated upon the encounter in a letter to the artist Thorvald Erichson on 26 August, saying they had met on 1 June. See Jean Colrat, 'Un visiteur oublié', in Paris 2011–12, p.152; and pp.150–3 for Hauge and his visit to Marlotte. Hauge's mention of a meeting on 1 June may have been a miswriting of 1 July, given the letter to Munch, and given the fact that Cézanne wrote to Henri Gasquet from Paris on 3 June.

20 Colrat in Paris 2011–12, p.152.

21 See Theodore Reff, 'Painting and Theory in the Final Decade', in New York–Houston 1977–8, p.29. Among the still lifes are FWN 844, 870 and 871. The complex spatiality of this work also relates it to *Boy with Skull*, while its high colour – as compared to the near monochrome of the 1899 portraits – associates it with *Man in a Blue Smock* of c.1897 (cat. 24.1).

22 The dimensions of this canvas, unlike those of the three other portraits discussed here, do not conform to a standard size. This raises the possibility that the repair of the corner was somehow connected with the painting having been even larger than it is now and later cut down.

CAT. 20.4
Portrait of a Man, 1898–1900 (P, L only)
National Museum of Art, Architecture and Design, Oslo; FWN 530

Portraits of a Man
with Crossed Arms

Cézanne had previously painted many pairs of paintings of the same subject, some mutually very similar, and some like these of the same size, but none before had quite given the sense of someone in the same pose but viewed from a marginally different angle. We may perhaps want to associate these two studies, and the effects of shifting vision, with the artist's statement that he could find continuing inspiration from a landscape motif by slightly altering his view of it.[1]

These paintings have been dated to c.1899 because their execution relates to that of the portrait of Ambroise Vollard (cat. 20.2), which was painted that year in Cézanne's studio on the rue Hégésippe-Moreau. Since it is uncertain whether the Vollard portrait was painted in the spring or autumn of 1899, it is therefore also uncertain whether these portraits were painted before or after it.[2] If we allow the possibility of the artist's self-projection in such portraits, it is tempting to place them in Aix in the autumn of 1899 and to associate their mournful, and even angry, demeanour to his distress at the forced sale in November of the Jas de Bouffan, his father's house, which had long been his own home.[3] They were certainly painted there. However, it had been clear for some two months that the Jas was going to be sold, and Cézanne was busy removing his paintings and possessions, so it is hard to believe he had much time, or the inclination, for making portraits. These two works could, in fact, have been painted much earlier.[4]

The artist and critic Erle Loran attributed what he perceived to be facial distortion in these works to the influence of El Greco, while the curator Françoise Cachin proposed that the subject had a physical deformity, accounting for the misdirection of his eyes.[5] Be that as it may, there is more affective expression, amounting to dark melancholy, in these works than in any of the recently preceding ones, apart from his late self-portraits and an anomalous canvas like the *Old Woman with a Rosary* (cat. 18.1). This is not only a matter of facial features and subdued tonality. The crossed-arm pose in both paintings is disturbing in that the man's left hand is unnaturally distant from the end of the sleeve to which it belongs; and, while the fingers of his right hand may be assumed to tuck beneath the adjacent elbow, the image of the abbreviated hand with only the thumb visible is also uncanny. A similar and even more grotesque treatment of the hands appears in a portrait of a seated peasant made around the same time (fig. 73).

In the Guggenheim painting (cat. 21.1), both hands and the lower contours of the arms are outlined with a dense mass of dark blue lines that lie on top of the paint film. In the companion work (fig. 74), the hands are more decisively, flatly painted, all but filling the spaces of white canvas that Cézanne had left to accommodate them, the hand-with-thumb set down in confident parallel bands running along its length. Moreover, the colour in the Guggenheim canvas is the less bright and more muddied of the two. These differences suggest that the Guggenheim canvas was made first, and then revised while or after its companion was painted.

Three other features of the Guggenheim canvas may or may not reinforce that suggestion.

First, the lower part of the man's costume could well have been left unfinished. However, a similar turpentine-wash looseness characterises the lower part of the dress in the final-of-four paintings of *Madame Cézanne in a Red Dress* (cat. 14.4); in both cases, the effect is somewhat to dematerialise that section and thereby give buoyancy to the figure.

Second, adjacent to the man's left elbow is a group of non-depictive marks, which may have been the result of Cézanne testing his brush. However, there are earlier paintings in which it is clear that he was satisfied to leave such marks as part of the composition.[6]

And third, Cézanne chose not to include in what would be the second canvas the palette and other signs of his studio that he placed in the bottom left corner

CAT. 21.1
Man with Crossed Arms, *c.*1899
Solomon R. Guggenheim Museum, New York; FWN 528

FIG. 73
Seated Peasant, *c.*1899
Metropolitan Museum of Art, New York;
FWN 526

of the Guggenheim painting. He had included similar elements in the contemporaneous painting of the seated peasant; the absence of their distraction gives a more commanding presence to the figure. So does the change in posture. In both works, the subject looks out beyond the left edge of the painting, but in the Guggenheim painting he also turns in that direction, whereas in the companion painting his body is in the same plane as the surface, so that costume, body, paint and canvas support seem as one.

Vollard catalogued these works as portraits of peasants. However, the artist's son described one of them as 'a picture also known as "The Clockmaker"'.[7] While his information is often unreliable, it is true that the subject's long hair, cravat and waistcoat suggest not a peasant but the elegance of an artisan or bohemian.[8] The art historian Linda Nochlin may be exaggerating when she says that Cézanne was 'preoccupied' with class in his late paintings,[9] but he did notice and record class differences. JE

1 Cézanne to his son, 8 September 1906.
2 For the dating of the Vollard portrait, see p.180, note 8. Since that portrait was such a demanding project, and Cézanne was working on one of his large Bathers compositions when Vollard was not posing for him, it is hard to believe that he would have taken on two additional portraits at the same time.
3 See Danchev 2012, pp.322–3.
4 The setting seems similar to that of other portraits made at the Jas de Bouffan, among them FWN 523, 526 and 533, which have been dated to the 1897–8 period.
5 Loran 1943, pp.90–1; Paris–London–Philadelphia 1995–6, cat. 179, p.426.
6 Most famously, at the right side of *Small Houses in Pontoise*, 1873 (FWN 82).
7 Venturi 1936, vol.1, no.689, p.213.
8 Paris–London–Philadelphia 1995–6, as note 5.
9 Nochlin 1996, p.24.

FIG. 74
Man with Crossed Arms, *c.*1899
Private collection, New York; FWN 527

5 Last Years
1900–6

Paul Cézanne outside his studio at Les Lauves, Aix-en-Provence, 1906
Photograph by Gertrude Osthaus

CÉZANNE ENTERED the twentieth century a celebrated artist. There was an increasingly strong market for his canvases, and growing interest in his exhibitions. He also attracted young painters and critics to his studio in Aix, and corresponded with them to expound his 'theories'. At the same time, his life became more and more like that of an eccentric nineteenth-century rural landowner: mostly solitary except for his young visitors; tended by his housekeeper Madame Brémond and a gardener named Vallier; his accounts kept by his sister Marie; very rarely visiting Paris; his wife and son more often in Paris than Aix. But he painted almost daily, right up to the eve of his death at the age of sixty-seven, on 23 October 1906. His final self-portrait, painted around 1900, already shows a fragile, prematurely aged, but vehement figure.

Of the almost 100 paintings he made in the years that remained to him, most are landscapes, and the majority of these are an extraordinary, final run of paintings of Mont Sainte-Victoire. He was also deeply engrossed in three large Bathers compositions, which took precedence over other canvases that needed to be painted indoors, namely still lifes and portraits. As a result, there are only around twenty portraits from this period, seven of which were actually painted outside.

As in the portraits painted in Aix after 1890, the subjects are local men, women and children. Again, we see agricultural workers, but now also people closer to Cézanne: the pair of portraits of a woman in blue may be of his sister Marie; five canvases are certainly of Vallier.

In the later 1890s, Cézanne's palette with regard to his portraits had darkened, while his landscapes and still lifes began to alternate between lighter and darker tonalities. However, even the darkest of these never quite reached the near black-out of the three Vallier portraits, painted indoors; nor their material density, which approximates that of the portraits of the 1860s. By contrast, the Vallier portraits painted out of doors are as light, and in areas as transparent, in colour as any of his landscapes. JE

Final Self-Portraits

If the self-portraits are about 'taking inventory', as Joseph Rishel suggests, what might the artist have found in this final group?[1] In his sixties, afflicted with diabetes, Cézanne suggests an advancing state of enfeeblement, particularly in the pathetic Boston painting (cat. 22.1). Wearing a floppy, oblong beret, whose clean contours and dark monochrome set off the pallid features of the artist's face, he looks small and wan. In contrast to the intense gaze of so many earlier self-portraits, and even to the apprehensive yet direct glance of a contemporaneous sketch of the artist seen behind a canvas (fig. 75), his eyes appear as small round spots beneath pinched brows, hazed over as if impaired by cataracts. The figure recedes, the lights have gone out, the spirit extinguished – a disturbing finale to Cézanne's singular work in self-portraiture.

The earlier Tokyo painting (fig. 76) is its precursor, both less resolved and less melancholic. There is still life in the artist's eyes, achieved through a direct gaze, but his head is hunched down into his shoulders and his hat seems to press from above, as ghostly shapes in the background, lozenges familiar from the wallpaper in earlier compositions, float in and out of view around his head. Dark patches across the wall, like the stains of fleeting shadows, further dissolve the background. Raw stretches of unpainted canvas around the edges and spackled across his coat indicate a more summary level of 'finish'.

If, as the philosopher Maurice Merleau-Ponty famously has it, Cézanne's oeuvre addresses the fundamental ambiguity of perception, and, in the case of the self-portraits, of self-perception, these late works are a kind of epitome. Cézanne's incessant interrogation of visual reality and of his own reflection in the mirror exposes a central anxiety articulated by theories of modernity: the instability of the self and the erosion of faith in solid reality.[2] These most personal paintings suggest that the artist's struggle to gain the upper hand on sensorial and psychological chaos was far from abating. MM

FIG. 75
Self-Portrait with Beret, c.1899
National Gallery of Art, Washington, D.C.

---

1 Joseph R. Rishel in Paris–London–
   Philadelphia 1995–6, p.210.
2 See Dombrowski 2013 and Shiff 1994.

FIG. 76
Self-Portrait with Fedora, 1894
Ishibashi Foundation, Bridgestone Museum of Art, Tokyo; FWN 511

CAT. 22.1
Self-Portrait with Beret, 1898–1900 (see also detail, p.188)
Museum of Fine Arts, Boston; FWN 529

Portraits of a Woman in Blue

The sitter in these two paintings is characterised so differently from one painting to the other that scholars have wondered if Cézanne had put the same dress on two different women.[1] However, as with the pairs and groups of paintings of his wife that encompass a range of 'likenesses', it is more likely here that Cézanne has painted one woman twice, to very different effect.

In *Seated Woman in Blue* (cat. 23.1) the sitter is rather formally dressed in a tailored suit with triple-puffed sleeves that were fashionable in the late 1890s; a matching hat, decorated with flowers, sits high on her head.[2] John Rewald suggests that she is Madame Brémond, Cézanne's housekeeper in Aix-en-Provence, strongly dismissing Lionello Venturi's suggestion that she is the artist's wife, Hortense. It has also been suggested, and this is perhaps more likely, that she is Cézanne's sister, Marie, with whom he remained close, and whose affluent and conservative social station more closely matches the attire.[3]

The Hermitage painting is larger by a third than that in the Phillips Collection (cat. 23.2), and the composition is more architecturally ambitious. It is structured by means of diagonals that merge in and out of pyramidal and diamond shapes, tilting shards that Cézanne arranges into a dynamic equilibrium. The woman looks aside and slightly down, and seems lost in thought (Lawrence Gowing's characterisation of her as 'transfixed' seems a little intense).[4] In addition to the orange, green and gold table cover, the painting shares much with the earlier *Young Italian Woman* (fig. 65). The pictures are of identical scale, with the figures arranged around intersecting diagonals, pressed up to the picture plane, and just over three-quarter-length in view. In both, the figure supports

herself against a table, her gaze oblique and downcast, her contours reinforced by dark blue and black lines. The *Young Italian Woman* conveys very little psychologically, however, as her face is more mask-like than the sitter in the Hermitage painting. One senses a more sympathetic, familiar rapport with the woman in blue.

The Phillips Collection painting is strikingly dark in comparison, not only in hue but also in affect. The table has gone and the tapestry curtain has moved up to hang behind the sitter. She reclines in her chair, and her head, which seems larger beneath a heavier hat than in the Hermitage picture, is cocked back, perhaps resting against the wall. Her mouth is down-turned, and the flesh sags from her cheekbones down around her jaw line. Indeed, she seems older and certainly more resigned, closed, perhaps disdainful. The blue suit has lost its tailored shape. Whereas in the Hermitage picture it accentuates the sitter's small waist and allows for the curve of her bust, here the fabric bunches around her middle and falls in wrinkled folds to the floor. The sleeves are more sharply modelled, her left arm as if sheathed in metallic armour.

FIG. 77
Apples and Oranges, *c.*1899
Musée d'Orsay, Paris; FWN 871

CAT. 23.1
Seated Woman in Blue, *c.*1904 (see also detail, p.192) (P only)
State Hermitage Museum, St Petersburg; FWN 541

CAT. 23.2
Seated Woman in Blue, 1902–4 (see also detail, p.193)
Phillips Collection, Washington, D.C.; FWN 540

Gowing views the two pictures as pendant bookends to the 'great still-lifes' of 1899,[5] such as *Apples and Oranges*, *c*.1899 (fig. 77). This work and the Hermitage portrait share the same patterned cloth; both are structured by means of a diagonal thrust that reaches up from lower left to upper right, where it is met by stabilising verticals. The Phillips picture, however, may have more resonance with later, more melancholic paintings such as the haunting *Old Woman with a Rosary* (cat. 18.1) and some of the more sinister views of the gothic ruin, the Château Noir (fig. 78). MM

FIG. 78
Château Noir, 1900–4
National Gallery of Art,
Washington, D.C; FWN 359

1 Theodore Reff, 'Painting and Theory in the Final Decade', in New York–Houston 1977–8, p.22, and Albert G. Kostenevich, *French Painting, Mid-Nineteenth to Twentieth Centuries*, trans. Valery G. Derevyaghin, Valery A. Fateyev and Yuri A. Kleiner (Iskusstvo, Moscow, 1991), p.68. Kostenevich also thinks they were painted in different periods, with the Hermitage picture closer to *Old Woman with a Rosary and Young Italian Woman* than the Phillips version.

2 This, according to Rewald 1996, p.489.

3 Reff, in New York–Houston 1977–8, p.22, suggests that the sitter may have been one of the artist's sisters.

4 Lawrence Gowing, 'The Logic of Organized Sensations', in New York–Houston 1977–8, p.64. Françoise Cachin places the Hermitage picture in the studio at Les Lauves, which Cézanne moved into in 1902. Denis Coutagne places both pictures in Les Lauves. Cachin, in Paris–London–Philadelphia 1995–6, pp.446–8, and Coutagne, 'The Major Works in the Lauves Studio', in *Atelier Cézanne, 1902–2002: Le centenaire* (Société Paul Cézanne, Aix-en-Provence, 2002), p.58. Jayne S. Warman has the Hermitage picture in the living quarters at rue Boulegon in Aix, and closer to 1900, with the Phillips painting possibly later. Email with the author, February 2017.

5 Quotation marks are Gowing's, without reference. Gowing 1977, p.64.

Late Portraits of Peasants

Cézanne made his earliest portraits of peasants at the beginning of the 1890s in his studio at the Jas de Bouffan and in a farmhouse on its estate. There, he also worked on his Card Players compositions, for which some of these portraits served either as studies or complementary, independent works. (Examples of these are discussed on pp.149–53.) In and after the mid-1890s, as the genre compositions were completed, Cézanne turned his attention mainly to other portrait subjects, notably friends and acquaintances in both Paris and Aix-en-Provence, and women more than men in the latter venue. It is thought to be in the later 1890s that he returned to making portraits of peasants, producing some half-dozen in the years through to 1904 or 1906.

The subject of the earliest of the three portraits discussed here, *Man in a Blue Smock* (cat. 24.1), has been

identified by art historian Nancy Ireson as probably Père Alexandre, a farm worker from the Jas de Bouffan, who appears in the background of two of the *c.*1890–2 Card Players compositions (see fig. 79),[1] and is also the subject of a related contemporaneous portrait study (fig. 80). However, the *Man in a Blue Smock*, a more complex portrait, is clearly a later work with less of the solidity of the early 1890s peasant works, and appears to belong to a small group of portraits with slivers of unpainted canvas. Among these are a companion painting of the same subject (fig. 81) and *Joachim Gasquet* (cat. 20.1). In fact, as Ireson and others have pointed out, this is most likely the canvas that Gasquet saw in the artist's studio at the Jas de Bouffan, and described in an article published in March-April 1898 as being of a peasant who, 'in his blue smock, adorned with his red

FIG. 79
The Card Players, 1891–2
Metropolitan Museum of Art,
New York; FWN 680

CAT. 24.1
Man in a Blue Smock, *c.*1897
Kimbell Art Museum, Fort Worth, Texas; FWN 524

neckerchief, arms dangling, is impressive in his roughness, like the conception of a patch of earth that has suddenly taken form in coarse and magnificent flesh, sunbaked and whipped by the wind'.[2]

If this sounds condescending as well as hyperbolic, Cézanne's painting is far from being either. Gasquet's view of Provençal peasants as shaped by the land in which they were born was not far from Cézanne's nostalgic, Arcadian attachment to his native landscape and its people. (It is also reminiscent of Vincent van Gogh's view of the local inhabitants of Arles.) But if the portrait has a thematic connotation, it is suggested by the decorative, pseudo-eighteenth-century screen in front of which the artist posed his model and to which he had, as a young man, added some figures of his own.[3] The juxtaposed depictions of an actual late-nineteenth-century peasant and a fictional pastoral scene do two things. First, the woman with the parasol on the actual screen (fig. 82, detail) is looking at an elegant admirer, part of whose arm is all that Cézanne shows of him here, so she may be thought to be looking instead at a simple peasant dressed for a holiday outing in his Sunday best.[4] Second, notwithstanding this humorous invocation of Père Alexandre's roughness, the juxtaposition also has the opposite effect, imbuing him if not quite with Rococo delicacy, then with a quietly meditative feeling reminiscent of Cézanne's admired anti-Rococo, eighteenth-century painter, Chardin.

The *Seated Peasant* (cat. 24.2) – we do not know who he is – painted about two years later has some of that same feeling, but none of the wry humour. The background, far from being a delicately painted screen, is a somewhat lurid version of the tear-drop patterned wallpaper of portraits painted at the Jas de Bouffan in 1886–8.[5] And, although Cézanne posed the figure in a not dissimilar way to Père Alexandre, he turned him to face forward: a frontal mass, as solid and sober as any he had previously painted, with enormous hands and a tiny head. The big pyramid shape, pushed up close to the surface, recalls the *Woman with a Cafetière* (cat. 17.2), as does the almost perfect symmetry of the pose, reinforced here by the walking stick that drops down in parallel to the central axis of the figure, the tip of its

FIG. 80
Man with Pipe, 1891–2
Nelson-Atkins Museum of Art, Kansas City, Missouri; FWN 678

FIG. 81
Seated Peasant, *c.*1897
Hiroshima Museum of Art; FWN 523

FIG. 82
The Environs of Aix-en-Provence, *c.*1859 (detail)
Folding screen with Arcadian scenes and ornaments
Findlay Galleries, Inc.; FWN 560

handle marking the axis itself. Two other portraits are related to this one. The sense of a figure almost perched in the air associates it with the *Portrait of a Man* (cat. 20.4); and the symmetrical bent arms, forming a big diamond shape between them, causes the figure to seem as immovable as Gustave Geffroy in his portrait (cat. 17.1).

The painting was preceded by a watercolour (fig. 83), whose role in the composition of the canvas was described by the art historian Lawrence Gowing:

> In the watercolor, the key of blue modulating into yellow and pink formed a conventional system for the notation of the actual bulk. When the lumpy shapes of the model had been elucidated on paper Cézanne could proceed to the pyramidal formulations from which he built the structure on canvas … The painting, which appears more 'real', with a more objective and material reference, is in fact more schematic … Only when the complex solidity had been grasped were the schematic structure and indeed the naturalness within reach. In this case the imposing simplicity of the painting was evidently arrived at in two stages.[6]

This is very much to the point. However, while Gowing is correct in saying that the canvas reached a naturalness absent in the watercolour, it did not quite reach the level that inhabits other schematic portraits, even *Woman with a Cafetière*; the sheer force of the schematic structure producing such disproportionate parts prevents that happening.[7] In any event, Cézanne, having painted nothing quite like it before, would not do so again.

Compared to *Seated Peasant*, the *Portrait of a Peasant* (cat. 24.3), thought to have been made within the last few years of Cézanne's life, is schematic in an extremely

FIG. 83
Seated Peasant, *c.*1900
Kunsthaus, Zurich

CAT. 24.2
Seated Peasant, c.1900–4
Musée d'Orsay, Paris; FWN 535

natural, relaxed manner. We do not know the sitter in the painting,[8] but the pose is almost identical to a trio of portraits – two of the artist's gardener and general factotum Vallier, and one of an unknown man – presumed to have been painted just after it (cats 26.1–26.3). They are posed on what looks like the chair used for this work, and sit on the terrace of Cézanne's new studio at Les Lauves, where the artist began painting in 1902. It is just conceivable that he began this portrait outside,[9] but it was certainly completed in the studio itself; another trio of larger portraits of Vallier that he made inside the studio at Les Lauves share a similar background (cats 25.1, 25.2; fig. 84).[10] Here, it comprises two simple zones, each featureless except for the meticulously woven pattern of their hatched brushstrokes – hardly the record of a landscape – carefully brought up to surround the shape of the figure.

At least, the background is featureless except for a rectangle behind the sitter on the right-hand side of the painting. It is most likely a small canvas, which would associate this work with a few other late portraits in which Cézanne placed studio materials.[11]

Unlike the studio portraits of Vallier, which were extensively revised throughout, only the overcoat of the sitter in *Portrait of a Peasant* is heavily reworked with multiple, dense, dark blue contour lines creating built-up tracks of paint. Even so, the result does not approach the dense darkness of those Vallier canvases; its comparative lightness contributes to its effect of relaxed naturalness. So does the fact that the face and hands are gently, summarily painted in 'those slender films of colour' that Geffroy remarked upon in his portrait.[12] However, the unfinished eyes, when noticed, are unnerving. Having only sketched in the facial features, Cézanne was probably saying to himself, as with Geffroy's portrait, 'We'll leave that for the end.' But, as Geffroy said, 'sadly, there was no end' – no last session to complete the painting, as was often the case.[13] JE

1 London–New York 2010–11, p.147, in a discussion of this portrait to which my account is indebted, as it is to Rewald's earlier study in R 826. The Card Players composition not illustrated here is FWN 681.

2 Joachim Gasquet, 'Le sang provençal', *Les Mois dorés*, March–April 1898, pp.379–80, most fully discussed in the context of Gasquet's nationalist and regionalist beliefs, though not of this painting, in Athanassoglou-Kallmyer 2003, pp.215–20; and more broadly on Cézanne's Arcadian ethos, pp.187–231. Rewald, in R 826, associates this description with the painting.

3 See Theodore Reff, 'Cézanne's Early Paravent and the Jas de Bouffan', in *Jas de Bouffan* (Société Cézanne, Aix-en-Provence, 2004), pp.57–67.

4 Christina Feilchenfelt in Vienna–Zurich 2000, p.29, and Athanassoglou-Kallmyer 2003, p.189, offer similar readings to this one.

5 If this background was painted in situ, it means that it presumably must have been painted before the forced sale of the Jas de Bouffan in November 1899, possibly well before that date, since it had been clear for some two months that the Jas was going to

be sold, and Cézanne was busy removing his paintings and possessions. See Danchev 2012, pp.322–3. (It is commonly dated to 1900 or later.) However, Jayne S. Warman makes the excellent point, in an email dated 7 February 2017, that this background is so summary and so mechanically regular that Cézanne may well have used a memory of the Jas wallpaper when thinking of how to treat this area; and it clearly does serve as a visual distraction that draws attention away from an extremely static figure.

6 Lawrence Gowing, 'The Logic of Organized Sensations', in New York–Houston 1977–8, p.60.

7 Its somewhat smaller-than-usual size among these paintings – a standard canvas size 20 (72 cm high), as opposed to the size 25 (81 cm high) of the preceding work and the size 30 (92 cm high) of the following one – also contributes to the density of its structure.

8 The sitter bears a general resemblance to a figure that appears in the Card Players compositions, identified as a gardener at the Jas de Bouffan named Paulin Paulet. (See Nancy Ireson and Barnaby Wright in London–New York 2010–11, pp.16–17.)

However, none of the figures who posed for the Card Players wore a string tie; this painting was made about a decade later than those compositions; the Jas had been sold; and Cézanne was now working at his new studio at Les Lauves.

9 The heavy coat over a jacket together with the sturdy hat of this figure allows the possibility that it was begun outside on the terrace in the autumn or winter on an overcast day, in the pale grey light that Cézanne liked – see Doran 1978, p.30. n.3; Doran 2001, p.225, n.3 – then brought inside unfinished to be reworked. (The subjects of the related paintings definitely wore summer clothes out of doors, and were painted in dappled sunlight.)

10 So does a still life, FWN 875.

11 See fig. 81; also cat. 21.1 and FWN 526. If the painting was begun outside, this rectangle could conceivably be the head of a long-handled gardening tool akin to the spade hoe held by a gardener in an earlier portrait (FWN 673), but that seems unlikely.

12 See p.157.

13 Ibid.

CAT. 24.3
Portrait of a Peasant, 1904–6 (see also detail, p.198) (P, W only)
National Gallery of Canada, Ottawa; FWN 542

CAT. 25.1
The Gardener Vallier, 1902–6
National Gallery of Art, Washington, D.C.; FWN 543

Indoor Portraits of Vallier, the Gardener

The sitter in these imposing paintings has been identified as a man named Vallier, who helped Cézanne in the garden and around the studio at Les Lauves, Aix. In addition to three oils (see cats 26.2, 26.3; fig. 85) and three watercolours of Vallier in a straw hat (see figs 86, 87) presumably made in the summer,[1] Cézanne painted three oil portraits of him in colder weather, with a shorter beard and wearing a wool coat and cap. Of the latter three, two are slightly larger, of equal dimensions and of very similar composition (cats 25.1, 25.2). Indeed, they look like exact copies, the only instance of such replication in Cézanne's oeuvre. These two paintings of Vallier in profile have added strips of about 14 cm along the bottom and 10 cm along the right side of each canvas to elongate and enlarge the composition, adding monumentality. The paint surface is inordinately thick, requiring Cézanne to wait for under-layers to dry fully before adding more.[2] He cultivates an impacted look by dragging dry but loaded brushes across already dry paint, allowing the under-strata to remain visible. In some passages, paint gathers in lumps, such as at the sitter's temples. Final strokes in a thin, translucent dark blue resembling ink reinforce contours. These are particularly evident in the added strip, perhaps to ensure the integrity of the whole.

The relationship between the two pictures is puzzling. Why make two when neither one of them had a designated 'client' and both would remain in the studio? If one was a second version of the other, why would the artist not start with a canvas of the revised dimensions rather than again adding a strip at the bottom? Were they instead developed simultaneously? And yet so laboured, each one?

The literature on the Vallier pictures cannot answer these questions and, in fact, is rather bedevilled by either vague philosophising or a recitation of mundane details about Vallier's and Cézanne's final days.[3] Indeed, these pictures are among the least legible in Cézanne's oeuvre. As with most of his portraits, he has largely displaced emotional expression from the conventional site of the face to the formal elements of colour, shape, composition and touch.

There is a tendency to see these paintings as a final statement, a last gasp from the artist before he dies. They are also read with unusually autobiographical references, a kind of conflation between this crusty old gardener and the increasingly antisocial, cranky old painter.[4] The artist's friend Joachim Gasquet even suggested that when Vallier could not sit, Cézanne himself would don the man's coat and hat and continue painting from a mirror. With characteristic poetic flourish, Gasquet wrote, 'And thus, by a strange transference, a mystical substitution – which was perhaps intentional, he mingled together in his profound paintings the features of the old beggar with those of the old artist, both their lives at the confluence of the same void and the same immortality.'[5]

In fact, the letters from Cézanne's final years are riddled with ruminations on ageing and death, and these paintings are quite moving when read as meditations on old age. There is a forbidding grandeur and haunting introversion in these encrusted images of Vallier, his face shadowed by the visor of his cap, cheeks sunken beneath his beard.[6] In the two similar versions, his hands lie in his lap in a strange, gaping gesture, as if holding an illegible pipe or grasping

CAT. 25.2
The Gardener Vallier, 1902–6 (P, W only)
Private collection; FWN 544

FIG. 84
The Gardener Vallier, 1902–6
Private collection, Geneva; FWN 545

something that has disappeared. In the third version (fig. 84), he faces forward, legs apart, the heavy coat thrown over his shoulders and left side, covering his left hand. His face is animated by an unsettling, nervous energy.

The most extraordinary aspect of these pictures, however, is their densely worked surfaces, and the strange colour effects afforded by building up layers of pigment in this way. They have an arduously laboured

look, and indeed there are accounts of Cézanne having started a portrait of Vallier as early as 1902, and that he was still working on one within days of his death in 1906.[7] If his oeuvre was a life-long struggle, one senses in this last group an artist with diminished energy and eyesight but undiminished ambition, thrashing through the 'realisation' of his 'sensations' to achieve something satisfying. In his own mind, however, success evaded him, and he died still striving. MM

1 FWN 547, 548 and 549 are the oils; the watercolours are RW 639, 640 and 641. There is another oil and a watercolour (cat. 26.1, RW 638) of a man, sitting in the garden, with legs crossed and wearing a boater, which could also be Vallier.

2 Conservation report, National Gallery of Art, Washington, D.C., 1992.

3 See, for instance, *Cézanne: Finished – Unfinished* (Hatje Cantz, Berlin, 2000) in which one of the entries cites Jean Royère's 1912 description of the Vallier portraits as having to do with the harmony between nature and human beings: 'He [Cézanne] desired an ardent connection between them, a deep concordance, so that the picture, despite fragmentary handling, would

reveal a superior essence' (p.196). Rewald claimed to be struck speechless by the Vallier paintings, following the lead of Roger Fry, who, as recounted in Virginia Woolf's biography, was struck dumb by one of Cézanne's later works while giving an art history lecture. See John Rewald, in New York–Houston 1977–8, p.407.

4 Françoise Cachin in Paris–London–Philadelphia 1995–6, p.511.

5 Gasquet 1991, p.132.

6 For more on the emotional impact of these pictures, see Nochlin 1996, pp.22–3, and Heather McPherson, *The Modern Portrait in Nineteenth-Century France* (Cambridge University Press, Cambridge, 2001), p.139. For Cézanne's own musings on emotional

expression in painting, see his letter to Louis Aurenche, 25 January 1904.

7 Jean Borély reports a picture descriptive of one of the Vallier portraits on a visit in 1902, in 'Cézanne à Aix', p.491. From Theodore Reff 's essay in New York–Houston 1977–8, p.22. Francis Jourdain saw one of the portraits on Cézanne's easel in 1903, and again in 1904. R.P. Rivière and J.F. Schnerb report seeing one of the Valliers in 1905 in 'L'Atelier de Cézanne', *La Grande revue*, 5, no.24, 25 December 1907. He was working on one of these the day before he died, according to a letter from his sister. Marie Cézanne to his son Paul, 20 October 1906. Rewald 1978, p.333. Rewald claims that the final picture was FWN 549, in Rewald 1978, p.92.

Outdoor Portraits of Vallier, the Gardener

Cézanne hardly ever painted portraits out of doors until he moved into his studio at Les Lauves, Aix, in September 1902; lack of privacy, or the distractions of the countryside, or both, must have made it hard to concentrate on the sitter. In front of the Lauves studio, though, there was a quiet terrace, shaded by a single linden tree, with views down a sloping garden that opened onto a distant panorama that included many of the sites he had painted earlier. There, Cézanne painted six portraits including, in 1905–6, *Seated Man*, a portrait of an anonymous local inhabitant wearing a straw hat, and three paintings of his gardener and general factotum, Vallier.[1] These four portraits form a distinct series: all were painted on a standard size canvas, figure 15 (approximately 65 × 55 cm); and all were prepared for by means of watercolours each identical in size (48 × 31 cm). As was customary with Cézanne at this point, the water-colours are relatively naturalistic in their drawing but schematic in their choice of colour, whereas he reversed the equation with the oils, painting in earthy naturalistic colours shaped by more schematic drawing.[2]

Seated Man (cat. 26.1) and two of the Vallier portraits (cat. 26.2, fig. 85) show a full-length figure, seated with legs crossed, on the same chair. The first work shows the sitter posed in front of a low parapet with the foliage of the garden behind him. Its colours are based around the contrast of ochre with touches of brick-red and a set of hues ranging from violet through blue to dark green. The rhythmic sequences that Cézanne observed in the motif (as indicated by the preparatory watercolour) he made straighter, and the planes between them flatter. The parapet is close to horizontal, while above and especially below it the subject has been reshaped into a mosaic of abutted, interpenetrating and overlapping patches. And the drawing of the figure sets up counterpoised movements through the painting: the slender, tree-like vertical to the right of the man's head is echoed in the shapes of his walking stick and the legs of his chair. Cézanne similarly repeated an opposed curving movement in waves

FIG. 85
The Gardener Vallier, 1905–6
Foundation E.G. Bührle Collection, Zurich; FWN 548

CAT. 26.1
Seated Man, 1905–6 (see also detail, p.215) (W only)
Museo Thyssen-Bornemisza, Madrid; FWN 546

that descend from the tree at the left, to the man's elbow and hand, and down to his right leg that points to the lower right corner.

The two full-length oils of Vallier (cat. 26.2, fig. 85) show the gardener seated not in front of a parapet but against a wall overgrown with foliage; therefore, although it is likely, it is not certain that they were also made on the terrace at Les Lauves. The Zurich canvas is less developed than the London work; quieter and more uniform in its articulation, with floating filaments of drawing indicating areas for potential further development. And the upper part of the figure, including the head, is unfinished. The London painting, although also unfinished in places, is denser, more strongly coloured and more decisively drawn; and Cézanne had begun to develop a narrow vertical feature at the right of the canvas to speak to the vertical bands of sky and ochre wall at the left.

The final watercolour (fig. 87) and oil (cat. 26.3) are commonly assumed to comprise the last portraits in watercolour and oil that Cézanne made. They show the gardener much closer, at half-length, and in profile facing right. The watercolour follows the method of the full-length paintings of Vallier, notably the one in Berlin (fig. 86), in leaving blank white paper for most of Vallier's body and surrounding it with a cloak of dense, multi-coloured washes. In the Berlin work, this produces a disembodied, spectral figure. In the final watercolour, though, the blank paper is given a sense of enormous volume owing to the parallel, dark grey filaments of tonal drawing, floating within paler grey washes with touches of pink and ochre, that carry on down Vallier's right sleeve before coming to rest at an unnaturally huge hand. These are matched by a swarm of more animated rivulets that spill down from the shoulder, from behind the neck, and down his profile to merge the opposite side of the figure with the dark ground. The figure is at once tranquil and flowing with movement; a massive bodily presence conjured up by the lightest of touches and washes of watercolour; and an affectionate image of dignified old age.

FIG. 86
The Gardener Vallier, 1905–6
Museum Berggruen, Berlin

CAT. 26.2
The Gardener Vallier, 1905–6 (see also detail, p.210)
Tate, London; FWN 547

The marvel of the accompanying painting is how Cézanne exaggerated the darkness of the ground, while allowing sufficient light to glow through the pigment, and thereby increased the contrast between the figure and ground. He was thus able to maintain for a figure in opaque paint a brightness equivalent to that of the figure formed of white paper in the watercolour.

Cézanne mustered colours used for painting his late landscapes to compose Vallier's jacket; the gardener's face and hands are the colour of rocks in the Bibémus quarry; and the bits and pieces of drawing that describe folds and contours of both cloth and flesh have the look of tracks and crevices in convex natural forms. Pulling the figure to the left, as compared to the watercolour, allowed Cézanne to reshape its profile with greater clarity and economy; it flows from face to beard to shoulder, falls, turns, turns again, and then flattens out as a path does, again reinforcing the gardener's link to the organic world. The thinness of the pigment, with flecks of white canvas showing here and there, suffuses the entire figure with luminosity; Vallier glows as if illuminated by the setting sun in an analogy to his age – watching and waiting with the open, dark space in front of him.[3]

It has been said that Cézanne, on occasions when his model was unavailable, dressed in his gardener's clothes and painted himself as Vallier, or Vallier as himself.[4] Since this painting and its accompanying watercolour are the only images of Vallier posed as Cézanne almost always posed in order to paint himself in the mirror, it is tempting to consider them his final self-portraits. JE

---

1 The other paintings were FWN 537, 538.
2 The watercolours are RW 638, for the *Seated Man*; RW 639, 640, for the two full-length portraits of Vallier (not one for each, but two that lead, one after the other, to the pair of oils); and RW 641, for the half-length portrait of Vallier. For reasons of space, only the final two watercolours are discussed here.
3 Schapiro 1962, p.126, offers a fuller, very beautiful exegesis of this painting.
4 Gasquet 1921, p.67; Gasquet 1991, p.132.

FIG. 87
The Gardener Vallier, 1906
Private collection, Chicago

CAT. 26.3
The Gardener Vallier, 1906 (W only)
Private collection; FWN 549

Posthumous Portraits

This publication and the exhibition it accompanies have held fast to an understanding of Cézanne's portraits as comprising paintings of individuals who posed for him, and his own self-portraits (including the two based on photographs). Excluded, therefore, have been paintings of imaginary figures; copies of other artists' portraits; multiple-figure compositions with identifiable people; depictions of individuals at work or at leisure; all but one double portrait; and nudes. Nonetheless, we felt that it would be fitting to include, by way of conclusion, what may be described as a posthumous portrait representative of the end awaiting us all.

This canvas is one of six still lifes with a skull, or skulls, that Cézanne painted, in addition to a portrait of a boy seated next to a skull (fig. 62). The portrait and one of the still lifes (FWN 838), made around 1896–8, preceded four of the other still lifes (FWN 872–5), which date from around 1898 to 1904, two years before Cézanne's death aged sixty-nine. Unsurprisingly, and reasonably, these memento mori works have been associated with his awareness of his own mortality.

One of them, showing a single skull with a candlestick, reprises a canvas that Cézanne painted around 1866 (FWN 707), when he was only twenty-seven, one of a sequence of early, morbid compositions. The present canvas is the only work to focus on a single unaccompanied skull: painted around 1885, it can be associated with neither youthful ghoulishness nor premonitions of imminent death. For those wishing to give it a biographical reference, the choice is a stark one: either Cézanne's miserable time in 1885 following an unconsummated love affair at the age of forty-six; or his resigned acceptance of a less-than-passionate private life leading to his marriage to Hortense Fiquet a year later (see p.111).

This painting was preceded by a watercolour (fig. 88), which reveals the naturalistic source of the unusual geometry in the background. These interlocking planes relate it to the artist's so-called proto-Cubist paintings of Gardanne, made in 1886, therefore supporting the second association. But that cannot be thought definitive; and, besides, the Gardanne landscapes are cool and objective. If we are to relate this canvas to any other Cézanne works, it should perhaps be to his *Self-Portrait with Palette* (cat. 12.2), surmounted by an alarmingly gaunt head and painted around the same time. JE

CAT. 27
Still Life with Skull, *c*.1885 (w only)
White House Collection, Washington, D.C.; F W N 805-TA

Dramatis Personae

ALEX DANCHEV

The fact is one doesn't paint souls. One paints bodies; and
when the bodies are well painted … the soul, if there is one, of every
part of the body blazes and shines through!

Cézanne to Joachim Gasquet, from Joachim Gasquet, *Cézanne*, 1921

Much as he might have wished, Cézanne continues to
elude his expositors. Many aspects of his life and work
remain mysterious, including the identity of his sitters.
Of over thirty sitters represented in this exhibition,
at least ten are unidentified; and there are several
more of whom we know practically nothing, other than
what Cézanne chooses to reveal to us, among them
such characters as the gardener Vallier or the obliging
Uncle Dominique.

As so often, he began with his family and friends.
His father, **Louis-Auguste Cézanne** (1798–1886) (fig. 89),
was a formidable figure, both cutting and overbearing,
with whom Cézanne had an ambiguous relationship
throughout his life but especially in his youth.
Otherwise known by his son as *le papa*, or, more wryly,
'the author of my days', he was a true paterfamilias,
much caricatured then and since.

Louis-Auguste was in many ways the archetypical
self-made man; archetypically, too, he believed that his
son should follow suit, in his own image. He himself
had made his way in hats, and then in money-lending,
in Aix-en-Provence. In the fullness of time he became
a banker, by the simple expedient of buying the bank.
He prided himself on his potency, in every sense – he
was still making advances to one of the maids at the
age of eighty. And yet he was a more complex character
than he at first appears. He cannot be dismissed simply
as a crude reactionary. He was socially conservative
but politically progressive, strongly republican and
viscerally anti-clerical – for father and son alike, the
emperor, Napoleon III, was a tyrant. He was instinctively
cautious, or canny, with miserly tendencies, but
was also capable of acting magnanimously and far-
sightedly, with surprising generosity, as he proceeded
to demonstrate with his son, though attended by
great trouble and strife.

Louis-Auguste wanted the best for his son, as he
saw it. First of all, this meant a good education and
a suitable profession, which in his book narrowed
the field to a single acceptable course of action. He
considered law to be eminently suitable; anything else
was not. Cézanne had no interest in the profession, but
had no better idea of his own. In 1858, he duly embarked
on a degree in law at the University of Aix. After
barely eighteen months, he found he could not stand
it. He abandoned the law, and the University of Aix,
and determined to go to Paris and become an artist,
if he could. After a struggle, his father acquiesced.
Moreover, he underwrote it. He authorised an open-
ended stay in Paris on a monthly allowance of 125
francs, 25 francs more than Cézanne's friend Emile
Zola was earning at the Librairie Hachette. Thanks
to *le papa*, Cézanne was on his way.

It is hardly an exaggeration to say that the
father of the artist underwrote not only Cézanne's
daily existence in Paris but also his whole life.

Cézanne, Pissarro and
friends in Pissarro's garden,
Pontoise, photographer
unknown, *c*.1874
LEFT TO RIGHT Alfonso
(medical student and painter),
Cézanne (seated), Lucien
Pissarro, Aguiar (Cuban painter
and doctor), Camille Pissarro

FIG. 89
Louis-Auguste Cézanne,
the artist's father, photographer
and date unknown

The open-ended commitment was to last twenty-five years. It ended only with Louis-Auguste's death, in 1886, when Cézanne was forty-seven, a legend in his own lifetime, but hardly able to make ends meet. Papa did indeed provide. Cézanne came into a substantial inheritance. For the first time in his life, he was free of material worry and paternal scrutiny. From now on there would be no more financial panics, no frantic need to find a means of supplementing his allowance, no call upon his friend Emile Zola for support. He could paint, and live, as he pleased.

When it came to living, his anxieties centred chiefly on his wife and son. Cézanne met **Hortense Fiquet** (1850–1922) (fig. 90) in Paris around the beginning of 1869, when he was thirty and she was barely nineteen. They began living together the following year. In 1872 they had a son, also christened Paul. Cézanne's relationship with Hortense was at first clandestine and then at arm's length. Neither was cut out for joint housekeeping. For many years she was kept out of sight and hidden from Cézanne's father for fear of paternal disapproval and disinheritance. Hortense was not openly avowed, nor Paul formally legitimised, until 1886, when the couple finally married, shortly before Louis-Auguste's death.

Hortense was a woman of humble origins who had had to fend for herself from an early age. Historically, she lacked friends. She was patronised by Cézanne's circle as 'La Boule' (the ball, or the dumpling), and by his family as 'La Reine Hortense' (Queen Hortense). She has fared little better at the hands of art historians, who tend to treat her as lumpen at best, as a gold-digger at worst. She was plainly not Cézanne's intellectual equal (few were); she seems to have had no great regard for him as a painter; understandably, perhaps, she developed a taste for the good life, but not in Aix. 'My wife likes only Switzerland and lemonade,' he said, half-seriously, reflecting on a brief visit in 1890, which he had hated. It is widely believed that she and Cézanne did not have much in common, apart from their son,

and that soon enough she came to mean little to him. Against that prejudiced account, however, should be set twenty-eight or twenty-nine portraits of her, painted by Cézanne over a period of twenty years. Absent or present, no one ever took her place. Hortense was at once more capable and more delicate than is generally allowed; Switzerland was not merely a play-ground but a health resort. She has been considerably underestimated. But not by Cézanne.

Paul Cézanne *fils* (1872–1947), nicknamed 'Le Boulet' (little dumpling, or the ball-and-chain), eventually became effectively his father's agent. He had no other role in life, unless it was as a drifter, or fritterer, or companion for his mother. Cézanne doted on him, and encouraged him unstintingly by letter, though he was not blind to his manifold shortcomings. 'My son, now in Paris, is a *great philosopher*,' he wrote in characteristic fashion to the painter Charles Camoin in 1903. 'By that I don't mean the equal or the emulator of Diderot, Voltaire or Rousseau.... He is rather touchy, *incurious*, but a good boy. As a go-between he will ease the difficulty I have in coping with life.'[1]

Cézanne's mother, **Elisabeth Aubert** (1814–97), had worked in Louis-Auguste's hat business. It is difficult to catch her voice above the noise made by her domineering spouse. However deferential she may have been, or felt obliged to be, she was no pushover. She had 'temperament', as Cézanne would have said, approvingly. She was close to her younger brother, **Dominique Aubert** (b. 1817), a bailiff, who did not object to dressing up for his portraits, and turned out to be one of Cézanne's best early models. Elisabeth's relations with other members of the family, however, were sometimes strained, in particular with **Marie Cézanne** (1841–1921) (fig. 91), her elder daughter, who never married and became increasingly pious and pernickety with age. 'Paul will be eaten up by painting,' Louis-Auguste liked to say, 'Marie by the Jesuits.'[2]

Cézanne and his mother were fundamentally in sympathy. He was her favourite. She was privy to

FIG. 92
Emile Zola, looking at
a painting in his study in
Médan, photograph by
Dornac (Paul François
Arnold Cardon), c.1880

FIG. 91
Marie Cézanne, the artist's sister,
photographer unknown, c.1870

almost as many of his secrets as Zola (even that of his secret family). She counted as one of his moral supports: the vanishing breed he sought all his life.

Elisabeth was on good terms with her son's friends. His first and best friend, **Emile Zola** (1840–1902) (fig. 92), would visit her every so often, even after he had left Aix for Paris. Cézanne and Zola grew up together in Aix, in the same cradle, as Zola once put it. Theirs was one of the seminal artistic liaisons: as intimate, as vexed, as steadfast, as fascinating and as fathomless as any in the annals of modernism. The two men loved each other, it is tempting to say, like brothers. They continued to do so, in spite of everything that came between them, in spite of Zola's worldly success, even after the publication of *L'Oeuvre* (1886), Zola's novel about a failed painter who bears a striking resemblance to Cézanne. This was the work that is supposed to have caused a fatal rupture, but in fact did nothing of the kind, as a recently discovered letter of 1887 from Cézanne to Zola serves to underline.[3] Their feelings for each other were anchored in shared experience, in self-disclosure, in coming of age as artist-creators against the grain, armed to the teeth with the tools of their trade (the pen and the palette knife), and armoured with – temperament. Cézanne characterised his own early manner as *couillarde*, or 'ballsy'. His ideal Zola was the Zola of *Mes Haines* (My Hates), the courageous comrade-in-arms, the ballsy brother-artist. 'If you ask me what I'm going to do in the world,' Zola declared, 'me, an artist, I will answer you: "I am going to live out loud".'[4]

Their mutual friend, the writer **Paul Alexis** (1847–1901) (fig. 93), dubbed 'Zola's shadow', aspired to be Zola's Boswell. He was a minor novelist but an appealing caricaturist. His work *Madame Meuriot* (1890) features an eccentric painter called Poldex (Paul d'Aix), 'a kind of colossus, gauche and bald, an old child, naïf, inspired, at once timid and violent'. Alexis highlights Poldex's temperament, his awkwardness and his

FIG. 93
Paul Alexis, drawing by Fernand Desmoulin, *c*.1880

FIG. 94
Antony Valabrègue, photographer and date unknown

inner struggle. 'Engrossed in the problems of his art, everything he could never capture, the miseries of the métier, banging his fist on the wall, he repeated endlessly, *Nom de Dieu! Nom de Dieu!*'[5] Cézanne was used to seeing his own character in print. He read such scenarios with remarkable equanimity.

In a sense, he asked for it. Most of his friends were writers. **Antony Valabrègue** (1844–1900) (fig. 94) was a poet and art critic, who studied in Aix. Sharing a garlicky meal with Fortuné Marion and Valabrègue – Marion, the cook, had put in some twelve to fifteen cloves – Cézanne poked fun at 'Citizen Valabrègue', who called garlic 'the truffle of the proletariat'. Valabrègue was something of a wit. He was fascinated by Cézanne – they all were – but did not really understand him. 'Every time he paints one of his friends,' he observed, good naturedly, 'it seems as though he were avenging himself for some hidden injury.'[6]

Fortuné Marion (1846–1900) was a bad cook but a brilliant scholar, whose passion was the rocks and soil, the flora and fauna of Provence. A precocious Darwinist (recognised even by Darwin himself), a renowned Professor of Zoology, and later the Director of the Museum of Natural History in Marseille, he was steeped in the geology and palaeontology of the area around Aix, in particular Mont Sainte-Victoire, the mountain that Cézanne made his own. Marion also liked to paint. Borrowing the palette knife, he executed a view of the village church in Aix (1866–70), now in the Fitzwilliam Museum, Cambridge, which has been taken for a Cézanne.

Cézanne and Marion discovered a real intellectual affinity, based on a shared love of their native land. They went on painting expeditions together; they shared their latest finds. Some indication of their free-wheeling discussions may be found in one of Cézanne's early sketchbooks, where cartoon-like studies of soldiers and greybeards are overlaid with diagrams of geological eras (Permian, Cambrian and such like), annotated in Marion's hand. The Cézannian era was yet to come. The fervour of their friendship cooled, but the lessons they learned together stuck. Many years later, Cézanne recalled Marion on 'the psychology of the earth' for Joachim Gasquet.[7]

DRAMATIS PERSONAE

Joachim Gasquet (1873–1921) (fig. 68) was a poet and critic, a mover and shaker in the literary world of Aix (and beyond), who praised 'the blood of Provence', and who evolved into a rightist, a royalist and in his own high-flown way something of a racist. He wrote rapturously of Cézanne's *Old Woman with a Rosary* (cat. 18.1) as a Provençal racial symbol, and did his best to represent the artist as a kind of penitent Dostoevsky. That effort was doomed to failure; but Gasquet cannot be ignored. He was undoubtedly close to Cézanne for a few years (*c*.1896–9); he had a rare insight into the great soul reminiscent. What is more, Cézanne wrote him some fascinating letters. Gasquet's account of that experience, replete with extensive conversations reproduced verbatim, is one of the prime sources on the life of the artist – Cézanne straight from the horse's mouth, as it seems – and also one of the most problematical.[8]

Gasquet had an unbeatable entrée – he was the son of Cézanne's boyhood friend Henri Gasquet,

a baker – and he was not without a certain allure. He may have reminded Cézanne of his youth, spent with Zola; they revisited some of the old haunts. He may have conjured a brighter image of Cézanne's son, now ensconced in Paris. Gasquet was twenty-three when they met, two years younger than Paul *fils*, but more vivid, more accomplished, more intelligent, more curious. But there were limits. Cézanne admired intellectual seriousness (and passion), but any hint of preciousness repelled him. Gasquet was preciousness personified, at once superior and ingratiating. His viewpoint was little more than the glorification of a bygone age, and essentially narcissistic. Cézanne may have lived in the past, as he himself acknowledged, but he was not backward-looking. There was work to be done.

Perhaps the only one of his contemporaries at the School of Drawing in Aix, which he attended in 1857, for whom he had real respect as an artist was **Achille Emperaire** (1829–98) (fig. 95). 'I still have a good friend

FIG. 95
Portrait of Achille Emperaire (see cat. 4.2), one of two paintings rejected by the Salon jury of 1870, here held aloft by Cézanne in a caricature by Henri-Charles Stock

227

FIG. 96
Ambroise Vollard, photograph
by Rogi André, 1936

from that time,' he wrote to Gasquet forty years later. 'Well, he has not been successful, which does not prevent him from being a damn sight better painter than those good-for-nothings with their medals and decorations that bring one out in a sweat.'[9] Emperaire was *très fort* – the best, high praise. Cézanne was always fond of him, and even tried to look after him, though he was impossible to look after, even when he did not have a sou to his name. Emperaire dreamed of glory; his big eyes were pools of melancholy and mad fantasy. Alas, it never came true. He ended his days selling pornographic prints to the students of Aix.

Cézanne was apt to be uncompromising in his assessment of his peers, but he was always ready to encourage beginners, especially if they were serious. 'I think the young painters are much more intelligent than the others,' he remarked in his last letter to his son. 'The old can only see in me a disastrous rival.'[10] Belying his insular reputation, he would sometimes seek them out. **Alfred Hauge** (1876–1901) (fig. 72) was a young Norwegian painter to whom Cézanne introduced himself one day at dinner in the hotel where they were both staying in Marlotte, near Fontainebleau, in 1899, enquiring politely if he was a painter, too; evidently he already knew the answer. Hauge was flabbergasted – he thought Cézanne was dead. He was sufficiently unnerved to say so. He recovered from this unpromising beginning, however, and the two of them took their meals together, painted watercolours together, exchanged work, and even selected the same motif out of doors as the subject of their canvases.

Little is known of Hauge, but he was not a complete innocent. In 1895–6 he shared a studio and an apartment with Edvard Munch. On 14 April 1900 he had the means with which to buy a Fantin-Latour from Ambroise Vollard for 1,200 francs.

Ambroise Vollard (1866–1939) (fig. 96) was Cézanne's dealer, and in some measure the maker of his reputation, or perhaps the guarantor of his rise to world status. For about a decade, coinciding with the last ten years of Cézanne's life, Vollard acquired an effective monopoly on his work. According to the catalogue raisonné of his paintings, no fewer than 678, more than two-thirds of his lifetime production, passed through Vollard's hands – almost certainly a significant underestimation, given the prevalence of off-the-record transactions and the impenetrable character of the dealer's books. In 1899, Vollard emptied the artist's studio of an enormous cache of paintings and watercolours, snapped up any unconsidered trifles, propositioned every Cézanne owner he could find, and established a remarkably close relationship first with Cézanne's son and then with Cézanne himself, a relationship never broken. In time, this relationship made Vollard's fortune.

It was Vollard who gave Cézanne his first one-man show, in 1895, when he was already fifty-six, and more or less invisible, though not yet dead. The show was held in the Galerie Vollard, a boutique in the rue Laffitte, off the boulevard Haussmann in Paris, where some 150 works were displayed in rotation, a disorderly jumble in the confined space – more Cézannes than anyone had ever seen. Apart from the spectacle of Degas and Renoir drawing lots to see who should carry off a small still life (a watercolour),[11] perhaps the most extraordinary aspect of this revelatory show was that Cézanne and Vollard had not yet met. Their relationship was sealed only after the exhibition had opened.

In a curious way they were made for each other. 'Cézanne was the great romance of Vollard's life,' as Gertrude Stein said.[12] The dealer also wrote about the artist: Vollard's *Paul Cézanne* (1914) is in effect the

first biography, masquerading as a kind of celebrity memoir, or rather a celebrity memoir masquerading as a biography.[13] Like Gasquet's *Cézanne* (1921), it has been pillaged ever since. Cézanne for his part had faith in Vollard – more than in most of humankind – and would not hear of parting from him, as he made clear to Charles Camoin: 'I believe absolutely in Vollard as an honest man. Since your departure, the Bernheims and another dealer have been to see me. But I remain faithful to Vollard, and am only sorry that my son has left him with the impression that I might take my canvases elsewhere. I am having a studio built on a piece of land that I acquired for the purpose, and Vollard will certainly continue to be my intermediary with the public. He's a man of tremendous flair, good bearing and sense of propriety.'[14]

Cézanne lacked patrons. Uniquely, **Victor Chocquet** (1821–91) (fig. 97) became both a patron and a friend. Chocquet was not a rich man. He was a customs official. He was also a born collector: in his own unemphatic fashion, one of the most important private collectors of the nineteenth century. He was introduced to Cézanne by Renoir, in 1875, but it was Delacroix who brought them together. 'Renoir tells me that you like Delacroix?' hazarded Cézanne. 'I adore Delacroix,' replied Chocquet. 'We'll look together at what I have of him.'[15] What he had eventually amounted to over eighty paintings, drawings and watercolours. Cézanne venerated Delacroix. Baudelaire's homage in *L'Art romantique* (1868), 'The Life and Work of Eugène Delacroix', was his constant study. So were the Delacroixs hanging in the Louvre. Poring over Chocquet's collection, on hands and knees, the works strewn across the floor, was one of Cézanne's greatest pleasures.

As Cézanne began to paint Chocquet, Chocquet began to collect Cézanne. In fifteen years he amassed

FIG. 97
Victor Chocquet, portrait photograph
by Cézanne, *c*.1860

an outstanding collection of thirty-five works. At the same time he became a moral support: a confidant, and also a kind of gauge. Cézanne was in the habit of weighing and assaying his own moral character (as he called it), measuring himself against other men, where he identified suitable models. Chocquet was one. Cézanne was very touched when the collector wrote to congratulate him on his marriage. He replied: 'Now, I should not like to weigh too heavily on you, morally I mean, but since Delacroix served as an intermediary between us, I will permit myself to say this: that I should have liked to have your stable outlook, which allows you to reach the desired end with certainty. Your kind letter … testifies to a great balance of human faculties.… Fate has not endowed me with an equal stability, that is the only regret I have about the things of this earth.'[16]

If not exactly a moral support, **Gustave Geffroy** (1855–1926) (fig. 98) was another key ally. However, in his case, puzzlingly, something went wrong. After an almost ideal introduction and courtship, the relationship abruptly soured. Cézanne turned against him, for reasons that are still not entirely clear. Geffroy was an influential writer and critic. He was the author of the first substantial article on Cézanne, a kind of profile, in *Le Journal*, in 1894.[17] Typically, Cézanne read it the day it came out, and wrote to express his appreciation. Monet invited them both to lunch at Giverny. Cézanne himself proposed a portrait, which proceeded very amicably – until the moment he abandoned it. In itself, that was not unusual; something similar happened with Vollard's portrait a few years later. Soon enough, however, Cézanne could be found cursing 'the Geffroys and the other scoundrels who have drawn the attention of the public to me, for the price of a fifty-franc article'. This smacks of betrayal; and Gasquet goes so far as to speak

of Cézanne's 'loathing' of Geffroy, which sounds as though he might be exaggerating, but for a letter from the artist to Vollard, written in such strong language that it was in effect censored by the dealer – deleted from the public record – until 1993. Describing Geffroy's *Le Coeur et l'esprit*, a collection of five stories of which he singles out 'Le Sentiment de l'impossible' as one of some 'very fine things', he goes on to say: 'How has such a distinguished critic reached such a complete castration of feeling? He's become a businessman.'[18]

What caused this volte-face? The traditional explanation provides not so much a reason as the repetition of a sort of dogma. It is predicated on the assumption of a fundamental ideological schism between a progressive unbeliever, like Geffroy, and a reactionary old codger, like Cézanne, his nose buried in the Catholic newspaper *La Croix*, his faith a rock, his church a haven, his politics an instinctual mix of blood and soil and chauvinism. The unreconstructed Catholic reactionary is a myth, but the line peddled by Vollard, and later by others, seems oblivious to any contradictions. Whatever the cause of his disillusion with Geffroy, there was no ideological schism. '*Homo sum*,' Cézanne quoted splendidly to a young friend, '*nihil humani a me*.'[19] I am a man, nothing human is foreign to me.

For the remainder of Cézanne's subjects, all is speculation, or legend. Gasquet spun a fantastic tale of the *Old Woman with a Rosary* as a renegade nun, homeless and destitute, taken in by a charitable Cézanne. The artist himself stated plainly that she was a former servant of the lawyer Marie-Joseph Demolins, Gasquet's friend and collaborator on the literary journal he created as a mouthpiece for his views, *Les Mois dorés*.[20] The gardener Vallier was more than a gardener. Legend has it that he had been to sea; traditionally, some of the portraits are known by the

FIG. 98
Gustave Geffroy in his study,
photographer unknown, c.1894

DRAMATIS PERSONAE

alternative title *Le Marin* (The Sailor). Cézanne relied upon him for practically everything – even a massage, contrary to another legend that no one was permitted to touch him. His presence was providential. Vallier was Cézanne's secret sharer.

Louis Guillaume was the son of Cézanne's friend and neighbour in Paris, Antoine Guillaume, a cobbler. Louis was of an age with the artist's son; the two used to play together. The *Boy in a Red Waistcoat* (cat. 15.1) is **Michelangelo de Rosa**, a marvellous name for a young Italian model – exceptionally for Cézanne, a professional model. The portraits of men – standing, sitting and smoking – are very likely of workmen in Cézanne's employ, as gardeners or labourers. The women and children may well be their womenfolk and offspring. The *Man with Pipe* (cat. 16.1) is sometimes said to be

'Père Alexandre'. *The Smoker* (cat. 16.2) is most probably Paulin Paulet, a gardener, who was also enlisted to pose as a card player, along with his daughter Léontine. Father and daughter were paid five francs and three francs, respectively. Léontine remembered interminable sittings and being scared when Cézanne stared at her. But on the day of her first communion he gave her a two-franc piece and told her to go and buy whatever she wanted. With workers or peasants he was always affable and *bon enfant*, or good-natured. His familiars in Aix were all traditional craftsmen of one sort or another: the baker Gasquet, the locksmith Rougier, the gardener Vallier. With these men there was never any acting up or acting out. There was only a scrupulous courtesy, an utter lack of pretension, and a palpable sense of solidarity.

The author has drawn on his own works, *Cézanne: A Life* (Profile, London, 2012) and *The Letters of Paul Cézanne* (Thames & Hudson, London, 2013).

1 Cézanne to Camoin, 22 February 1903.
2 Marthe Conil, 'Quelques souvenirs sur Paul Cézanne, par une de ses nièces', *Gazette des beaux-arts* 56, 1960, p.301.
3 Cézanne to Zola, 28 November 1887. On the controversy and the relationship, see Danchev 2012, ch.9. For a re-examination of the relationship in the light of the letter, see Lethbridge 2016, pp.126–42.
4 Emile Zola, *Mes Haines* [1866], in *Ecrits sur l'art* (Gallimard, Paris, 1991), p.46.
5 Alexis 1890, pp.311–12.
6 Valabrègue to Zola, 2 October 1866, in Danchev 2012, p.36.
7 Gasquet [1921] 2002, p.243. The sketchbook is in the Louvre. The relevant pages are reproduced in Danchev 2012, pp.96–7.

8 Among the problems are such issues as slippages in time, smuggled borrowings from other sources (notably Zola's novels) and the author's own intrusive voice. There is also the question of the narrow window of Gasquet's witness, or first-hand knowledge. He saw a lot of Cézanne for three years, 1896–9, but not thereafter. And then there is a time lag. According to Gasquet's wife, his account was written in 1912–13 (some six years after Cézanne's death); but it was not published until 1921. It was belatedly translated into English as *Joachim Gasquet's Cézanne* (1991), subtitled 'a memoir with conversations'. The conversations only fuel the evidential controversy. A selection appears in Michael Doran's invaluable collection, *Conversations with Cézanne* (2001), in an inferior translation.
9 Cézanne to Gasquet, 30 April 1896.
10 Cézanne to son Paul, 15 October 1906.
11 *Three Pears*, 1888–90; see Danchev 2012, pl.52.

12 Gertrude Stein, *The Autobiography of Alice B. Toklas* [1933] (Penguin, London, 1966), p.35.
13 See Vollard [1938] 2005.
14 Cézanne to Camoin, 11 March 1902.
15 Vollard [1914] pp.57–60.
16 Cézanne to Chocquet, 11 May 1886. The letter continues to develop this theme even more poignantly.
17 The article is printed in full in Paris–London–Philadelphia 1995–6, exh. cat., pp.29–30.
18 Cézanne to Gasquet and Vollard, 30 April 1896 and 9 January 1903.
19 Cézanne to Louis Aurenche, 20 November 1901, apparently quoting from memory, from *The Self-Tormentor* by the Roman playwright Terence. The actual quotation reads 'Homo sum; humani nihil a me alienum puto'.
20 See Cézanne to Gasquet, 12 May 1902.

Chronology

JAYNE S. WARMAN

I could paint for a hundred years, a thousand without stopping,
and I would still feel as though I knew nothing.

Cézanne to his art dealer Ambroise Vollard, *c*.1896,
from Ambroise Vollard, *Paul Cézanne*, 1914

1839
Paul Cézanne is born in Aix-en-Provence (19 January),
the son of Louis-Auguste Cézanne (a seller of hats
turned banker) and Elisabeth Aubert (a native of Aix).

1841
Marie Cézanne, the artist's sister, is born (4 July).

1844
Cézanne's parents are married (29 January), so
legitimising their children.

1850
Hortense Fiquet, the daughter of Claude-Antoine
Fiquet and Catherine Desprez, and Cézanne's future
wife, is born in Saligny, Jura (22 April).

1850–2
Cézanne registers at the Catholic Ecole Saint-Joseph,
where he befriends Henri Gasquet (fig. 69). In 1852
Cézanne enters the Collège Bourbon. An excellent
student, he wins many prizes and meets Emile Zola.

1854
Rose Cézanne, the artist's second sister is born (1 June).

1857
Cézanne registers at the Ecole Gratuite de Dessin, Aix,
where he draws after the live model, as well as the
plaster casts and marble originals in the Musée d'Aix.

1858
Zola goes to Paris to live with his widowed mother;
he writes often to Cézanne and encourages the
aspiring artist to join him. In December Cézanne
registers at the law school in Aix and is enrolled
the following year.

1859
Louis-Auguste acquires the Jas de Bouffan,
a country property of about fifteen hectares on
the outskirts of Aix.

1860–1
Cézanne is determined to go to Paris to learn to
paint. Louis-Auguste finally agrees, contingent upon
Cézanne continuing his law studies, and together
they leave Aix for Paris (April 1861). Cézanne studies
at the Académie Suisse, where he meets fellow artists
Camille Pissarro, Antoine Guillemet and Achille
Emperaire. Failing to qualify for the Ecole des
Beaux-Arts, he returns to Aix (September).

1862–4
By early November 1862 Cézanne has returned to
Paris and stays until July 1864. He again studies at
the Académie Suisse and meets Pierre-Auguste Renoir.
He paints a self-portrait after a photograph (cat. 1.1),
the earliest known portrait of the artist. In 1863 he
may have exhibited at the Salon des Refusés. Death
of Eugène Delacroix is announced (13 August 1863).

Cézanne setting out to paint
sur le motif, **near Auvers**,
photographer unknown, *c*.1875

FIG. 99
Chestnut Trees and Farm at Jas de Bouffan, *c.*1876
Private collection; FWN 90

1865

Cézanne paints himself looking very much the young radical (FWN 397). He spends the winter in Aix, working at the Jas de Bouffan, where he paints a mural of his father on the walls of the *grand salon* (fig. 19).

1866

From mid-February to mid-August Cézanne is in Paris, where he meets Edouard Manet and Claude Monet. In April he submits to the official Paris Salon a still life and a large portrait of his friend, the poet Antony Valabrègue (cat. 3.1), both of which are rejected. Spending the summer in Bennecourt, a village north-west of Paris, he paints the 70-year-old *père* Rouvel, father-in-law of the local innkeeper (probably fig. 17), but by mid-August he is back in Aix, where he remains until the following February. During this period he paints his family, including a life-size portrait of his father reading a newspaper (cat. 4.1), and begins a portrait of his 12-year-old sister Rose (FWN 401), known only from a sketch on a letter. Later that year the Provençal naturalist Antoine-Fortuné Marion and Valabrègue pose for Cézanne (fig. 100), a study 'done from nature' for a larger composition never completed. A sketch of the work (C 153) appears on a letter to Zola,

dated autumn 1866. Cézanne also paints his uncle, Dominique Aubert, in different guises (cats 2.1–2.6, figs 22–5), an image of himself (FWN 403), and begins a likeness of his sister Marie (cat. 1.3 recto), followed in 1867 by a portrait thought to be of his mother (cat. 1.3 verso), all executed with a palette knife, a technique that the artist favours at this time.

1867

In February Cézanne is living in Paris, where he works at the Académie Suisse on a powerful image of a popular black model, *The Negro Scipio* (FWN 422). Early June finds him back in Aix, painting 'some truly beautiful portraits; no longer [executed] with a palette knife, but just as vigorous' (so writes Marion to the musician Heinrich Morstatt), possibly *Portrait* (FWN 416) and *Young Man Leaning on his Elbow* (FWN 420). He makes two portraits of Emperaire, one a mural on the wall of the *salon* at the Jas de Bouffan (FWN 421), the other a full-size likeness on canvas (cat. 4.2).

1868

Cézanne alternates between Paris (January–May) and Aix (mid-May to mid-December), ending the year in Paris at 53, rue Notre-Dame-des-Champs.

1869

At the beginning of the year he meets the 19-year-old Hortense Fiquet, with whom he forms a personal relationship, a liaison hidden from his father. Cézanne divides his time between the Midi in the south and the Ile-de-France. He begins another portrait of Valabrègue (cat. 3.2) and between September and July 1870 he works on two double portraits of Zola and the writer Paul Alexis, painted at Zola's rue La Condamine apartment in Paris (FWN 601; cat. 3.3).

1870

In April Cézanne submits to the official Paris Salon his 1867–8 portrait of Emperaire (cat. 4.2) and a reclining nude, now lost (FWN 595), both of which are refused by the jury. The two canvases are caricatured in a cartoon by Stock (fig. 95). In July France declares war on Prussia (which continues until February 1871) and Cézanne avoids conscription by taking refuge in L'Estaque, where Hortense joins him. He depicts her with unbound hair (FWN 627). Visiting Aix on a regular basis, he paints his childhood friend Gustave Boyer (FWN 427–9), his father (FWN 430), his mother (cat. 1.3, verso) and possibly begins a portrait of Marion (cat. 1.2).

1871

'Bloody Week' in Paris (21–8 May) sees the army suppress the radical government of the Paris Commune. Cézanne and Hortense decide to return to Paris in July; in December the couple moves to 45, rue Jussieu.

1872

Paul *fils* is born (4 January), the couple's only child. Cézanne paints Hortense nursing their baby son (FWN 618). That summer the family stays in Saint-Ouen-l'Aumône, north-west of Paris. Cézanne paints *en plein air* with Pissarro, who has settled nearby in Pontoise. At the end of year the family rents a 'shack' in Auvers-sur-Oise, where a number of artists live and work. Here, Cézanne meets Dr Paul Gachet, known to Louis-Auguste since 1858, who befriends many of the artists in the area.

1873

The family spends the year in Auvers. The artist often walks to Pontoise to paint with Pissarro, who introduces him to Julien Tanguy, Cézanne's first picture dealer.

FIG. 100
Marion and Valabrègue Setting Out for the Motif, 1866
Private collection, Mexico City; FWN 400

1874

Back in Paris, Cézanne submits three paintings to the first Impressionist exhibition (15 April–15 May).

1875

During the year, Cézanne paints himself (cats 5.1, 5.2; FWN 435) and Paul *fils* (Introduction, fig. 7). By mid-April the family is settled at 67, rue de l'Ouest, an apartment that they retain until early 1880. Towards the end of 1875, through Renoir, Cézanne meets Victor Chocquet, a collector and admirer of Delacroix. Chocquet becomes a close friend and early patron, eventually acquiring nearly forty paintings and watercolours.

1876

Cézanne spends the summer painting landscapes in the fishing village of L'Estaque and in Aix,, but by the end of August he is back in Paris, where he begins work on a head of Chocquet (cat. 6.1).

1877

During 1877 he paints Hortense in their rue de l'Ouest apartment (FWN 441; cats 7.1, 7.2), two portraits of Chocquet in the collector's rue de Rivoli apartment (fig. 37; cat. 6.2), and at least one self-portrait (fig. 35). He exhibits seventeen works in the third Impressionist exhibition (4–30 April), including the portrait of Chocquet begun the previous year (cat. 6.1) and one of Hortense (FWN 441). The Chocquet, in particular, is vilified by a negative press.

1878

In early March Cézanne and Hortense leave for the Midi. But while Cézanne lives at the Jas de Bouffan, Hortense and young Paul reside in three different locations in Marseille until September. From November to December, while Hortense is in Paris, Cézanne is with his son, now aged six, in L'Estaque, where he makes sketches of young Paul (such as C 732 [a drawing] and Introduction, fig. 6 [one of two small oil sketches]).

FIG. 101
House of Père Lacroix, Auvers-sur-l'Oise, 1873
National Gallery of Art, Washington, D.C.; FWN 77

FIG. 102
Still Life with Compotier,
1879–80
Ny Carlsberg Glyptotek,
Copenhagen; FWN 781

1879

From early April until the end of March 1880 Cézanne is based in Melun, south-east of Paris, at 2, place de la Préfecture. Here he paints the son of a family friend, Louis Guillaume (cat. 9.1), and begins a portrait of Hortense (fig. 42), which he reworks later.

1880

In April the family is living at 32, rue de l'Ouest, their residence in Paris until at least the end of August 1885. While here, Cézanne paints a self-portrait (cat. 8.1) and probably starts several canvases of Hortense (such as cat. 9.3) and son Paul (FWN 458, 469–70; cat. 9.2). For the month of August he visits Zola in Médan, west of Paris, and possibly executes a self-portrait there (fig. 39), which he may have begun the previous June.

1881

From May until late October Cézanne and family stay in Pontoise. The artist again paints with Pissarro. On this visit, or one made the following May, Cézanne leaves a copy of a pastel portrait of himself drawn by Renoir (Introduction, fig. 11). In October Louis-Auguste has a studio built for his son at the Jas de Bouffan.

1882

From March to October Cézanne is back in Paris. In May his first and only painting is accepted for the Paris Salon, *Portrait of M.L.A...* (cat. 4.1) is accepted for the Paris Salon, for the first and only time. The artist and his family spend the summer with the Chocquets in Hattenville, Normandy, where Cézanne focuses on landscape.

1883

On 30 April the death of Edouard Manet is announced. Cézanne divides his time during the year between Aix and L'Estaque, where he spends May to September with Hortense and Paul *fils*. He possibly makes loosely drawn sketches of Hortense here (such as FWN 467, 468).

1884

Cézanne spends most of the year in Aix.

1885

From mid-June to end July the family stays with the Renoirs at La Roche Guyon, Ile-de-France, but Cézanne then leaves for Aix, Hortense for Paris. By the end of August he is working in Gardanne, near Aix; in November the family joins him and they stay here until October the following year. Around this time Cézanne paints Hortense (cats 11.1, 11.2) and several self-portraits (cats 10.1–10.3).

1886–7

March sees the publication of Zola's novel *L'Oeuvre*, the story of a brilliant but failed artist, who resembles Cézanne and other contemporaries. On 28 April Cézanne and Hortense are married in Aix, followed some six months later by the death of Louis-Auguste (23 October), who leaves his son a considerable inheritance. Cézanne now lives at the Jas de Bouffan with his mother, while Hortense and Paul *fils* live in Aix at 10 *bis*, Cours Sextius. During this time he paints Hortense at the Jas de Bouffan (cats 13.1–13.3) and possibly Paul *fils* (cat. 12.1).

1888

In February Cézanne and Hortense move back to Paris. Now living at 15, quai d'Anjou, they keep this address until 1890. While here, he paints Hortense wearing a red dress (cats 14.2–14.4) and begins a series of canvases of model Michelangelo de Rosa (figs 50–2; cat. 15.1; RW 375–6). He also rents a studio on the rue du Val de Grâce, where he works on a series of Harlequin studies (FWN 669–70; fig. 54; C 938–41; RW 295) and a large composition titled *Mardi Gras* (FWN 668), for which Paul *fils* and Louis Guillaume are the models. From July to November Cézanne is in Chantilly, outside Paris, to be alone and to paint landscapes.

1889

In June the Cézannes stay with the Chocquets once more in Hattenville, where the artist paints his friend Victor, seated in his garden (FWN 498). From July to November Cézanne is back at the Jas de Bouffan. The year end is marked by the death of Claude Fiquet, Hortense's father (13 December).

1890

From mid-May to mid-November the Cézannes travel to Emagny to settle Claude Fiquet's estate and then on to Switzerland, a family trip that the artist can barely tolerate. Hortense returns to Paris; Cézanne to the Jas de Bouffan. The artist starts to suffer from diabetes, which makes him irritable.

1891

In February 1891 Cézanne moves Hortense and Paul *fils* to 9, rue de la Monnaie in Aix. He continues to live at the Jas de Bouffan, where he paints Hortense's portrait (FWN 483–5, 509). On 7 April Chocquet dies. In late December 1891 the Belgian painter Eugène Boch buys the large portrait of Emperaire (cat. 4.2) from Tanguy for 800 francs.

FIG. 103
Gardanne, *c.*1885
Barnes Foundation, Philadelphia; FWN 224

1891–6

While in Aix, over the next five years Cézanne works on a series of individual portraits and studies of farm-workers at the Jas de Bouffan (cats 16.1, 16.2; figs 56–7, 59, 80; FWN 508, 679, 682–3), many of which form the basis for his six (multi-figure) Card Player compositions (figs 55, 79; FWN 681, 684). He also works on portraits of a young girl here (cat. 19.1; fig. 66).

1892–3

Cézanne travels in and around Aix, Paris and Fontainebleau. In October 1893 a self-portrait (probably cat. 10.3) is exhibited at the Paris gallery, Le Barc de Boutteville.

1894

Cézanne is in Maisons-Alfort and Melun, outside Paris, painting landscapes along the Marne. In November, while visiting Monet in Giverny, he works on a self-portrait (fig. 76), which he abandons. In December his *Madame Cézanne in a Striped Dress* (cat. 9.3) is published in *Le Coeur* (the first time a portrait of Cézanne's is published), in an article on the artist written by Emile Bernard.

1895

From April to mid-June the artist works on a portrait of the writer and critic Gustave Geffroy (cat. 17.1). He does not 'finish' it, but leaves it with the sitter. From the end of June (to May 1896) he is back at the Jas de Bouffan, during which time he executes several portraits (cats 17.2, 18.1). In November Ambroise Vollard, who becomes Cézanne's dealer, exhibits some 150 paintings on a rotating basis in his rue Laffitte gallery, Paris, Cézanne's first solo show. Although no catalogue was issued, at least fifteen portraits can be identified, most of them bought by Cézanne's artist friends: Monet (FWN 422; fig. 52); Edgar Degas (fig. 37; FWN 450); Pissarro (fig. 35) and Geffroy (figs 63, 64). The American expatriate Egisto Fabbri buys the first of thirty-six Cézannes (cat. 15.1).

1896

In late winter (or early spring 1897) Cézanne undertakes portraits of his childhood friend, Henri Gasquet (fig. 69), and his son the poet Joachim (cat. 20.1), both executed at the Jas de Bouffan. The family spends June in Vichy and July and August in Talloires, on the shores of Lac d'Annecy. Cézanne makes sketches of the gardener's young son at the Hôtel de l'Abbaye (C 1085) and paints his portrait (cat. 19.2).

FIG. 105
Maurice Denis, **Homage to Cézanne**, 1900
Musée d'Orsay, Paris

1897–9

Cézanne again depicts workmen at the Jas de Bouffan (cat. 24.1; fig. 81). From June to September he rents a cottage in Le Tholonet, just outside Aix, to work *sur le motif*. Hortense then joins him in Aix. The following month Cézanne's mother dies (25 October).

1898

January finds Cézanne back in Paris, where he rents a studio at 15, rue Hégesippe-Moreau. In May the couple moves to 31, rue Ballu, their home for the next six years. The artist probably paints his last self-portrait, wearing a beret (cat. 22.1), in this apartment. Vollard exhibits sixty paintings by Cézanne, five of which are portraits (9 May–10 June).

1899

Auguste Pellerin, the 'margarine king', buys the first of thirty-four portraits by Cézanne (cat. 2.5). His legendary collection, which eventually includes over 100 works by the artist, is visited by many painters and writers. Cézanne paints Vollard's portrait (cat. 20.2) at his Paris studio over a period of many sittings. The estate of Chocquet's widow is auctioned at the beginning of July: Galerie Durand-Ruel buys *Mardi Gras* (FWN 668) and

two portraits (cat. 6.2; FWN 498); Galerie Bernheim-Jeune buys a portrait of Victor Chocquet (cat. 6.1). Cézanne spends July and August in Marlotte, near Fontainebleau, where he meets a young Norwegian artist, Alfred Hauge, and paints his portrait (cat. 20.3). He later slashes it in a fit of pique. In November the Jas de Bouffan is sold. Cézanne takes an apartment at 23, rue Boulegan in Aix and has a studio built under the eaves, where he paints a young Italian woman the following year (fig. 65).

1900

Cézanne's reputation begins to take hold, especially among younger artists. Maurice Denis paints his *Homage to Cézanne* as a manifesto for the new generation of painters (fig. 105). The Bruno and Paul Cassirer gallery, Berlin, presents the first exhibition of Cézanne's paintings in Germany (2 November–1 December). Four portraits are shown.

FIG. 106

**Mont Sainte-Victoire,
View from Les Lauves,**
1902–6
Metropolitan Museum of Art,
New York; FWN 356

1901

A self-portrait (cat. 5.1), belonging to the Dutch collector Cornelis Hoogendijk, is shown at the first International Exhibition (May–June) in The Hague. In November Cézanne buys a plot of land at Les Lauves, in the hills above Aix, and plans to build a studio there (completed September 1902). Hortense is in Aix, too, from end November to May 1902; she now visits Aix for a few months each year.

1902

On a visit to Aix, art dealers Josse and Gaston Bernheim-Jeune buy a self-portrait (cat. 8.1) from the artist (February or March). Zola's death is announced (29 September), which grieves Cézanne deeply. At Les Lauves the artist begins a series of portraits of his gardener, Vallier (cats 25.1, 25.2, 26.2, 26.3; figs 84–7), which he pursues until 1906, together with views of Mont Sainte-Victoire seen from the hills behind the studio.

1903

Works from Zola's estate are auctioned (9–13 March); Vollard, Pellerin and the dealer Jos Hessel buy Cézanne portraits (FWN 395, 403, 601 respectively). Death of Pissarro (13 November).

1904

An entire room is devoted to Cézanne's work at the Salon d'Automne (15 October–15 November); ten portraits in oil are shown, as well as photographs of nine others (see Introduction, fig. 1). The Russian collector Sergei Shchukin buys *Mardi Gras* (FWN 668) – of the nine Cézannes in his collection, five are portraits. In December the American expatriates Leo and Gertrude Stein purchase a portrait of Madame Cézanne (fig. 42) from Vollard for 8,000 francs.

1905

Cézanne's paintings appear for the first time in London at the Grafton Galleries in an exhibition organised by Durand-Ruel (January–February).

1906

On 15 October, while painting *sur le motif* in the rain, Cézanne collapses and is brought home in a laundry cart. The following day he returns to his studio to work on Vallier's portrait, but is very weak. By the morning of 23 October Cézanne has died at his rue Boulegon apartment. He is laid to rest at the Cimetière Saint-Pierre, Aix.

1907

Vollard and the Galerie Bernheim-Jeune buy the contents of the artist's Lauves studio. Among these works are the portrait of Louis-Auguste (cat. 4.1) and three portraits of Vallier (cats 25.1, 25.2; fig. 84). Later in the year a major retrospective of Cézanne's work is shown at the Salon d'Automne (1–22 October 1907), comprising fifty-seven works, with loans primarily from Pellerin, Cézanne *fils* and Vollard. Leo Stein succinctly summed up the artist's life and work when he said: 'Hitherto Cézanne had been important only to a few … At the Autumn Salon of 1905 people laughed themselves into hysterics before his pictures, in 1906 they were respectful, and in 1907 they were reverent. Cézanne became the man of the moment.'

Postscript

In the years following Cézanne's death the artist's reputation has continued to grow and remains influential today among painters who still draw inspiration from his example. His paintings have entered many important private and public collections across the globe and have been widely exhibited in major retrospectives in the twentieth and twenty-first centuries. However, the only exhibition devoted entirely to Cézanne's portraiture was held over 100 years ago in 1910 at Vollard's gallery in Paris. *Cézanne Portraits* (Paris, London and Washington, D.C.), 2017–18, focuses again on this genre in a complete survey.

FIG. 108
The Large Bathers, 1906
Philadelphia Museum of Art;
FWN 981

Select Bibliography

The works listed below are those specific to Cézanne that were consulted in the preparation of the present volume, and are referred to in abbreviated form in the notes to the texts. (Publications on broader or other subjects are described fully at first mention.) For the benefit of those wishing to study Cézanne's portraits further, this bibliography offers a brief guide to the more important references.

INDIVIDUAL WORKS

The online catalogue raisonné by Feilchenfeldt, Warman and Nash is now the essential reference on Cézanne's paintings and provides full details of provenance, exhibition history and literature for all the artist's works illustrated in the present volume. It does not contain descriptive catalogue entries on individual works; for these, Rewald's 1996 catalogue raisonné should be consulted, along with the exhibition catalogues (with the exception of that devoted to still lifes) listed in the final section of this bibliography. Among the general references, those by Adriani, Schapiro and Stokes comprise plates with accompanying commentaries, some devoted to portraits; while those by Athanassoglou-Kallmyer, Dombrowski, Fry and Lewis discuss portraits within the context of their respective subjects; and Reissner's 2008 publication, and Hales' essay in New York 2014–15, are important studies by conservators.

LETTERS, EARLY DOCUMENTS AND BIOGRAPHIES

The artist's letters are best consulted in the original French in Rewald 1978 and in English translation in Danchev 2013. The early first-hand accounts of Cézanne's life and work by Vollard and Gasquet (Vollard 1914, 1923, 1937; Gasquet 1921, 1991, 2002) are as essential as they are often unreliable.

Rilke 2002 contains the poet's 1907 letters on the artist's work. Doran 1978 and 2001 are impeccable anthologies of early documents, in French and English respectively. They may be supplemented by Wechsler 1975, an anthology of earlier and

later critical studies. And Fry 1927, the earliest English-language study, is at once an important historical document and a still relevant piece of criticism. Danchev 2012 is the most recent and up-to-date biography.

THE PORTRAITS

The present volume is the first to be devoted to Cézanne's portrait paintings. There is a catalogue raisonné of the portrait drawings, Andersen 1970; but, for the paintings, the few substantial works are on specialised categories: the self-portraits (Platzman 2001) and the portraits of Hortense Fiquet (Butler 2008, Sidlauskas 2009, New York 2014–15). Also worth consulting are the general studies of nineteenth-century French portraiture listed in note 3 of the Introduction to the present volume, some of which include specific discussions of Cézanne's portraits.

CATALOGUES RAISONNÉS

Wayne Andersen, *Cézanne's Portrait Drawings* (MIT Press, Cambridge MA and London, 1970)

Adrien Chappuis, *The Drawings of Paul Cézanne: A Catalogue Raisonné*, 2 vols (New York Graphic Society, Greenwich CT, 1973)

Walter Feilchenfeldt, Jayne S. Warman and David Nash, *The Paintings of Paul Cézanne: An Online Catalogue Raisonné*; www.cezannecatalogue.com/catalogue/index.php

John Rewald, *Paul Cézanne: The Watercolours: A Catalogue Raisonné* (Little, Brown, Boston, and Thames & Hudson, London, 1983)

John Rewald, with Walter Feilchenfeldt and Jayne S. Warman, *The Paintings of Paul Cézanne: A Catalogue Raisonné*, 2 vols (Harry Abrams, New York, 1996)

Lionello Venturi, *Cézanne: Son Art, Son Oeuvre*, 2 vols (Editions Paul Rosenberg, Paris, 1936)

Letters, early documents and biographies

ALEXIS 1890
Paul Alexis, *Madame Meuriot: Moeurs Parisiennes* (Bibliothèque-Charpentier, Paris, 1890)

BERNARD 1904
Emile Bernard, 'Paul Cézanne', *L'Occident* 6, July 1904

BERNARD 1907
Emile Bernard, 'Souvenirs sur Paul Cézanne et lettres inédites', *Mercure de France* 69, no.247, 1 October 1907

CALLOW 1995
Philip Callow, *Lost Earth: A Life of Cézanne* (Ivan R. Dee, Chicago, 1995)

DANCHEV 2012
Alex Danchev, *Cézanne: A Life* (Profile Books, London, 2012)

DANCHEV 2013
Alex Danchev, *The Letters of Paul Cézanne* (Thames & Hudson, London, 2013)

DENIS 1910
Maurice Denis, 'Cézanne', translated by Roger Fry, *Burlington* 16, no.83, February 1910

DORAN 1978
Michael Doran, *Conversations avec Cézanne* (Macula, Paris, 1978)

DORAN 2001
Michael Doran, *Conversations with Cézanne* (University of California Press, Berkeley, 2001)

GASQUET 1921
Gasquet, Joachim, *Cézanne* (Editions Bernheim-Jeune, Paris, 1921)

GASQUET 1991
Joachim Gasquet, *Cézanne: a Memoir with Conversations*, trans. Christopher Pemberton (Thames & Hudson, London and New York, 1991)

GASQUET [1921] 2002
Joachim Gasquet, *Cézanne* (Encre marine, Fougères, 2002)

REWALD 1941
John Rewald (ed.), *Paul Cézanne: Letters* (Cassirer, London, 1941)

REWALD 1948
John Rewald, *Paul Cézanne: a Biography* (Simon & Schuster, New York, 1948)

REWALD 1959
John Rewald, *Cézanne, Geffroy et Gasquet, suivi de Souvenirs sur Cézanne de Louis Aurenche et de lettres inédites* (Quatre Chemins-Editart, Paris, 1959)

REWALD [1941] 1976
John Rewald, *Paul Cézanne: Letters* (Da Capo Press, New York, and Bruno Cassirer, Oxford, 1976)

REWALD 1978
John Rewald (ed.), *Paul Cézanne: Correspondance* (Grasset, Paris, 1978)

REWALD 1986
John Rewald, *Cézanne: A Biography* (Harry N. Abrams, New York, 1986)

RILKE 2002
Rainer Maria Rilke, *Letters on Cézanne*, ed. Clara Rilke, trans. Joel Agee (North Point Press, New York, 2002)

RIVIÈRE and SCHNERB 1907
R.P. Rivière and J.F. Schnerb, 'L'atelier de Cézanne', *La Grande revue*, 25 December 1907

VOLLARD 1914
Ambroise Vollard, *Paul Cézanne* (G. Grès, Paris, 1914)

VOLLARD 1923
Ambroise Vollard, *Paul Cézanne: His Life and Art*, trans. Harold L. Van Doren (Nicholas Brown, New York, 1923)

VOLLARD [1923] 1937
Ambroise Vollard, *Paul Cézanne: His Life and Art* (Crown Publishers, New York, 1937)

Cézanne's portraits

BUTLER 2008
Ruth Butler, *Hidden in the Shadow of the Master: The Model-Wives of Cézanne, Monet and Rodin* (Yale University Press, New Haven, 2008)

NOCHLIN 1996
Linda Nochlin, 'Cézanne's Portraits', Geske Lectures, College of Fine and Performing Arts, University of Nebraska, Lincoln, 1996

PLATZMAN 2001
Steven Platzman, *Cézanne: The Self-Portraits* (University of California Press, Berkeley, 2001)

SIDLAUSKAS 2009
Susan Sidlauskas, *Cézanne's Other: The Portraits of Hortense* (University of California Press, Berkeley, 2009)

General references

ADRIANI 1993
Götz Adriani, *Cézanne Paintings* (Harry N. Abrams, New York, 1993)

ATHANASSOGLOU-KALLMYER 2003
Nina M. Athanassoglou-Kallmyer, *Cézanne and Provence. The Painter in his Culture* (University of Chicago Press, Chicago and London, 2003)

DOMBROWSKI 2013
André Dombrowski, *Cézanne, Murder, and Modern Life* (University of California Press, Oakland, 2013)

FRY 1927
Roger Fry, *Cézanne: A Study of his Development* (Hogarth Press, London, 1927)

LETHBRIDGE 2016
Robert Lethbridge, 'Rethinking Zola and Cézanne', *Journal of European Studies*, no.46, 2016

LEWIS 1989
Mary Tompkins Lewis, *Cézanne's Early Imagery* (University of California Press, Berkeley, 1989)

LEWIS 2000
Mary Tompkins Lewis, *Cézanne* (Phaidon, London, 2000)

LORAN 1943
Erle Loran, *Cézanne's Composition* (University of California Press, Berkeley, 1943)

MEIER-GRAEFE 1927
Julius Meier-Graefe, *Cézanne*, trans. J. Holroyd-Reece (Ernest Benn, London, 1927)

REISSNER 2008
Elizabeth Reissner, 'Ways of Making: Practice and Innovation in Cézanne's Paintings in the National Gallery', *National Gallery Technical Bulletin*, vol.29, 2008

REWALD 1936
John Rewald, *Cézanne et Zola* (Editions A. Sedrowski, Paris, 1936)

REWALD 1954
John Rewald, 'Un article inédit sur Paul Cézanne en 1870', *Arts* (Paris), 21–7 July 1954

REWALD 1969
John Rewald, 'Chocquet and Cézanne', *Gazette des Beaux-Arts*, vol.74, July–August 1969

REWALD 1971
John Rewald, *Cézanne and His Father*, Studies in the History of Art, vol.4, 1971–2

SCHAPIRO [1952] 1962
Meyer Schapiro, *Cézanne* (Harry N. Abrams, New York, 1952); 2nd edn 1962

SHIFF 1984
Richard Shiff, *Cézanne and the End of Impressionism* (University of Chicago Press, Chicago, 1984)

SHIFF 1994
Richard Shiff, *Paul Cézanne* (Rizzoli, New York, 1994)

STOKES 1947
Adrian Stokes, *Cézanne* (Faber & Faber, London, 1947)

VOLLARD [1938] 2005
Ambroise Vollard, *En Écoutant Cézanne, Degas, Renoir* (Grasset, Paris, 2005)

WECHSLER 1975
Judith Wechsler (ed.), *Cézanne in Perspective* (Prentice-Hall, Englewood Cliffs, 1975)

Exhibition catalogues

NEW YORK–HOUSTON 1977–8
Cézanne: The Late Work, Museum of Modern Art, New York, 1977–8; Museum of Fine Arts, Houston, 1978

AIX-EN-PROVENCE 1984
Cézanne au Musée d'Aix, Musée Granet, Aix-en-Provence, 1984

LONDON–PARIS–WASHINGTON, D.C. 1988–9
Cézanne: The Early Years, 1859–1872, Royal Academy of Arts, London, 1988; Musée d'Orsay, Paris, 1988–9; National Gallery of Art, Washington, D.C., 1989

PARIS–LONDON–PHILADELPHIA 1995–6
Cézanne, Musée d'Orsay, Paris, 1995–6; Tate Gallery, London, 1996; Philadelphia Museum of Art, Philadelphia, 1996

VIENNA–ZURICH 2000
Cézanne. Finished and Unfinished, Kunstforum, Vienna, and Kunsthaus, Zurich, 2000

LONDON–NEW YORK 2010–11
Cézanne's Card Players, Courtauld Gallery, London, 2010–11; Metropolitan Museum of Art, New York, 2011

PARIS 2011–12
Cézanne et Paris, Musée du Luxembourg, Paris, 2011–12

NEW YORK 2014–15
Madame Cézanne, Metropolitan Museum of Art, New York, 2014–15

HAMILTON–PHILADELPHIA 2014–15
The World is an Apple. The Still Lifes of Paul Cézanne, Barnes Foundation, Philadelphia, 2014; Art Gallery of Hamilton, Ontario, 2014–15

List of Lenders

List of Works

The National Portrait Gallery would like to thank the copyright holders for granting permission to reproduce works illustrated in this book. Every effort has been made to contact the holders of copyright material, and any omissions will be corrected in future editions if the publisher is notified in writing. Dimensions of works are given height × width (mm), where available.

All works are by Paul Cézanne unless otherwise noted.

EXHIBITION WORKS

CAT. 1.1
Self-Portrait, c.1862–4
Oil on canvas; 440 × 370 mm
Private collection, New York

CAT. 1.2
Antoine-Fortuné Marion, 1870–1
Oil on canvas; 406 × 325 mm
Kunstmuseum, Basel
Photograph © Kunstmuseum Basel –
Martin P. Bühler

CAT. 1.3 (recto)
Marie Cézanne, the Artist's Sister, 1866–7
Oil on canvas; 535 × 370 mm
Saint Louis Art Museum, Missouri;
Museum Purchase (34:1934)

CAT. 1.3 (verso)
The Artist's Mother, 1867
Oil on canvas; 535 × 370 mm
Saint Louis Art Museum, Missouri;
Museum Purchase (34:1934)

CAT. 2.1
Uncle Dominique in Profile, 1866–7
Oil on canvas; 395 × 305 mm
Lent by the Syndics of Fitzwilliam
Museum, Cambridge
© The Provost and Scholars of
King's College, Cambridge

CAT. 2.2
Uncle Dominique, 1866–7 (w only)
Oil on canvas; 403 × 315 mm
Private collection, Boston
Photograph © 2017 Museum of
Fine Arts, Boston

CAT. 2.3
Uncle Dominique in a Turban, 1866–7
Oil on canvas; 440 × 370 mm
Private collection

CAT. 2.4
Uncle Dominique, 1866–7
Oil on canvas; 480 × 350 mm
Private collection
Photograph © Christie's Images/
Bridgeman Images

CAT. 2.5
Uncle Dominique as a Lawyer, 1866–7 (P only)
Oil on canvas; 650 × 545 mm
Musée d'Orsay, Paris
Photograph © RMN-Grand Palais
(Musée d'Orsay)/Hervé Lewandowski

CAT. 2.6
Uncle Dominique in Smock and Blue Cap,
1866–7
Oil on canvas; 797 × 641 mm
Metropolitan Museum of Art, New York,
Wolfe Fund, 1951; acquired from Museum of
Modern Art, Lillie P. Bliss Collection (53.140.1)

CAT. 3.1
Antony Valabrègue, 1866
Oil on canvas; 1160 × 980 mm
National Gallery of Art, Washington, D.C.
Collection of Mr and Mrs Paul Mellon,
1970.35.1

CAT. 3.2
Antony Valabrègue, 1869–70
Oil on canvas; 600 × 502 mm
J. Paul Getty Museum, Los Angeles
Digital image courtesy of the Getty's Open
Content Program

CAT. 3.3
*Paul Alexis Reading a Manuscript to
Emile Zola*, 1869–70
Oil on canvas; 1300 × 1600 mm
Museu de Arte de São Paulo Assis
Chateaubriand

CAT. 4.1
The Artist's Father, Reading L'Evénement, 1866
Oil on canvas; 1985 × 1193 mm
National Gallery of Art, Washington, D.C.;
Collection of Mr and Mrs Paul Mellon,
1970.5.1

CAT. 4.2
Achille Emperaire, 1867–8 (P only)
Oil on canvas; 2000 × 1220 mm
Musée d'Orsay, Paris
Photograph © RMN-Grand Palais
(Musée d'Orsay)/Hervé Lewandowski

CAT. 5.1
Self-Portrait, c.1875
Oil on canvas; 640 × 530 mm
Musée d'Orsay, Paris; Gift of Jacques
Laroche, 1947
Photograph © RMN-Grand Palais
(Musée d'Orsay)/Hervé Lewandowski

CAT. 5.2
Self-Portrait, Rose Ground, c.1875
Oil on canvas; 660 × 550 mm
Musée d'Orsay, Paris; Gift of
Philippe Meyer, 2000
Photograph © RMN-Grand Palais
(Musée d'Orsay)/Michèle Bellot

CAT. 6.1
Victor Chocquet, 1876–7 (w only)
Oil on canvas; 460 × 360 mm
Private collection
Photograph © Bridgeman Images

CAT. 6.2
Victor Chocquet, 1877
Oil on canvas; 457 × 381 mm
Columbus Museum of Art, Ohio; Museum
Purchase, Howald Fund (1950.024)

CAT. 7.1
Madame Cézanne in a Red Armchair, c.1877
Oil on canvas; 724 × 559 mm
Museum of Fine Arts, Boston;
Bequest of Robert Treat Paine, 2nd
Photograph © 2017 Museum of
Fine Arts, Boston

CAT. 7.2
Madame Cézanne Sewing, 1877
Oil on canvas; 600 × 497 mm
Nationalmuseum, Stockholm
Image © Erik Cornelius/
Nationalmuseum, Stockholm

CAT. 8.1
Self-Portrait, 1880–1
Oil on canvas; 347 × 270 mm
National Gallery, London; Bought,
Courtauld Fund, 1925
© National Gallery, London

CAT. 8.2
Self-Portrait in a White Bonnet, 1881–2
(P, L only)
Oil on canvas; 555 × 460 mm
Neue Pinakothek, Munich
Photograph © bpk, Berlin/Bayerische
Staatsgemäldesammlungen

CAT. 8.3
Self-Portrait, c.1882 (P only)
Oil on canvas; 460 × 380 mm
Pushkin State Museum of Fine Arts, Moscow
Photograph © Bridgeman Images

CAT. 9.1
Louis Guillaume, 1879–80 (w only)
Oil on canvas; 559 × 467 mm
National Gallery of Art, Washington, D.C.;
Chester Dale Collection (1963.10.101)

CAT. 9.2
The Artist's Son, 1881–2
Oil on canvas; 340 × 375 mm
Musée de l'Orangerie, Paris
Photograph © RMN-Grand Palais
(Musée de l'Orangerie)/Franck Raux

CAT. 9.3
Madame Cézanne in a Striped Dress,
1883–5 (w only)
Oil on canvas; 565 × 470 mm
Yokohama Museum of Art

CAT. 10.1
Self-Portrait, c.1885
Oil on canvas; 550 × 463 mm
Carnegie Museum of Art, Pittsburgh;
acquired through the generosity of
the Sarah Mellon Scaife Family

CAT. 10.2
Self-Portrait with Bowler Hat, 1885–6
Oil on canvas; 445 × 355 mm
Ny Carlsberg Glyptotek, Copenhagen
Photograph: Ole Haupt

CAT. 10.3
Self-Portrait with Bowler Hat, 1885–6
(P, L only)
Oil on canvas; 420 × 340 mm
Private collection

CAT. 11.1
Madame Cézanne, 1885–6 (w only)
Oil on canvas; 460 × 380 mm
Museum Berggruen, Berlin
Nationalgalerie, Staatliche Museen
zu Berlin
Photograph © akg-images

CAT. 11.2
Madame Cézanne, 1885–6
Oil on canvas; 467 × 389 mm
Philadelphia Museum of Art; Samuel S.
White 3rd and Vera White Collection
(1967-30-17)

CAT. 11.3
Madame Cézanne, 1885–6
Oil on canvas; 460 × 380 mm
Musée d'Orsay, Paris, on loan to
Musée Granet, Aix-en-Provence;
Gift of Philippe Meyer, 2000
Photograph © akg-images

CAT. 11.4
Madame Cézanne in a Striped Dress, 1885–6
Oil on canvas; 620 × 510 mm
Philadelphia Museum of Art; Henry P.
McIlhenny Collection in memory of
Frances P. McIlhenny (1986-26-1)

CAT. 12.1
Paul Cézanne, the Artist's Son, 1886–7 (w only)
Oil on canvas; 645 × 540 mm
National Gallery of Art, Washington, D.C.;
Chester Dale collection

CAT. 12.2
Self-Portrait with Palette, 1886–7 (P only)
Oil on canvas; 920 × 730 mm
Foundation E.G. Bührle Collection, Zurich

CAT. 13.1
Madame Cezanne, 1886–7
Oil on canvas; 470 × 390 mm
Musée d'Orsay, Paris
Photograph © RMN-Grand Palais
(Musée d'Orsay)/Hervé Lewandowski

CAT. 13.2
Madame Cezanne in Blue, 1886–7
Oil on canvas; 735 × 610 mm
Museum of Fine Arts, Houston; Robert Lee
Blaffer Memorial Collection, Gift of
Sarah Campbell Blaffer

CAT. 13.3
Madame Cezanne, 1886–7 (L, w only)
Oil on canvas; 1006 × 813 mm
Detroit Institute of Arts; Bequest of
Robert H. Tannahill
Photograph © Bridgeman Images

CAT. 14.1
Madame Cézanne in a Red Dress, 1888–90
(P, w only)
Oil on canvas; 810 × 650 mm
Fondation Beyeler, Basel
Photograph: Peter Schibli

CAT. 14.2
Madame Cézanne in a Red Dress, 1888–90
Oil on canvas; 810 × 650 mm
Art Institute of Chicago; Wilson L. Mead
Fund (1948.54)

CAT. 14.3
Madame Cézanne in Red, 1888–90
Oil on canvas; 890 × 700 mm
Museu de Arte de São Paulo Assis
Chateaubriand

CAT. 14.4
Madame Cézanne in a Red Dress, 1888–90
Oil on canvas; 1165 × 895 mm
Metropolitan Museum of Art, New York;
Mr and Mrs Henry Ittleson, Jr, Purchase
Fund, 1962 (acc.no. 62.45)

CAT. 15.1
Boy in a Red Waistcoat, 1888–90
Oil on canvas; 895 × 724 mm
National Gallery of Art, Washington, D.C.;
Collection of Mr and Mrs Paul Mellon, in
Honour of the 50th Anniversary of the
National Gallery of Art (1995.47.5)

CAT. 16.1
Man with Pipe, 1891–6 (L, w only)
Oil on canvas; 730 × 600 mm
Samuel Courtauld Trust,
Courtauld Gallery, London

CAT. 16.2
The Smoker, 1893–6 (L only)
Oil on canvas; 910 × 720 mm
Pushkin State Museum of Fine Arts, Moscow
© 2017. Photograph Scala, Florence

CAT. 17.1
Gustave Geffroy, 1895–6
Oil on canvas; 1160 × 890 mm
Musée d'Orsay, Paris; Gift of the
Pellerin Family, 1969
Photograph © RMN-Grand Palais
(Musée d'Orsay)/Hervé Lewandowski

CAT. 17.2
Woman with a Cafetière, c.1895
Oil on canvas; 1305 × 965 mm
Musée d'Orsay, Paris; Gift of
Mr and Mrs Jean-Victor Pellerin, 1956
Photograph © RMN-Grand Palais
(Musée d'Orsay)/Hervé Lewandowski

CAT. 18.1
Old Woman with a Rosary, 1895–6
Oil on canvas; 806 × 655 mm
National Gallery, London; Bought, 1953
© National Gallery, London

CAT. 18.2
Portrait of a Woman, c.1900
Oil on canvas; 650 × 540 mm
Private collection

CAT. 19.1
Girl with a Doll, c.1895
Oil on canvas; 920 × 730 mm
Private collection, New York

CAT. 19.2
Child in a Straw Hat, 1896
Oil on canvas; 690 × 580 mm
Los Angeles County Museum of Art; Mr and
Mrs George Gard De Sylva Collection (M.48.4)

CAT. 20.1
Joachim Gasquet, 1896 (P only)
Oil on canvas; 650 × 540 mm
National Gallery, Prague
Photograph © National Gallery, Prague 2016

CAT. 20.2
Ambroise Vollard, 1899
Oil on canvas; 1000 × 820 mm
Musée des Beaux-Arts de la Ville de Paris,
Petit Palais, Paris
Photograph © RMN-Grand Palais/
Agence Bulloz

CAT. 20.3
Alfred Hauge, 1899
Oil on canvas; 718 × 603 mm
Norton Museum of Art, West Palm Beach,
Florida; Gift of R. H. Norton (48.5)

CAT. 20.4
Portrait of a Man, 1898–1900 (P, L only)
Oil on canvas; 1025 × 755 mm
National Museum of Art, Architecture and
Design, Oslo; Given 1918 by the Friends of
the National Gallery, Norway (NG.M.01287)
© National Museum of Art, Architecture
and Design
Photograph: Anne Hansteen

CAT. 21.1
Man with Crossed Arms, c.1899
Oil on canvas; 920 × 727 mm
Solomon R. Guggenheim Museum,
New York (54.1387)

CAT. 22.1
Self-Portrait with Beret, 1898–1900
Oil on canvas; 633 × 508 mm
Museum of Fine Arts, Boston; Charles H.
Bayley Picture and Painting Fund and Partial
Gift of Elizabeth Paine Metcalf (1972.950)
Photograph © 2017 Museum of
Fine Arts, Boston

CAT. 23.1
Seated Woman in Blue, c.1904 (P only)
Oil on canvas; 885 × 720 mm
State Hermitage Museum, St Petersburg
Photograph © State Hermitage Museum/
Vladimir Terebenin

CAT. 23.2
Seated Woman in Blue, 1902–4
Oil on canvas; 660 × 498 mm
Phillips Collection, Washington, D.C.

CAT. 24.1
Man in a Blue Smock, c.1897
Oil on canvas; 800 × 635 mm
Kimbell Art Museum, Fort Worth, Texas;
Acquired in 1980 and dedicated to the
memory of Richard F. Brown

CAT. 24.2
Seated Peasant, c.1900–4
Oil on canvas; 720 × 585 mm
Musée d'Orsay, Paris
Photograph © Musée d'Orsay, Dist.
RMN-Grand Palais/Patrice Schmidt

CAT. 24.3
Portrait of a Peasant, 1904–6 (P, w only)
Oil on canvas; 908 × 756 mm
National Gallery of Canada, Ottawa

CAT. 25.1
The Gardener Vallier, 1902–6
Oil on canvas; 1074 × 745 mm
National Gallery of Art, Washington, D.C.;
Gift of Eugene and Agnes E. Meyer (1959.2.1)

CAT. 25.2
The Gardener Vallier, 1902–6 (P, w only)
Oil on canvas; 1070 × 724 mm
Private collection

CAT. 26.1
Seated Man, 1905–6 (w only)
Oil on canvas; 648 × 546 mm
Museo Thyssen-Bornemisza, Madrid
© Museo Thyssen-Bornemisza, Madrid

CAT. 26.2
The Gardener Vallier, 1905–6
Oil on canvas; 655 × 550 mm
Tate, London, Bequeathed by
C. Frank Stoop, 1933
Image © Tate, London, 2017

CAT. 26.3
The Gardener Vallier, 1906 (w only)
Oil on canvas; 650 × 540 mm
Private collection
Photograph © akg-images

CAT. 27
Still Life with Skull, c.1885 (w only)
Oil on canvas; 332 × 450 mm
White House Collection, Washington, D.C.
Image courtesy of the Board of Trustees,
National Gallery of Art, Washington, D.C.

OTHER WORKS

p.44
Paul Cézanne, photographer unknown, 1861
Musée d'Orsay, Paris; Vollard Archives
Photograph © RMN-Grand Palais
(Musée d'Orsay)/Rights reserved

p.80
Paul Cézanne, photographer unknown, c.1875
Photograph © Classic Image/Alamy

p.108
Paul Cézanne, photographer unknown, c. 1890
Photograph © Classic Image/Alamy

p.146
Paul Cézanne in his Paris studio, working
on *The Apotheosis of Delacroix*, 1894
Photograph by Emile Bernard
Silver gelatine print; 113 × 94 mm
Photograph © RMN-Grand Palais
(Musée d'Orsay)/René-Gabriel Ojéda

p.186
Paul Cézanne, outside his studio at
Les Lauves, Aix-en-Provence, 1906
Photograph by Gertrude Osthaus
Private collection
Photograph © Bildarchiv Foto Marburg/
Bridgeman Images

p.220
Paul Cézanne, Camille Pissarro and
friends, in Pissarro's garden, Pontoise,
photographer unknown, c.1874
Photograph © akg-images

p.234
Paul Cézanne, setting out to paint
sur le motif, near Auvers, photographer
unknown, c.1875
Photograph from John Rewald, in
collaboration with Walter Feilchenfeldt
and Jayne S. Warman, *The Paintings of
Paul Cézanne: A Catalogue Raisonné*, 1996

FIG. 1
A group of photographs of portraits
by Cézanne, exhibited at the Salon
d'Automne, 1904
Ambroise Vollard, *Paul Cézanne* (1914)
Photograph © Rob McKeever, 2017

FIG. 2
Portrait photographs of Eugène Chevreul
by Nadar (Félix Tournachon), 1886
Le Journal illustré, 5 September 1886

FIG. 3
Gustave Courbet, *Portrait of Champfleury*, 1855
Oil on paper, mounted on canvas; 463 × 381 mm
Musée d'Orsay, Paris
Photograph © akg-images

FIG. 4
Edouard Manet, *The Smoker*, 1866
Oil on canvas; 1003 × 813 mm
Minneapolis Institute of Arts, Minnesota;
Gift of Bruce B. Dayton
Photograph © Bridgeman Images

FIG. 5
Camille Pissarro, *Portrait of Paul Cézanne*, 1874
Oil on canvas; 730 × 597 mm
National Gallery, London; courtesy of
Laurence Graff OBE

FIG. 6
Portrait of the Artist's Son, c.1878
Oil on canvas; 210 × 152 mm
Private collection

FIG. 7
Portrait of the Artist's Son, 1875
Oil on canvas; 170 × 150 mm
Henry and Rose Pearlman Collection,
on loan to Princeton University Art Museum
Photograph © Bruce M. White, 2016
Henry and Rose Pearlman Collection/
Art Resource, New York/Scala, Florence

FIG. 8
Portrait of Victor Chocquet, c.1880
Oil on canvas; 200 × 155 mm
Simonow Collection, France
© CDPM32/Flaran-coll. Simonow
Photograph S. Bevan

FIG. 9
Portrait of Victor Chocquet
(after a photograph), 1880–5
Oil on canvas, 450 × 367 mm
Private collection

FIG. 10
Pierre-Auguste Renoir, *Portrait of
Cézanne*, 1880
Pastel on paper, 437 × 435 mm
Private collection
Photograph courtesy of Sotheby's, Inc. © 2012

FIG. 11
Portrait of Cézanne after Renoir, 1881–2
Oil on canvas; 570 × 470 mm
State Hermitage Museum, St Petersburg
Photograph © State Hermitage Museum/
Vladimir Terebenin

FIG. 63
Study for *Woman with a Cafetière*, c.1895
Oil on canvas; 360 × 385 mm
Private collection, New England
Photograph © Bridgeman Images

FIG. 64
Portrait of a Woman, c.1898
Oil on canvas; 932 × 730 mm
Barnes Foundation, Philadelphia
Photograph © 2017 Barnes Foundation

FIG. 65
Young Italian Woman, c.1900
Oil on canvas; 921 × 735 mm
J. Paul Getty Museum, Los Angeles
Digital image courtesy of the Getty's Open
Content Program

FIG. 66
Portrait of a Young Girl, c.1896
Oil on canvas; 550 × 460 mm
National Museum of Art, Bucharest
Photograph © akg-images

FIG. 67
Lac d'Annecy, 1896
Oil on canvas; 650 × 810 mm
Samuel Courtauld Trust,
Courtauld Gallery, London

FIG. 68
Joachim Gasquet, photographer and
date unknown
Photograph from John Rewald, in
collaboration with Walter Feilchenfeldt
and Jayne S. Warman, *The Paintings of
Paul Cezanne: A Catalogue Raisonné*, 1996

FIG. 69
Henri Gasquet, 1896
Oil on canvas; 562 × 470 mm
Marion Koogler McNay Art Museum,
San Antonio, Texas; Bequest of Marion
Koogler McNay (1950.22)
Photograph © 2016 McNay Art Museum/
Art Resource, New York/Scala, Florence

FIG. 70
Ambroise Vollard, photographer and
date unknown
Photograph from John Rewald, in
collaboration with Walter Feilchenfeldt
and Jayne S. Warman, *The Paintings of
Paul Cezanne: A Catalogue Raisonné*, 1996

FIG. 71
Ambroise Vollard, 1899
Graphite on off-white laid paper;
458 × 398 mm
Harvard Art Museums, Cambridge,
Massachusetts
Harvard Art Museums/Fogg Museum;
Gift of Mr and Mrs Frederick Deknatel
(1961.152)
Photograph: Imaging Department ©
President and Fellows of Harvard College

FIG. 72
Alfred Hauge, c.1899
Photograph from John Rewald, in
collaboration with Walter Feilchenfeldt
and Jayne S. Warman, *The Paintings of
Paul Cezanne: A Catalogue Raisonné*, 1996

FIG. 73
Seated Peasant, c.1899
Oil on canvas; 546 × 451 mm
Metropolitan Museum of Art, New York;
Walter H. and Leonore Annenberg Collection,
Gift of Walter H. and Leonore Annenberg,
1997, Bequest of Walter H. Annenberg, 2002
(1997.60.2)

FIG. 74
Man with Crossed Arms, c.1899
Oil on canvas, 546 × 451 mm
Private collection, New York
Photograph © Bridgeman Images

FIG. 75
Self-Portrait with Beret, c.1899
Lithograph; image 330 × 290 mm,
sheet 640 × 480 mm
National Gallery of Art, Washington, D.C.,
Gift of Mr and Mrs Burton Tremaine

FIG. 76
Self-Portrait with Fedora, 1894
Oil on canvas; 600 × 490 mm
Ishibashi Foundation, Bridgestone
Museum of Art, Tokyo
Photograph © akg-images

FIG. 77
Apples and Oranges, c.1899
Oil on canvas; 740 × 930 mm
Musée d'Orsay, Paris
Photograph © akg-images/Erich Lessing

FIG. 78
Château Noir, 1900–4
Oil on canvas; 737 × 966 mm
National Gallery of Art, Washington, D.C.;
Gift of Eugene and Agnes E. Meyer

FIG. 79
The Card Players, 1891–2
Oil on canvas; 654 × 818 mm
Metropolitan Museum of Art, New York;
Bequest of Stephen C. Clark, 1960

FIG. 80
Man with Pipe, 1891–2
Oil on canvas; 390 × 300 mm
Nelson-Atkins Museum of Art, Kansas City,
Missouri; Gift of Henry W. and
Marion H. Bloch

FIG. 81
Seated Peasant, c.1897
Oil on canvas; 550 × 460 mm
Hiroshima Museum of Art

FIG. 82
The Environs of Aix-en-Provence, c.1859
Folding screen with Arcadian scenes
and ornaments
Oil on canvas; 2500 × 4020 mm
Findlay Galleries, Inc.

FIG. 83
Seated Peasant, c.1900
Watercolour on white paper, 458 × 310 mm
Kunsthaus, Zurich, Grafische Sammlung
Photograph © 2017 Kunsthaus, Zurich

FIG. 84
The Gardener Vallier, 1902–6
Oil on canvas; 1003 × 813 mm
Private collection, Geneva
Photograph © Hans Hinz – ARTOTHEK

FIG. 85
The Gardener Vallier, 1905–6
Oil on canvas; 650 × 540 mm
Foundation E.G. Bührle Collection, Zurich

FIG. 86
The Gardener Vallier, 1905–6
Watercolour and pencil on paper;
480 × 315 mm
Museum Berggruen, Berlin
Nationalgalerie, Staatliche Museen, Berlin
Photograph © bpk/Museum Berggruen,
Privatbesitz

FIG. 87
The Gardener Vallier, 1906
Watercolour and pencil on paper;
380 × 320 mm
Private collection

FIG. 88
Still Life with Skull, c.1885
Watercolour over black chalk; 235 × 310 mm
Detroit Institute of Arts, Michigan;
Bequest of John S. Newberry
Photograph © Bridgeman Images

FIG. 89
Louis-Auguste Cézanne, the artist's father,
date unknown
Photograph © akg-images

FIG. 90
Hortense Fiquet (later Madame Cézanne)
Photographer unknown, c.1905
Photograph © Classic Image/Alamy

FIG. 91
Marie Cézanne, the artist's sister,
photographer unknown, c.1870
Photograph © Classic Image/Alamy

FIG. 92
Emile Zola, looking at a painting in
his study in Médan, c.1880
Photograph by Dornac (Paul François
Arnold Cardon)
Photograph © Archive Larousse, Paris/
Bridgeman Images

FIG. 93
Paul Alexis, c.1880
Drawing by Fernand Desmoulin
Photograph © akg-images/De Agostini
Picture Library

FIG. 94
Antony Valabrègue, photographer and
date unknown
Photograph from John Rewald, in
collaboration with Walter Feilchenfeldt
and Jayne S. Warman, *The Paintings of
Paul Cézanne: A Catalogue Raisonné*, 1996

FIG. 95
'Le Salon par Stock', 1870
Musée Carnavalet, Paris
Photograph © Roger-Viollet/Mary Evans

FIG. 96
Ambroise Vollard, 1936
Photograph by Rogi André,
Silver gelatine print
Photograph © Centre Pompidou, MNAM-CCI/
Dist. RMN-Grand Palais/Philippe Migeat

FIG. 97
Victor Chocquet, c.1860
Photograph by Paul Cézanne
Photograph © Tallandier/Bridgeman Images

FIG. 98
Gustave Geffroy in his study, photographer
unknown c.1894
Private collection
Photograph © Roger-Viollet, Paris/
Bridgeman Images

FIG. 99
Chestnut Trees and Farm at Jas de Bouffan,
c.1876
Oil on canvas; 495 × 650 mm
Private collection
Photograph © Christie's Images/
Bridgeman Images

FIG. 100
*Marion and Valabrègue Setting Out
for the Motif*, 1866
Oil on canvas; 404 × 320 mm
Private collection, Mexico City
Photograph © Christie's Images/
Bridgeman Images

FIG. 101
House of Père Lacroix, Auvers-sur-l'Oise, 1873
Oil on canvas; 613 × 506 mm
National Gallery of Art, Washington, D.C.;
Chester Dale collection

FIG. 102
Still Life with Compotier, 1879–80
Oil on canvas; 435 × 540 mm
Ny Carlsberg Glyptotek, Copenhagen

FIG. 103
Gardanne, c.1885
Oil on canvas; 635 × 990 mm
Barnes Foundation, Philadelphia
Photograph © 2017 Barnes Foundation

FIG. 104
Le Moulin brûlé, Maisons-Alfort, c.1894
Oil on canvas; 730 × 920 mm
Private collection

FIG. 105
Maurice Denis, *Homage to Cézanne*, 1900
Oil on canvas; 1800 × 2400 mm
Musée d'Orsay, Paris
Photograph © akg-images/Erich Lessing

FIG. 106
Mont Sainte-Victoire, View from Les Lauves,
1902–6
Oil on canvas; 572 × 972 mm
Metropolitan Museum of Art, New York;
Walter H. and Leonore Annenberg Collection,
Gift of Walter H. and Leonore Annenberg,
1997, Bequest of Walter H. Annenberg, 2002

FIG. 107
Three Skulls on an Oriental Rug, 1904
Oil on canvas; 545 × 650 mm
Kunstmuseum, Solothurn; Dubi-Muller
Foundation (1980)
Photograph © akg-images

FIG. 108
The Large Bathers, 1906
Oil on canvas; 2105 × 2508 mm
Philadelphia Museum of Art; Purchased
with the W.P. Wilstach Fund (1937)

Index of Cezanne's Works

Italic page numbers indicate illustrations.

General Index

Italic page numbers indicate illustrations.
'PC' indicates Paul Cézanne

255

Published in Great Britain by
National Portrait Gallery Publications,
St Martin's Place, London WC2H 0HE

Published to accompany the exhibition

Cézanne Portraits

MUSÉE D'ORSAY, PARIS
13 June to 24 September 2017

NATIONAL PORTRAIT GALLERY, LONDON
26 October 2017 to 11 February 2018

NATIONAL GALLERY OF ART, WASHINGTON, D.C.
25 March to 1 July 2018

This exhibition has been made possible by the provision of insurance through the Government Indemnity Scheme. The National Portrait Gallery, London, would like to thank HM Government for providing Government Indemnity and the Department of Culture, Media and Sport and Arts Council England for arranging the indemnity.

The National Gallery of Art, Washington, would like to thank the Anna-Maria and Stephen Kellen Foundation for its generous support of the exhibition in Washington.

Every purchase supports the National Portrait Gallery, London. For a complete catalogue of current publications, please write to the National Portrait Gallery at the address above, or visit our website at www.npg.org/publications

MANAGING EDITOR Christopher Tinker
PROJECT EDITOR Denny Hemming
PICTURE RESEARCH Mark Lynch
PRODUCTION MANAGER Ruth Müller-Wirth
DESIGN Philip Lewis
PROOFREADER Patricia Burgess
INDEX Christopher Phipps

ISBN 978 1 85514 547 4 hardback
ISBN 978 1 85514 731 7 paperback

A catalogue record for this book is available from the British Library.

10 9 8 7 6 5 4 3 2 1

Printed and bound in Italy by
Conti Tipocolor S.p.A.

Origination by Altaimage Ltd, London

Typeset in Absara Sans, Eva Pro and Geneo Pro